AF608625

Practicing Cooperation

Diverse Economies and Livable Worlds

Series Editors: J. K. Gibson-Graham, Maliha Safri, Kevin St. Martin, Stephen Healy

Urbanism without Guarantees: The Everyday Life of a Gentrifying West Side Neighborhood
Christian M. Anderson

Carving Out the Commons: Tenant Organizing and Housing Cooperatives in Washington, D.C.
Amanda Huron

Reimagining Livelihoods: Life beyond Economy, Society, and Environment
Ethan Miller

Fair Trade Rebels: Coffee Production and Struggles for Autonomy in Chiapas
Lindsay Naylor

Building Dignified Worlds: Geographies of Collective Action
Gerda Roelvink

Practicing Cooperation: Mutual Aid beyond Capitalism
Andrew Zitcer

PRACTICING COOPERATION

Mutual Aid beyond Capitalism

ANDREW ZITCER

Diverse Economies and Livable Worlds

University of Minnesota Press
Minneapolis
London

The University of Minnesota Press gratefully acknowledges the financial assistance provided for the publication of this book by Drexel University.

Copyright 2021 by the Regents of the University of Minnesota

All rights reserved. No part of this publication may be reproduced, stored in a retrieval system, or transmitted, in any form or by any means, electronic, mechanical, photocopying, recording, or otherwise, without the prior written permission of the publisher.

Published by the University of Minnesota Press
111 Third Avenue South, Suite 290
Minneapolis, MN 55401–2520
http://www.upress.umn.edu

ISBN 978-1-5179-0979-6 (hc)
ISBN 978-1-5179-0980-2 (pb)

A Cataloging-in-Publication record for this book is available from the Library of Congress.

Printed on acid-free paper

The University of Minnesota is an equal-opportunity educator and employer.

UMP LSI

CONTENTS

PREFACE AND ACKNOWLEDGMENTS

What is cooperation good for? This question formed the seed of an inquiry that led to this book, this moment. During my early adulthood in West Philadelphia, I became fascinated with a number of cooperative businesses around me that were democratically owned and controlled. At the time, it seemed they were doing things the hard way, with their staff collectives and boards of directors, with their calls for participation and membership, with their endless meetings. In the case of the local food cooperatives, I wondered why people did not just go to the new Whole Foods downtown if they wanted high quality, healthy food. Whole Foods did not ask for membership or a monthly commitment of labor. To me, it seemed these organizations were making things unnecessarily difficult on themselves.

I grew up in a time and place where corporate, capitalist economics ruled. As long as you had the money to pay for the goods and services you desired, it was so very easy to fulfill any consumerist whim. It was the land (and the era) of shopping malls. Looking at that time and place, I realized two things: the economy of the affluent suburbs is deeply unequal and marginalizes many who cannot afford the price of admission. It is a space of economic winners and losers, with the losers often out of the winners' sight or desperately working to keep up appearances so that they outwardly resemble those who are empowered and well-off.

Learning more about my local cooperatives, I saw how they were trying to build a different, more democratic economy and bring people along with their efforts. Still, my question remained: What were these co-ops good for? By this, I meant: What were they good *at*? How could they thrive amid capitalist competition? And I also meant: What were they good *for*? Why did they pursue a strategy seemingly so much more complicated and frustrating in order to manifest these alternative practices?

Little did I know that these questions about the nature of the good formed the basis of virtue ethics and moral philosophy. As I expanded my thinking, what seemed like mere operational matters took on depth, range, and urgency. I began to read about the traditions of liberalism and communitarianism, before stumbling on the work of philosopher

Alasdair MacIntyre, whose ideas form a core element of this book. MacIntyre spoke not only to the questions I had around food cooperatives, but he spoke to my long-standing fascination with narratives and tradition. I had found an intellectual lodestar to guide my project.

Around the same time, I discovered the work of economic geographers J. K. Gibson-Graham, who believe that a postcapitalist present already exists in the midst of an overweening emphasis on the capitalist status quo. Reading Gibson-Graham and other critical theorists awakened me to the important distinctions between the political economy I knew growing up and the one that I wanted to help build in maturity. I found that MacIntyre's devotion to ethical practices in the face of competitive individualism could be fruitfully placed in dialogue with Gibson-Graham's hopeful reading of economy as a site of transformation.

As I was busy reading, I was even more active at the cooperatives themselves, observing meetings, sitting on committees, conducting interviews. This process brought up just as many questions as it answered, proving to me that cooperation as a practice was worthy of serious scrutiny. Spending years thinking about Philly food cooperatives Mariposa and Weavers Way allowed me to come up with answers to these questions about goodness and cooperation.

As I wrapped up that project, I increasingly felt that cooperation was something bigger, more complex, and manifold than could be answered by looking only at food cooperatives. I realized that there were more cooperative projects in my midst, even if they were not necessarily capital-C cooperatives. I began to have the urge to build a more expansive theory of cooperation itself, both by looking at additional cases and by extending the scope of my reading. I was already connected to Headlong Dance Theater and the People's Organization of Community Acupuncture (the other two cases in this book). I realized that cooperation as a practice, in the sense MacIntyre meant it, in the sense I will describe in this book, could be found in any number of places in the political economy. I moved forward with this expanded project, seeking to locate cooperation not just in the cooperative movement but beyond it as well.

Along the way, I determined that the way to cultivate a healthy and robust practice of cooperation was to submit it to critical scrutiny. I observed what I call a paradox of exclusivity, in which cooperative projects need to be particularly careful about whom they include and how, as there is a danger of leaving people out on the basis of race, class, gender, ability, and other measures. Finally, I determined the best way to advance cooperation was to understand it as a process that occurs at multiple scales, so I started to read my data through a scalar lens. Cooperation needs attention at the level of the body, at the level of work and organization, at the level of community economy, and at the level of democracy in order to meet its greatest potential.

The journey started by that question about the good continues to intrigue me. I have much more to learn about cooperative practice, both in working alongside those who pursue it and in studying the various traditions of cooperation that exist around the world and over time. In particular, I continue to seek out voices of cooperators and theorists of color whose influence is present but insufficiently represented in my studies to this point. One of the greatest findings of this inquiry is the extent to which cooperation is a practice of resistance to the injustices of the status quo. That resistance has often been carried out by people who have been marginalized by systems of oppression. A transformation of our future will likewise be made possible with their vision and leadership, with supporters like myself joining the effort. Knowing that I am only partway concluded with this journey is just as exciting to me as the beginning of the journey a few years back.

Along the way, I have benefited from the wisdom and guidance of so many, and I want to acknowledge their mentorship and support. I thank the editors of the Diverse Economies and Livable Worlds series at the University of Minnesota Press for bringing me into the fold of this incredible project: Katherine Gibson, Stephen Healy, Maliha Safri, and Kevin St. Martin. Thanks also to Jason Weidemann, Zenyse Miller, Mike Stoffel, Ana Bichanich, and everyone at the University of Minnesota Press for their careful attention to this project and their kind answers to my many questions.

I thank Katherine Gibson, Jo McNeill, Katharine McKinnon, and the attendees of the 2019 Community Economies Theory and Writing Retreat in Bolsena, Italy, supported by the Julie Graham Community Economies Research Fund. The week I spent with all those brilliant minds in such beautiful environs led to a breakthrough in the writing process and a major boost to my confidence.

My experience as a doctoral student at the Edward J. Bloustein School of Planning and Public Policy gave me the critical perspective I needed to undertake this project. This book (and most of the other work I have done over the past decade) would not exist without the mentorship and friendship of Bob Lake, James DeFilippis, Kathe Newman, Julia Sass Rubin, Nicholas Klein, Juan Rivero, Akira Drake Rodriguez, Ryan Good, Katharine Nelson, Gina Bienski, Benjamin Teresa, Lee Polonsky, and Salvatore Pappalardo.

This book benefited tremendously from the feedback of developmental editor Sheri Englund, as well as constructive criticism from Bob Lake, Akira Drake Rodriguez, Nicholas Klein, and anonymous reviewers.

I thank the thoughtful individuals from Mariposa, Weavers Way, the other food co-ops, Headlong Dance Theater, and the many acupuncturists (POCA and beyond) who shared their stories with me. This book is a testament to your incredible and ongoing efforts.

Finally, I thank my friends and family for supporting this project over the past several years, in dissertation and now in expanded book form: Marc and Barbara Zitcer, Laura and Brian Lewis, Jessica and Joseph Fleischer, Norman and Adina Newberg, Fran and Jeremey Newberg, Liam Newberg, Philip and Jane Cantor, Daniel Cantor, and too many others to name. Finally, to Noga Newberg, Lev, and Liat—our cooperative family project—this book is dedicated to you. May we continue together the search for the good in this world.

INTRODUCTION

INCLUSION AND ITS DISCONTENTS

The corner of Greene Street and Carpenter Lane is a bustling intersection in Philadelphia's Mount Airy neighborhood. Shoppers pop in and out of the local businesses that line both sides of the street. Some chat at tables in front of the coffee shop; some browse books at the independent store across the way. Others pick up pet supplies or thumb through stacks of kids' clothing at the consignment boutique. It's a remarkably vibrant scene for an otherwise quiet residential area.

A steady stream of patrons visits the smaller businesses on Greene and Carpenter, but the busiest store stands out from the rest: Weavers Way Co-op, a community-owned grocer that has anchored this little corridor since the mid-1970s. Weavers Way has thousands of members, each owning a piece of a business they call their own. Many other patrons shop at the co-op without a membership. Weavers Way is open seven days a week, twelve hours a day, supplying its devotees with organic produce, artisanal cheeses, and sacks full of bulk grains from amaranth to quinoa. For its many fans, Weavers Way represents the best food you can buy, from a business that embodies the best of Mount Airy's communitarian values.

Not everybody at Greene and Carpenter sees the co-op as a little slice of utopia. First, it is pricey. The high cost is partly due to the quality of the food and partly because Weavers Way is a small business that pays its workers better than the supermarket competition. But the co-op is hardly a discount grocer, selling mostly organic goods at premium prices. Second, the food selection appeals to the palates of a fairly specific cultural demographic: the largely white, liberal/progressive, highly educated population that makes up the majority of its membership. Finally, there have been times the co-op has signaled to some of its neighbors that the store is not meant for them.

A story from the mid-1990s illustrates the challenges the co-op has faced in its attempts to serve everyone in the neighborhood. For decades, the co-op was only open to members. That meant people who wanted shopping privileges needed to make a $400 equity investment, as well as work a couple of hours per month stocking shelves or ringing up other members. There were a number of benefits to this arrangement: labor costs were reduced, as members did a lot of the work; fellow feeling among members was high, since people got to know one another during work shifts.

But the members-only policy was also restrictive. It kept out shoppers who did not have the ability to make a member equity investment. It also kept out shoppers who did not have the ability to commit to working monthly shifts in the store. And there was a group of hungry would-be customers right across the street from the co-op, at the C. W. Henry Elementary School. Schoolkids would rush over after school let out at 3 p.m., looking to buy snacks to fuel the next few hours of play. For a while, easygoing managers would let the kids shop under a guest-shopper policy, which had been designed for people who wanted to try out the co-op before joining as working members. But it was not easy to accommodate the kids in the tiny grocery store. A sudden influx of ten or twenty juvenile customers would overwhelm the aisles and the grown-up shoppers. Kids often had the wrong amount of change when they got to the register, causing long lines to snake into the store's center as the volunteer member cashiers tried to sort it all out. There were reports of shoplifting. Management was overwhelmed and unsure how to proceed.

The co-op's leaders took a proactive step. They decided to more rigorously enforce the members-only shopping policy during the after-school hours. Only children of members could shop. The co-op started to post a staff member as a sentry, standing at the co-op's door, asking each child, "Are you a member?" If the child's parents were co-op members, the child would be let in to shop. This checkpoint served as no impediment to many of the white children, as their parents were members of the co-op. They were able to go in and shop for their afternoon healthy treats. But many of the Black kids' parents were not members, so they were not allowed in.

According to a longtime board member at Weavers Way, this inadvertently racialized sorting process was not lost on the children. She recalled:

> One of my nephew's children, young son, came home and told his father—this is a mixed child, his father is African American, his mother is white—came home and said "Daddy, they won't let us in the co-op. They don't let the Black kids come in."[1]

She went on to explain how she was taken aback at the lack of support for all of the students at Henry Elementary: "We were busy selling the lettuce and the bread, the bottom line; we were busy taking care of the needs of the co-op, and the immediate community—we forgot that Henry School also was a neighbor." She admitted, "As a result of that comment, the board began to ask, 'Look at what hath we wrought?'"

The co-op's dilemma could not have been rendered in starker terms. Enforcement of Weavers Way's membership policy—something designed to foster deep community among members of the co-op—had a very undesirable effect: many of the children of members were white and many of the nonmember children were Black. Thus, each weekday afternoon, a white co-op manager stood at the door, turning away Black children. Co-ops need to maintain a certain sense of boundary in order to differentiate themselves from noncooperative businesses, creating a feeling of attachment and loyalty. But if the co-op starts to exclude people who want to participate, especially on the basis of race, class, gender, and the like, the democratic purpose of the co-op is crushed. This paradox of exclusivity, as I call it, is one of the biggest challenges cooperatives face.

To its credit, the leaders of Weavers Way reacted quickly. Co-op staff and members worked with Henry Elementary to create a miniature cooperative business inside the school, where students could take orders from their peers, purchase the snacks at cost from the co-op, and run a small business. Weavers Way employees taught kids at Henry how to sell food at a modest profit in their school, and the kids got to donate the profits to the charity of their choice. In doing so, the students learned about cooperation, entrepreneurship, and giving back, about having a stake in something of their own. This Marketplace program eventually spread to seven schools in Philadelphia through Weavers Way's nonprofit subsidiary organization, which it designed to advance the broader social objectives of cooperation. Years later, Weavers Way made membership and member labor optional, rather than required, opening the stores more broadly to the general public.

This story depicts a small moment in the annals of exclusivity, but it serves to introduce one of the key concerns of this book: cooperative practices have tremendous potential to transform the social, economic, and cultural lives of the people who participate. But they also run the risk of fostering elitism and exclusion. Sometimes that exclusion is intentional; sometimes it is the result of poor planning and a lack of awareness. It also begs the question of what constitutes a cooperative project, who is represented in the community, and who makes the decisions. And this story teaches that cooperation is a practice, a complex social activity that needs to be constantly revised and refined, its participants thoughtfully reflecting on the means and ends of cooperation in order to more fully realize the extent of its potential.

The Purpose of This Book

This evocative story from Weavers Way, and many others like it, form the core of this book. The practice of cooperation is built around the following assertion: the way to a more just and equitable society lies in the widespread adoption of cooperative practices. Cooperation will produce a more sustainable economy, infused with care, standing in stark contrast to the dominance of competitive market capitalism and individualism that strains the fabric of contemporary communities. Though competition and individualism have ruled the day for a long time, this is not a necessary course of events, and through careful work, these behaviors can be reversed and relegated to their rightful place. They can be replaced by a diverse set of economic behaviors designed to better support a community economy. Cooperation is perhaps the most long-standing and best known among these options to transform the economy and society.

This book aims to inspire current and potential cooperators across sectors and walks of life. Its deep investigation of the benefits and challenges of cooperation through the examination of diverse cases is designed to encourage introspection among readers about the issues they face in the work they do. The book takes its cases seriously, looking beneath the surface to see how they work and where they flounder. The book's sustained examination of particular practices of cooperation in particular settings begins to sketch a broader vision of what constitutes cooperative practice more generally. Along the way, the book poses the central question: What are the qualities of cooperation that make it ethical, effective, and sustainable?

This book has no patience for a simple, unreflective embrace of cooperation. I am not interested in cooperatives that serve merely as oppositional organizations, self-satisfied with both their achievements and their position standing outside the mainstream of the economy. These qualities, particularly true of some co-ops started in the 1960s as part of the New Left,[2] no longer feel relevant or productive when there is so much at potential for broader transformation. Nevertheless, I strive to advance cooperation that pushes against the boundaries of capitalist thinking, seeking to build a more ethical, sustainable, and just economy, rather than remaining satisfied with the status quo. This book takes as a challenge political scientist Jon Elster's question: "If cooperative ownership is so desirable, why are there so few cooperatives?"[3] I answer with an affirmative stance: there is so much cooperation going on, and so much cooperative potential to foster. The best path is to interrogate and bolster what is possible through sustained critical scrutiny.

Viewed one way, the scale of capitalism overwhelms cooperation. Increasing cooperative practice means trying to make real gains, striving toward ubiquity. In order to do so, it makes sense to take a broad view of cooperation, to look expansively at cooperative practices, looking, for example, at collectives, like the ones featured in this book: Headlong Dance Theater or the People's Organization of Community Acupuncture, a nontraditional multistakeholder cooperative. This book finds inspiration in the margins, like the cultural sector or the alternative health movement. Rather than focusing on large, established players in the cooperative movement (like the Mondragon cooperatives in the Basque region of Spain), I look to what is emerging from less expected spaces. It is in the margins where openings are available and have the potential to influence the mainstream, as the cases in this book are beginning to do to the sectors around them. Black feminist author bell hooks calls the margin a site of resistance. It is a "site of creativity and power, that inclusive space where we recover ourselves, where we move in solidarity to erase the category colonized/colonizer."[4] By examining how diverse organizations interpret the call to cooperation against competitiveness, it becomes possible to see how it might be promoted and strengthened.

In asserting the importance of cooperation, I make three arguments. The first argument is that cooperation is a practice—a form of complex, fraught project that requires constant interrogation and refinement. Practices are social by definition, and that quality renders them difficult to sustain, given the ways in which we fail to support goals of equity, efficacy, and justice in most of our social projects. A practice is also a complex and coordinated set of activities, working against the grain of contemporary economic and social activity.

Cooperation is a practice of organization in many ways. It organizes bodies in space and time; it organizes institutions; it organizes streets and towns; it has the potential to organize society at large. Whether a dance company searching for new paths to ask urgent aesthetic and political questions or a co-op grocer competing against corporate giants, the way to cooperative success is filled with uncertainty and no shortage of deterrents. And yet, if we value cooperation, it must be interrogated and critiqued so that it is in a better position to thrive.

The second argument is that cooperation occurs on many scales.[5] It is easy to notice cooperative businesses with main street store frontage or economic purchasing power that piques the interest of business bloggers. But I argue that cooperation begins somewhere much more intimate: at the scale of the body itself. It is within bodies and between bodies that cooperation starts, and ultimately returns. As much as it is social, cooperation is nevertheless a transformative act at the level of the individual. Cooperation also requires a kind of shared labor, so it is necessary to understand cooperative work at a scale that derives from the body but transcends it as well. Cooperative businesses have traditions of shared labor and mutual aid that deserve careful consideration. Beyond bodies working together, cooperation also exists on the streets and marketplaces that drive economies, and the scale of cooperative economies needs interrogation too. Can cooperative economics power local economies? I pay homage to pragmatist philosopher John Dewey's notion of creative democracy as the ultimate scale of cooperation. If all of these scales are fundamentally transformed to embrace cooperation as a practice, the effects will be extraordinary.

My final argument is that cooperatives need to be deeply and committedly inclusive and justice oriented. I discuss at length the paradox of exclusivity that co-ops have to overcome to achieve their potential. From racial and class exclusion, to lack of transparency, to dismissiveness of the broader society, cooperatives have to work diligently to make sure they are spaces of inclusion and not spaces of oppression. The way from marginality to mainstream lies through reckoning with this paradox: cooperatives need to be exclusive enough to generate a feeling of group connection and buy-in, but not so much that they leave different people out of the project. This is the challenge of cooperation as a practice.

HOW THE PROJECT STARTED

My project to formally understand cooperation began in 2009, when I began to think critically about the cooperative enterprises around me in Philadelphia: a cooperative grocer where I was a member, a dance collective whose show I helped produce at a community arts venue, and a community acupuncture clinic where I sought relief from migraines. I was not interested in these projects because they were cooperatives; I knew nothing of substance about cooperatives. They were just compelling projects that fit with my interest in grassroots ways of providing goods and services.

I embarked on a period of participant observation with all three organizations from 2009 to 2015, working as a member-owner at Mariposa Food Co-op and Weavers Way Co-op and serving on several committees; I volunteered with the collective Headlong Dance Theater, serving as a board member and facilitator; I observed and received treatments in a series of Philadelphia acupuncture clinics, as well as clinics in Portland, Oregon, and Providence, Rhode Island (members of the People's Organization of Community Acupuncture). Along the way, I conducted over one hundred in-depth interviews with a variety of stakeholders in and around these cooperative projects. I paid close attention to these conversations, recording, transcribing, and analyzing them to look for relevant themes and inspiring ideas. I learned that sustaining this work is incredibly hard, fraught with all manner of organizational challenges and pitfalls.

A note on methods: scholars, even critical scholars, often valorize a form of distance that approaches objectivity because of the lack of the researcher's personal stake in the relationships under scrutiny. While I think distanced relationships, if carefully navigated, are effective as a research tool, I nevertheless think a lot of research is driven by the life circumstances in which researchers finds themselves. The questions, curiosities, and commitments embraced by the researcher are fertile ground for a kind of engaged participatory research. This comes in a range of flavors, from observation to participatory action research; there is power in exploring these extant relationships to collectively get at the heart of what is being studied.

An important caveat: just because this kind of research takes place in partnership with those who are already part of the researcher's network—what researchers call a convenience sample, if you will—does not mean that differences of race, ethnicity, education, gender, age, ability, and more do not need to be reckoned with. The researcher should not make assumptions about agreement just because they are engaged with the research partners in a common project or struggle. In this sense, one could state that research is often "me-search"—cue the groans—

but I believe it is often the case. Owning up to this in my scholarly work and using the best of what it has to offer feels to me like a fertile ground for liberatory praxis. This is what I have tried to do in this work.

The focus of this book is on particular cases in the United States. Though I hope to inspire cooperators everywhere, my own experience and research on these domestic cases limits the scope of the claims I seek to make. The particular cultural, social, legal, and financial structure of the United States, with its emphasis on rugged individualism and competition, fits well for a study of this kind. For the most part, these cases have more or less national reach (the People's Organization of Community Acupuncture is a national organization, headquartered in Portland but with clinics in most of the United States; there are hundreds of food co-ops like Mariposa and Weavers Way spread around the country, and I did speak to representatives at co-ops in several states). Nevertheless, all of these cases had strong grounding in Philadelphia, the city where I live, teach, and participate in cooperative projects of my own.

Philadelphia is a city that both benefits mightily from cooperation and desperately needs more of it. It is home to a large number of cooperative and solidarity economy efforts across the region. Yet there is much work to be done, as these efforts often do not reach poor neighborhoods of color.[6] Philadelphia is the poorest city among America's large cities, with high rates of poverty and unemployment.[7] Each of the cases in this book works in its own way to try to bring light and to address the tremendous challenges and inequalities faced by Philadelphians.

This book is deeply grounded in the work of specific organizations in a specific place and time, with Philadelphia as a focus. Yet I want to be clear that the practice of cooperation, even when seemingly marginal, is widespread. Inspiring examples like the ones profiled in this analysis are all over the place. I pepper the book with examples beyond my core case studies to remind myself and the reader of this fact, particularly in my chapter on community economies. I am sure that many similar studies could be made of practices of cooperation in places all over the country where people strive for a more just economic future. Rather than detract from the importance of analyzing Headlong, POCA, and Weavers Way, I intend for these cases and this methodology to inspire others to get engaged in the cooperative practices in their own backyards. Participating in the work of these case studies in and beyond Philadelphia was inestimably beneficial to my understanding of the challenges of cooperation, and I recommend for readers to get connected to initiatives going on in their own communities.

I became connected to each of these cases at a pivotal movement in its organizational evolution, without knowing it in advance, and somewhat by coincidence. As I undertook this study, the food co-ops each expanded to new buildings and changed organizational structures, with one co-op opening—and quickly closing—a branch in a low-income Black neighborhood. The dance collective marked its twentieth anniversary with the departure from the organization of one of its three founding codirectors. The acupuncture co-op expanded massively around the United States yet struggled to chart a path to financial sustainability. As the research evolved, I wanted to document the challenges, shortcomings, and successes of these kinds of cooperative experiments. As I discussed this project with cooperators and scholars around the country, giving presentations on the work in progress, I have learned they have an appetite for a book that explores cooperation from the ground up, while placing it in a context informed by history, philosophy, and theory—a book that links everyday work to a broader understanding. *Practicing Cooperation* is a book for them.

I chose these cases, in part, because they were right there in front of me in Philadelphia. In that sense, they are a convenience sample. But I pursued them over all of these years because they are provocative and interesting projects that have a lot of things to teach us about the way our economy and society function. They also demonstrate diversity: in cooperative form, in sectors of the economy, and the scale on which they effect change. I selected these cases and concentrate on them throughout the book because of the importance of grounding theory in lived experience. In this case, it is both the lived experience of the cooperative subjects who told me their stories for this book as well as my own experience participating in their cooperative practice as both researcher and participant.

COOPERATIVE FOOD

I began my research with participant observation at two consumer-owned grocery cooperatives in Philadelphia. Cooperative grocers are one of the oldest forms of cooperatives, dating back to the 1840s in the north of England (more on this history in the chapter that follows). The provision of food has driven consumer cooperation for going on two hundred years, formally, and for millennia, when it comes to informal

FIGURE 1. Weavers Way Co-op is one of the longest established businesses in Philadelphia's Mount Airy Village. Photograph by Andrew Zitcer.

economic cooperation around the world.[8] Weavers Way Co-op and Mariposa Food Co-op were both founded in the early 1970s, and both experienced a wave of growth and renewal in the late 2000s.

Weavers Way Co-op has locations in the West Mount Airy and Chestnut Hill neighborhoods of Philadelphia, and another location in suburban Ambler, Pennsylvania. The co-op's efforts extend beyond selling high quality food, to its work in regional cooperative development, urban farming, and community engagement. Now in its fifth decade of operation, Weavers Way has become something of a regional and even national leader in the consumer cooperative movement. Over the years, and through its share of challenges, Weavers Way has emerged to become a political and economic force in Northwest Philadelphia and beyond.

Weavers Way has approximately 9,300 members, and thousands more shop without a membership. The members of Weavers Way Co-op are also owners of the co-op, by making onetime equity investments of $400 per household in the co-op. Members are eligible to vote in elections, to serve on the board of directors, earn rebates, and get member specials. If the co-op were ever to dissolve, members would receive a

FIGURE 2. In 2010, Weavers Way expanded to a second location in the Chestnut Hill neighborhood. Photograph by Andrew Zitcer.

payout. If members leave the co-op, they can ask for their equity investment to be returned.

The number of paid staff at Weavers Way is approximately 130. There is a member labor program in which paid staff work alongside member-owners, working shifts in the stores. As an employer, Weavers Way places a high priority on competitive compensation and offers health benefits to its employees.[9] Weavers Way's sales for 2017 exceeded $22 million; the co-op is profitable and recently offered a rebate to members, paid down debt ahead of schedule, and gave out staff bonuses.

The results of a recent member survey indicated that the membership of Weavers Way is overwhelmingly white, affluent, and highly educated. As with any voluntary survey, we have to take the results with a grain of salt, as it is unclear if these responses are representative of the membership or the shopper group as a whole. But from many visits there, I can confirm that it is largely, though by no means exclusively, a white liberal space in a diverse urban neighborhood. The importance of this observation is something I will explore in chapters to come.

One of Weavers Way's unique features is the co-op's commitment to its two production farms. One is a two-acre market farm that sells produce at farmers markets and at the co-op branches; the other, a 2.5-acre farm, produces food for a CSA. The co-op employs two farmers year-round and has several farm apprentices and interns during the growing season. Working members can work shifts at the farm instead of in the co-op stores. Weavers Way has a nonprofit arm called Food Moxie, which is responsible for farm education at the co-op's farms, as well as a community gardening program at Stenton Family Manor, a family homeless shelter.

The other long-standing food co-op in Philadelphia is Mariposa Food Co-op. It provides a counterpoint to Weavers Way in that it is smaller, more grassroots, and more focused on alleviating issues of racial and class-based injustice. For forty years, Mariposa was nestled in a tiny five-hundred-square-foot storefront at 4726 Baltimore Avenue in the Cedar Park neighborhood of West Philadelphia. Through most of its life, Mariposa served a small membership of a few hundred, with most members walking to the co-op to purchase groceries off the shelves or by bulk preorder.

In March 2012, Mariposa relocated to a considerably larger store at 4824 Baltimore Avenue, one block west of its original location, adaptively reusing an old bank building and renovating it using the latest in sustainable architecture. The co-op raised approximately $2.5 million for the relocation from a varied set of earned and contributed sources including: member loans, conventional bank loans, sale of the original co-op storefront, and grants and low interest loans from an array of funders, including other food co-ops in the region.[10]

The neighborhood around Mariposa, Cedar Park, is an ethnically and economically diverse streetcar suburb of downtown Philadelphia, with the central business district easily accessible by trolley and bus. The neighborhood is largely a population of renters, with a high transient population of students affiliated with area schools such as University of Pennsylvania, Drexel, University of the Sciences, and Walnut Hill College.[11] The area has gentrified in the past decade, with an influx of young families and professionals who have driven up property values.[12]

For most of its history, Mariposa existed in a relatively steady state, open a few days a week, with a few hundred members. It had a staff of three or four, and most of the business practices were nonstandard and ad hoc.[13] Books were kept by hand; there was no cash register; there were no personnel policies.

But in the mid- and late 1990s, Mariposa experienced significant

FIGURE 3. Mariposa Food Co-op is an anchor of the Baltimore Avenue commercial corridor in West Philadelphia. Photograph by Andrew Zitcer.

membership growth driven by the growing interest in local and organic food,[14] mistrust of large corporate retailers,[15] and the aforementioned popularity of the surrounding neighborhood. This pressure pushed Mariposa to expand staff, professionalize operations, and ultimately choose to expand and relocate.

Mariposa is committed to a participatory democratic structure, with consensus as its operating basis. This conviction, along with the radical activism of some of its most dedicated members, makes Mariposa different from many of the politically liberal but mainstream co-ops in the nation. Mariposa members are active on issues of food justice, gender and sexuality, antiracism, and more. The co-op devotes considerable staff and member resources to its activism, attempting to make the store an expression and outgrowth of these values. As the co-op grows larger and more financially successful, there is a concern among some members that the political agenda will be diluted or may disappear altogether.

In the past several years, Mariposa has made significant strides toward its goal of serving the broader West Philadelphia community. But the co-op is challenged by the debt it has taken on in the course of its expansion, the high cost of labor, potential burnout of key staff and volunteers, and the challenge of staying true to its ambitious mission of social justice and making the retail grocery store the nexus of a social and political transformation.

Mariposa had approximately 3,300 members as of the beginning of 2020, a sharp increase from a few years before. This increase is due to a membership drive prior to the relocation of the co-op, as well as the snowballing popularity of cooperatives and local and organic food.[16]

Membership entails a financial investment in the co-op. This investment of member equity is the member's ownership stake in the co-op; the collective equity of the membership forms the working capital of the co-op. The required contribution totals $200 per individual member and is billed in $25 quarterly installments paid over two years. Mariposa has nonmember shoppers but encourages patrons to become members. Nonworking members get periodic discounts and other perks, while the few remaining working members get a 10 percent discount off the posted shelf prices.

Members participate in the co-op through two primary means: work shifts and governance responsibilities. Work shifts happen in the store and earn members discounts on products. Work shifts include stocking shelves, helping with deliveries, processing bulk orders, and working in the back office. Members can also earn work shift credit by serving on a committee, attending a general membership meeting, or serving on the board of delegates. Member owners govern the co-op through their participation in general membership meetings and through the Mariposa board of delegates. Mariposa's member owners are eligible to run and vote in annual board elections, to serve on committees and working groups, and to participate in general membership meetings.

Mariposa projects its annual sales to climb to over $3 million, more than double the sales of the years prior to expansion. Though Mariposa realized a loss early on due to the costs of expansion, sales have been strong, and the new store is paying down debt faster than expected.

Weavers Way and Mariposa share a lot in common. They both began in the same era, with a similar founding ethos. They are both urban co-ops, though their host neighborhoods are quite different. Over the past decade, each has stabilized and professionalized. But they have taken different paths to get to where they are. In this book, I contrast the two co-ops, finding that Weavers Way represents a powerful and strong business entity with rather mainstream political and economic convictions. By contrast, Mariposa is a smaller and less economically and politically powerful player, but it holds fast to its radical commitment to changing the economy and society. I believe both co-ops have something to offer and the ways in which we can learn from both make it useful to examine them side-by-side.

COOPERATIVE HEALTH

Acupuncturists Lisa Rohleder and Skip Van Meter founded the first community acupuncture clinic in Portland, Oregon, in 2002, dubbing it Working Class Acupuncture. Today, they are the leaders of a cooperative movement that has two hundred clinics and gives over one million treatments per year. Acupuncture is the practice of placing needles into strategic points under a patient's skin in order to influence the flow of qi, commonly and roughly translated as "energy" or "life force." It has been proven effective in the treatment of a range of chronic and acute health conditions that are difficult and expensive to manage.[17] Acupuncture has been used for millennia in China, where it originated and first came into prominence. It came to the West as early as the mid-seventeenth century and was practiced in fits and starts here beginning in the nineteenth century. It has grown in popularity in the United States since the 1960s. Rohleder and Van Meter were inspired by experiences they had treating patients in a public health group setting. They quickly established the template that would later become the model for all the clinics in their co-op (dubbed the People's Organization of Community Acupuncture or POCA): a sliding payment scale of $15–35 per visit and treatment of multiple patients per hour in a group setting. The low-cost, high-volume model has roots in acupuncture traditions from China, as well as the radical praxis of the 1970s, and stands opposed to most acupuncture in the United States, where patients are seen—one at a time—at a cost that can exceed $75 per treatment.[18] Costly treatments, argue Rohleder and Van Meter, lead patients of limited means to undertake treatment less frequently and suffer with symptoms that can be alleviated by more acupuncture.[19] Rohleder, in particular, struggled with the gulf she perceived in the acupuncture world between boutique practices for the upper and middle class and public health acupuncture for poor addicts. As she puts it, "People who had functional lives and modest resources did not exist as potential patients. They were completely invisible. . . . If acupuncture clinics were restaurants, there would be only soup kitchens and four-star bistros, with nothing in between."[20]

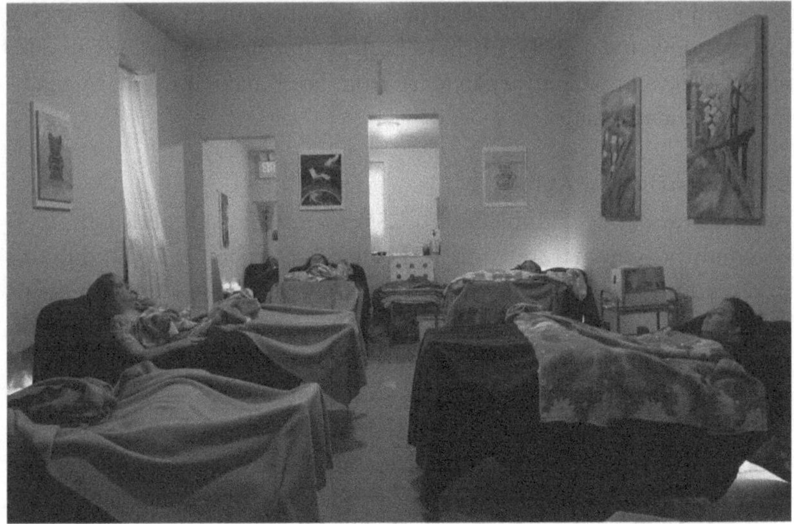

FIGURE 4. Patients recline as they receive treatments in a community acupuncture clinic. Photograph by Aaron W. Todd. Courtesy of West Philadelphia Community Acupuncture.

The low-cost, high-volume model proved successful, in that Rohleder and Van Meter were able to work full time in the clinic and make ends meet. Working Class Acupuncture began to attract attention from other acupuncturists who wanted to do something similar. Rohleder and Van Meter started to give workshops on how to administer community acupuncture, and Rohleder emerged as a spokesperson and evangelist for the model. She wrote for the main industry publication, *Acupuncture Today*. She self-published books on community acupuncture that the emerging community clinics distributed; these books combined practical advice, inspirational language, and fiery condemnation of the acupuncture establishment and the U.S. health-care system. By the end of 2006, 11 community acupuncture clinics were operating. By the end of 2008, the number was 32; by 2009, 115 clinics were open. The two hundredth community acupuncture clinic opened in 2011.[21]

Early on, Rohleder and Van Meter realized that franchising their Portland clinics did not make sense. They wanted to build a movement, not a business. Instead of thinking of the success of individual private practices, Rohleder sought the elevation of what POCA calls the Big Damn Clinic. As one of POCA's leaders explained to me in an interview: "Do you think of this business as your business? Or do you think of it as this entity outside yourself that you steward and that you're a part of, but that your goal is to bring more people into it? It's not your practice."[22] The Big Damn Clinic was a collection of small independent entities that needed to find a way to partner for growth and sustainability. To harness the power of this network of clinics, POCA was born in 2011. Lisa Rohleder writes that the community acupuncture movement stumbled on traditions of cooperation as a result of trying to comprehend what was already happening in the clinics: "By 2010 we recognized that there was a name for this phenomenon. It's called the principle of mutual aid, or the spirit of mutualism, and it is the cornerstone of the cooperative movement. Because none of us knew much about business, let alone cooperatives, it didn't dawn on us that what we were doing was more like a cooperative than it was like anything else."[23]

POCA is composed of four classes of members: individual acupuncturists (who may or may not be working in POCA clinics), acupuncture clinics, patients (though that term is self-defined), and companies who provide supplies like needles to POCA clinics. Members pay annual dues on a sliding scale. POCA is unlike most cooperative businesses: it does not run any clinics; it provides no direct income to practitioners or benefits to consumers. There are no dividends or rebates offered to members who participate financially. Nevertheless, POCA proudly claims the title of cooperative.

So how does POCA support community acupuncture as a cooperative? It hosts popular online forums and a series of videos where practitioners share information on everything from acupuncture practice to clinic administration to dealing with challenging patients. In this sense, it functions as something of a peer-to-peer support network, a kind of knowledge commons.[24] In addition, POCA offers microloans for clinics to start up or expand. It hosts a job board where clinics seek acupuncturists or new owners. It offers mini courses that provide continuing education credits to licensed acupuncturists. Videos and posts are geared toward patients as well, with a section devoted to patient testimonials. The goal is to attract a diverse group of members, not erect an intellectual and political monolith.

POCA's most ambitious project is the movement's own accredited acupuncture school, POCA Tech, which enrolled its first class of eleven students in 2014. The goals of POCA Tech are twofold: to provide more community-minded acupuncturists to fill roles at POCA clinics and to foster a radical acupuncture education that teaches social justice alongside traditional Chinese medicine. POCA Tech charges significantly lower tuition than most acupuncture schools, in order to not saddle graduates with high levels of debt. POCA's commitment to working-class ideology influenced its choice to brand POCA Tech as a technical school, in contrast to the acupuncture establishment's long-standing goal of standardizing a professional doctorate. In order to facilitate this low-cost degree, POCA Tech runs on a lot of volunteer labor and a lean paid administration, which may prove difficult to sustain over time.

POCA governs itself using the principles of sociocracy, a system based on collaboration and mutual consent.[25] Developed in the 1970s, sociocracy is a systems theory for organizations that emphasizes collaborative, consent-based decision-making. Sociocracy is based on the delegation of decisions to a set of semiautonomous subgroups of circles or teams. Rather than hewing to the letter of the sociocratic law, POCA sees itself as inspired by and in conversation with the sociocratic model, much like its eclectic relationship with the cooperative movement. One of the things that hampers POCA's governance is the relatively small pool of people who shoulder most of the work. The POCA leader explained that there are probably only forty people at the head of a national movement with hundreds of member clinics. The risk of burnout is real, and for a movement that promotes cooperation and mutual aid, leadership development and succession should be a serious ongoing concern.

COOPERATIVE ART

Headlong Dance Theater was founded in 1993 by codirectors David Brick, Andrew Simonet, and Amy Smith. After graduating from Wesleyan University, the trio relocated to Philadelphia. In the 1990s, Philadelphia was in the midst of a time of cultural experimentation and expansive thinking about the arts. Galleries and experimental performance spaces appeared, centered around the Old City neighborhood, east of the central business district.

Headlong pursues the following mission:

> Headlong is an activator of performance research, of cultural inquiry and of overlapping layers of communities. We incubate projects by supporting and sponsoring artists and we engage audiences by asking people to participate in the work. Headlong fosters the creative ecosystem by providing educational opportunities, financial advice and

FIGURE 5. Andrew Simonet, Amy Smith, and David Brick (left to right) are the founding codirectors of Headlong Dance Theater. Photograph copyright Jacques-Jean Tiziou / www.jjtiziou.net.

> strategic planning as well as by asking the questions that shape the cultures in which we live.[26]

Headlong's work is inspired by practices of structured choreographic improvisation, especially the work of Richard Bull and Cynthia Novack. Headlong does not rely on a single movement style or dance tradition; it is purposefully eclectic and pragmatic in its approach to movement. Similarly, Headlong dancers come in all shapes, sizes, ages, and genders, not conforming to any given stereotype about an ideal dancer body. Many of their early pieces used humor and cultural critique in ways that broke from the formalism and virtuosity of other contemporary experimental dance companies. Some early pieces include "Car Alarm" (1997), a folk dance set to the music of a car alarm. Another, "Pusher" (2000), involved an audience member meeting a dealer on a city street corner and being sold a dance, which unfolds around the audience member in an undisclosed location in downtown Philadelphia.

Over time, Headlong's pieces grew in complexity and ambition. In collaboration with noted choreographer Tere O'Connor, Headlong developed "More" (2009), a piece that unpacked and upended their collaborative approach to choreography. Instead of working together as a team, each of the three codirectors created separate pieces on the same set of dancers. Then the codirectors struggled collectively to unite these three separate pieces into something that spoke with one choreographic voice. One of the last pieces they crafted as a trio was "This Town Is a Mystery" (2012), in which Headlong collaborated with four diverse Philadelphia households to set dances in their living rooms, inviting experimental arts audiences to neighborhoods at the farthest reaches of Philadelphia. After these nonprofessional dancers finished each performance, the dancers and the audience shared a potluck dinner.

At the heart of Headlong's approach is a collective commitment on the part of the three founding codirectors to lead the organization artistically and administratively. In most arts organizations, save for the smallest ones, artistic leadership is separate from management, marketing, and fundraising. In Headlong's case, the codirectors trained themselves as arts administrators, striving to equally share the work of advancing the company on all fronts. Though not a cooperative in a formal sense, Headlong functioned as a collective of founding administrators. The work of sustaining a democratic practice was not always easy, for two reasons. The first is that it is never possible to share labor absolutely equally, and there have been times when resentment arose about who was doing the lion's share of the administrative or choreographic labor. Second, the addition of paid administrative staff and a company of dancers led to questions about whether the collective consensus-seeking structure of Headlong included others beyond the three founding codirectors.

On the eve of Headlong's twentieth anniversary, founding codirector Andrew Simonet left Headlong to pursue a career as an author and to run an artist-support organization. From his departure in 2013 until late 2019, the work was shared by David Brick and Amy Smith, with assistance from administrative support staff. Amy Smith departed Headlong in 2019, leaving it in the care of David Brick and a small staff. The substance of my analysis focuses on the years leading up to and including Simonet's departure, as Headlong struggled with organizational growth, artistic priorities, and financial sustainability.

Unlike the food co-ops, which serve a clear geographic community and membership, or POCA, which is a spatially diffuse but bounded virtual entity, Headlong has been important to a number of constituencies. Over the years, it has expanded the audience for contemporary dance. It has also incubated and fostered the careers of a number of peer and protégé artists. And since 2012, it has run its own training program for young artists, the Headlong Performance Institute, in conjunction with Bryn Mawr College. This book examines Headlong's relationship to the artist community in Philadelphia and how the communal spirit and generosity of Headlong led to artists making work in its wake. It will also examine the creative tension between artists who cut their teeth with Headlong and sought to make a career of their own apart from the organization.

MOVING FORWARD

In order to advance the book's central argument that cooperation is a practice that occurs on many scales, I will examine cooperation as it affects practices from spaces as intimate as the body all the way to society at large. Before delving into this material, I will first explain more about cooperatives and their history. Chapter 1, "The Social Imperative of Cooperation," places cooperation and cooperatives in context by situating them within the debates of the so-called sharing economy and other current economic trends. It asks the big questions about cooperative relevance, the connections between cooperation and capitalism, and the scale of the cooperative economy. The chapter also discusses the history of cooperatives, both in terms of cooperative philosophy and cooperative history dating back to the eighteenth and nineteenth centuries.

Chapter 2, "Tools for the Journey," collects key insights from moral philosophy, economic geography, political science, and sociology to be used as tools throughout the journey of this book. Rather than serving as a deep dive into abstruse theoretical debates, these ideas and thinkers are meant to illuminate the analysis of the cases and the book's main themes. These ideas are meant as tools to use, and they will travel with the reader throughout the book as a means of understanding the material as it comes into play. This chapter revisits classic debates about the nature of the self, contrasting individualistic, feminist, and other understandings. It introduces the idea of diverse and community economies as new, generative ways of thinking about life beyond a capitalist context. And it fleshes out the idea of practices, which is central to the discussion of cooperation as something achievable and sustainable.

Chapter 3, "Practices of the Body," begins the book's engagement with questions of scale, arguing that cooperation begins among bodies and starts with the orientation of the body and self toward others.

Indeed, a lot of cooperative theory talks about scaling up, replicating cooperatives above the level of the single cooperative firm. I believe we need to talk about scale below (and beyond) the level of the firm as well. These ideas about the body are illustrated by stories from the cases: dancers performing intimate choreography that deeply implicates the emotional terrain of their personal and artistic relationships; acupuncturists confronting their fears, biases, and antipathies toward bodies that differ from theirs; and the deep imbrication of food, bodies, and identities in the grocery cooperatives. This chapter firmly establishes the body as a site of cooperative practice, which leads to discussions about ethics and the politics of care, and the importance of embodiment and emotion in forming the cooperative body.

Chapter 4, "Practices of Work and Organization," is undergirded by an exploration of the value of labor and the place of work in the political economy and how this affects, and is affected by, the cooperative movement. The case studies offer ample evidence of the challenges cooperative workplaces face, from controversies around the use of hierarchical management in all of the cases, to cooperative member-labor specifically at the food co-ops, to the development of young artists-as-entrepreneurs spinning off from the dance company. It explores different ways of valuing work, as well as some of the schemes cooperatives use to manage their workplaces.

Chapter 5, "Practices of Community Economy," is framed by an exploration of the political assumptions undergirding community economy. It looks to the cases for community that occur at different scales: at the level of the main street commercial corridor, in the case of the food co-ops; at a local arts scene, in the case of the dance co-op; and in the case of a virtual web of hundreds of acupuncture clinics around the United States practicing mutual aid and helping one another succeed in business. It explores the notions of community economy put forth by J. K. Gibson-Graham. It also explores the notoriously fuzzy concept of community; this chapter reviews the dangers in assuming things about the community a cooperative strives to serve. The chapter also revisits the paradox of exclusivity in which cooperative projects seek to be broadly inclusive but often signal their exclusivity to people of different cultural, economic, and racial backgrounds.

Chapter 6, "Practices of Democracy," is concerned with the creation of what John Dewey called creative democracy. What would it look like if the cooperative project were to succeed in moving from the margins to the center? How can cooperation (in all its guises) achieve more than a modest contribution to the cultural and political economy? What are the contours of such a society? The cases all speak to the transformative potential: from a food system democratically managed and controlled, with economic democracy as its guiding principle; to the health of all bodies and the provision of health care to all; to the validation of the artistic impulse we all share (and many of us deny) and the creation of art in a loving community. This chapter addresses the widest scale of cooperative success and is the most idealistic. It draws on theories of democracy and justice from a variety of sources. This chapter ends on a note of ambition and hope for a cooperative future.

In the Conclusion, I recapitulate the themes of the book and review in a streamlined way the importance of cooperation as a practice that occurs at multiple, interconnected scales. I offer guidance to the various movements that seek to embrace cooperation and to cooperatives themselves, including concerns about exclusivity, more productive ways to interface with capitalism, and organizational sustainability. It also reflects back to the work of diverse economy scholars, exploring the work that can be done to situate cooperation within the broader agenda of that project and relate it to other forms of economic representation. It ends with a direct exhortation to cooperators and would-be cooperators to embrace the challenging practice of cooperation and persist in remaking the world along cooperative lines.

THE SOCIAL IMPERATIVE OF COOPERATION

There are many unsettling things about the United States economy in the twenty-first century. Despite several years of a strong stock market and overall growth, many suffer from the effects of rampant income inequality, stagnant wages, and tax cuts for the rich. This is not an economy that was built to support the majority of the people. Therefore, I was excited when I first heard the term *sharing economy.* I pictured people bartering, working together, and generally doing what it takes to live by the rules many of us learned in kindergarten. Maybe all of society's advanced technology has finally enabled new ways to subvert multinational corporate power and the race to the bottom that power represents. And yes, advanced technology has made some of that possible. That, I thought, must be the cause of all the buzz about the sharing economy and how it is transforming the way we live our lives.

The sharing economy is not that, for the most part. The sharing economy, also known as the gig or platform economy, represents a new wave of services performed by people who "share" their cars, their homes, or their skills working for companies like Uber, Airbnb, and TaskRabbit. The companies involved see themselves as brokers who take a commission rather than employers with responsibilities to those they hire. Instead of hiring employees who receive reliable hours, compensation, benefits, and sick days, sharing economy labor is contingent and precarious. These companies come to a city and produce staggering effects on everything from traffic to wages to housing costs. In order to enter and disrupt legacy industries like taxicabs and hotels, some companies deliberately skirt local laws and regulations, figuring that they will be able to undercut competitors and outmaneuver stodgy regulators. It often works, and it is big business. A recent Brookings Report notes that the sharing economy is estimated to grow to $335 billion in revenues by 2025.[1]

To be fair, there are those who claim the term *sharing economy* to signify things closer to my own vision of cooperation and mutual aid. In the taxonomy of sharing economy services, collaborative consumption practices like Freecycle, the no-cost gifting exchange, is very different than the delivery of goods by flexible workers through something like Instacart.[2] Different platforms in the sharing economy occupy different places on a market-to-gift spectrum, with some advancing possible social solidarity.[3] Some scholars count alternative economic practices such as food swaps and time banking as part of the sharing economy, while still noting the challenges of openness and equity that inhere in those practices.[4] The problematic side of the sharing economy is when corporations exploit economic precarity and marginality to persuade people to exploit their own labor in service of others' profits, while calling the sacrifice shared.

Sharing economy companies have been embraced by liberals and conservatives alike. To boosters, this represents a freer way to work than the traditional forty-hour week; they see these opt-in, low-barrier-to-entry jobs as a means for workers to make their own schedules and supplement other income. In an era where wages from regular employment do not cut it (assuming regular, full-time employment is even an option), gigging can help make ends meet.[5] But what does that say about the way our economic deck is stacked for workers? It says that work is increasingly unpredictable, and workers simply have to roll with it. In the case of many sharing economy jobs, pay can suddenly shift when the company decides to slash prices for the consumer. Or it might start directing clients to some favored workers, leaving the rest out of the loop and pitting wage workers in competition against one another. This means that a job that looks promising at first might become increasingly risky, and the worker may have taken on significant expenses—for example, leasing a car through Uber and staking her future on a meaningful income from a company that sees her as expendable.

The transformation the sharing economy represents is merely a culmination of logics that have unfolded over hundreds of years under capitalism. Workers have the nominal freedom to sell their labor on an open market, but the conditions are set for them by forces beyond their control. This was the impetus for both the cooperative movement and broad labor organizing in the first place. But the same vested interests who sought to marginalize workers since the Industrial Revolution have used each successive economic shock to push back on labor protections. In a sense, the technology that powers the sharing economy is a smoke screen for a continued effort to de-skill and delegitimize wage earners. A few decades ago, philosopher Michel Foucault lamented that man was becoming "an entrepreneur of himself."[6] Today, we are being asked to accept a radically new economic premise as a given: "It's just the way things are: Your home is a hotel, your car is a taxi, and your bike is not for recreation anymore."[7] The external costs of these conditions are massive and just beginning to be revealed: Airbnb not only causes rents to rise in gentrifying neighborhoods where people realize they can make more by renting their rooms than living in them, it also squeezes hotel employees who have fought hard for good wages and benefits through collective organizing. Ride-sharing services like Uber and Lyft cause wages to plummet for taxi drivers and have caused an increase in congestion in inner cities because, unlike taxis, they are unregulated, and their low prices threaten public transportation. And the push for workers to fight for that extra dollar has had fatal consequences, as in the case of Pablo Avendano, who was killed in Philadelphia in 2018 while doing food delivery by bicycle in hazardous weather conditions.[8]

The sharing economy does not fully live up to the premise of its name. Whatever you call it, it represents a turn toward unprecedented levels of competition, between workers competing for paying jobs, but also between consumers (who are encouraged to pursue low prices above all other considerations) and workers, who literally risk their lives to deliver fast food. In the face of this hypercompetition, there is a social imperative to advance an alternative to these kinds of economic and social conditions. To me, the most promising alternative is the practice of cooperation, something so powerful it can challenge the logics of contemporary capitalism.

To possess a real understanding of cooperation, we need to first understand why such an Orwellian doublespeak use of the word *sharing* could be used to describe something so fundamentally exploitative. The confusion is caused by a misapprehension of the very nature of our social and economic relationships. It is based on a problematic way of seeing the human as an atomized individual, and the roots of this misapprehension go quite deep.

In the rest of this chapter, I offer cooperation as another way forward, a parallel path that has its own inspiring history. This chapter sets up another paradigm of practice and explains its historical and geographic origins, as well as the principles that underlie the cooperative movement. The examples I profile are meant to contextualize the case studies presented in the rest of the book and establish that they participate in a rich and complex set of cooperative traditions. By situating the cases in the thick of the cooperative movement, it is possible to envision a hopeful future by learning that such a robust alternate tradition exists and persists. Cooperatives deserve considerably more visibility, and more critical scrutiny, if we want to see more of them in the world. That kind of scrutiny is what this book is here to offer. I round out the chapter by offering a series of examples of contemporary cooperative practices from around the world that offer us hope for a different social and economic future. In the chapters that follow, I will present evidence from my case studies about how they strive to cooperate in more thorough and more just ways.

WHAT IS A COOPERATIVE?

There are two good definitions for the term *cooperative.*[9] According to the International Co-operative Alliance (ICA), a co-op is an "autonomous association of persons united voluntarily to meet their common economic, social, and cultural needs and aspirations through a jointly-owned and democratically controlled enterprise."[10] The second definition comes from the United States Department of Agriculture (USDA), which assists rural cooperatives. It is a bit more succinct than the ICA definition: "A cooperative is a user-owned, user-controlled business that distributes benefits on the basis of use."[11] This definition (while missing the crucial concept of workplace democracy) succinctly conveys the key notions that co-ops are owned and governed by their members. Co-op members invest in equity shares and can receive rebates based on how much they shop (called patronage rebates) and dividends on their equity investment when the co-op is profitable. The financial rewards of co-op membership are calculated based on how much each member patronizes the co-op, not from the extent of one's ownership stake.

The cooperative movement significantly affects the quality of life for poor and disenfranchised people all over the world, moving them into positions of economic agency. They advance a third way of participating in a market economy, that is neither nonprofit nor for-profit. Cooperatives build momentum around shared political economic goals and local economic development.[12] Across the world, more than 1.2 billion people—1 out of 6—participate in cooperatives. Ten percent of the planet's employed population depend on co-ops for their livelihood.[13] Cooperatives are found everywhere, from massive agricultural co-ops in Japan and India, to the storied Mondragon worker cooperatives in the Basque region of Spain, to a network of credit unions and cooperative grocers across the United States. In New Zealand, the Netherlands, France, and Finland, co-ops account for more than 10 percent of the gross domestic product.[14] It is difficult to determine the exact number of cooperatives in the United States, since no one body keeps statistics on them. But according to the most recent estimates from the Center for Cooperatives at the University of Wisconsin, U.S. co-ops account for over two million jobs and more than $3 trillion in assets.[15]

A cooperative organization meets its members' needs by adhering to several key principles first formulated in the 1840s and revised periodically by the International Co-operative Alliance. The cooperative principles are an incredible testament to the values that undergird cooperative enterprise: co-ops are the world's original social enterprises. The cooperative principles include membership that is open to anyone, which was radical in the 1840s but remains an important reminder not to practice the politics of exclusivity. Co-ops are governed by a one-person, one-vote governance scheme, so that the amount of equity someone holds in a co-op does not determine her share of the decision-making power. That power is distributed evenly throughout the co-op. In cooperatives, surplus earnings are distributed according to the amount the member patronized the co-op, unlike publicly traded companies, where it is based on the number of shares owned. Beyond the internal operations of the co-op, the principles advance education and training for members, as in the case of worker cooperatives that invest in training their own workers for advancement. The cooperative principles also encourage support for other co-ops. At conferences and in regional associations, cooperatives freely share business plans, human resource strategies, and market analyses. For about a decade, Philadelphia co-ops have participated in a multistate Mid-Atlantic Food Cooperative Alliance, as well as a cross-sector local Philadelphia Area Cooperative Alliance. Finally, the international cooperative principles urge concern for the broader community. Cooperatives are not self-serving islands, trying to raise the quality of life for members alone. They participate in a local community, from the work of Weavers Way in urban farming and nutrition education, to the effect some co-ops have as conveners of business associations and commercial corridor revitalization.[16]

There are a number of different cooperative types.[17] The categories I use are consumer co-ops, worker co-ops, producer co-ops, and multi-stakeholder co-ops. These various types of co-ops, despite their different compositions, all issue a profound challenge to the status quo of the neoliberal political economy and dominant organizational paradigms. They go beyond the for-profit/not-for-profit binary and open up spaces of socially grounded enterprise that help to complicate and queer the dominant understanding of the economy.[18]

Consumer co-ops are set up by their members to provide needed goods such as housing, utilities, or natural foods. Examples of consumer cooperatives include housing co-ops, health care co-ops, and food co-ops like Weavers Way and Mariposa. Credit unions, an important part of the U.S. financial landscape, are a subset of the consumer co-op designation. Consumer co-ops are by far the most prevalent in the United States today: 97 percent of the 350 million cooperative memberships held by Americans are in consumer cooperatives.[19]

Worker co-ops are set up when the enterprise is owned by its workers, who collectively make decisions and share profits. The Arizmendi bakery chain in California is a well-known example of a successful retail business owned and run by its workers. Worker co-ops are distinct from their better-known, worker-owned cousins, businesses run under employee stock ownership plans (ESOPs). But ESOPs are often successors to privately owned businesses bought out by their workers, rather than businesses chartered as worker-owned.[20] And ESOPs may be worker-owned but not democratically controlled, because of unequal share ownership among employees.[21] Worker cooperation has experienced a renaissance of interest in the United States recently, buoyed by the support of the U.S. Federation of Worker Cooperatives and the Democracy at Work Institute.

Producer cooperatives differ from worker cooperatives because independent producers come together with products that are already finished. They cooperate in the marketing and distribution of finished goods. Agricultural production often uses this form of cooperative. Cabot Creamery and Ocean Spray are examples of producer co-ops in the United States.

Multistakeholder cooperatives are a newer form of cooperative organization, originating in Quebec two decades ago, in which more than one type of member cooperate to advance a shared purpose.[22] For example, the People's Organization of Community Acupuncture, profiled in this book, is a multistakeholder cooperative, since clinics, individual acupuncturists, and patients can all join the co-op and support POCA's development. Because these co-ops attempt to unite members with different needs, they are challenging to operate but potentially more powerful in overcoming difficult business environments.

Cooperation takes all of these forms, along with several minor variations. As much as I am interested in formal cooperative organizations—those incorporated as cooperatives and officially run as such—not all of the projects profiled in this book are capital-C Cooperatives. They do not necessarily see themselves as part of the cooperative movement stretching back to the eighteenth century, although some do. I am more interested in the practice of cooperation than in the creation of businesses that are formally cooperatives. And I do not want to be reductionist or doctrinaire about what counts as a co-op. Worker cooperative scholar Marcelo Vieta advances a framework of new cooperativism, recognizing that some of today's new cooperatives do not always necessarily manifest as formally constituted cooperatives. New cooperativism makes visible diverse forms of collective economic practices rooted in mutual aid that prefigure new sociopolitical arrangements.[23] This book aims to expand the purview of what constitutes a cooperative to embrace a greater number of emancipatory projects that critique capitalism, exclusion, and individualism. Therefore, it is important to connect the case studies in this book to the cooperative project to show the lines of influence that may not always be apparent.

The organizations I researched that are most closely aligned with the formal cooperative movement are food co-ops Mariposa and Weavers Way. As I highlighted in the Introduction, they are both products of New Left social movement organizing in the late 1960s and 1970s. This organizing project yielded a plethora of alternative organizations, from housing cooperatives, to worker-owned businesses, to grocers, and beyond.

The People's Organization of Community Acupuncture is a multistakeholder co-op where acupuncturists, clinics, and patients all hold memberships. By combining the interests of multiple stakeholders in a given sector (the provision of affordable acupuncture, in this case), POCA is able to communicate, share resources, and organize to strengthen its efforts to democratize acupuncture in the United States. POCA did not intend to organize in the vanguard of cooperative governance—indeed, its precursor organization was a traditional nonprofit—but it learned of the multistakeholder model and took a chance on it, finding that this model was more representative of POCA's actually existing mode of operation than any other form of organization. So, while some might question whether POCA is a real co-op, I argue that what matters more is that POCA achieves its programmatic objectives using the tools offered by cooperatives.

Last, Headlong is not a cooperative in a legal sense. Like most arts organizations in the United States, it is registered as a nonprofit corporation, meaning that it receives special tax treatment and can accept charitable donations. But Headlong's collective orientation to management and artistic creation is a clear echo of the same social movement organizations that animated the New Left in the 1960s and 1970s. Headlong's founders were clearly influenced by utopian or even hippie schemes, though the founders maintain a critical relationship to those traditions.

COOPERATIVE ADVANTAGES AND CRITIQUES

There are many in the movement who proselytize about a cooperative advantage. Some of the frequently cited elements of the cooperative advantage include the ability to overcome market failure through mutual aid; a more ethical and democratic workplace; a tighter connection between the enterprise and the local community; and grassroots economy development and poverty alleviation.[24] To their supporters, co-ops have the potential to be more just, more equitable, and more inclusive. Attempts to measure and quantify such an advantage are underway but in their infancy.[25] As an advocate, I agree with the premise of a cooperative advantage, but I do not believe such an advantage automatically adheres to any group claiming the cooperative mantle. Instead, the advantages need to be earned through hard work and continual introspection. They are a horizon to pursue, not the birthright of every cooperative.

Despite the faith of many in the cooperative movement, detractors deploy a cluster of critiques of cooperatives. Since the earliest days, cooperators' enthusiasm for their own movement has sometimes been met with disdain from both the left and the right. Reckoning with those critiques is an important step forward in building an argument for the enlargement of cooperative practice. Before moving on, I want to raise and engage those critiques. I will answer them not with platitudes or assurances but with examples of actually existing cooperative practice around the world.

Let us review some of the critiques leveled at the cooperative movement. One critique is that the cooperative economy will never be powerful enough to challenge capitalism. Karl Marx writes that the cooperative system would be restricted to "dwarfish forms."[26] (Marx and, especially, Engels contradict themselves on cooperatives; sometimes praising them, sometimes finding them lacking.) British socialist reformers Beatrice and Sidney Webb lament that worker cooperatives have no plan to replace capitalism, are beholden to a faulty economic analysis, and often degenerate over time, straying from their initial principles and adopting a capitalistic management strategy.[27]

Still other critics find co-ops hopelessly utopian and unrealistic in their goal of building a cooperative economy. Yet, utopianism alone should not be a disqualification for an economic paradigm. According to economist David Ruccio, all economic thought is utopian. Neoclassical economics (which imagines a friction-free, unfettered market) is just as utopian as communism.[28] Compared with cooperative economics, neoclassical economics is possibly even more utopian in that it is reductionist in the extreme, leaving out so many factors that complicate its implementation in the real world. Rather than seeing cooperation as a drive toward utopia, Ruccio suggests that it take advantage of its "utopian moment," the alternative vision it proposes as a ruthless critique of the existing order.[29]

The fact that cooperatives have been critiqued or dismissed by elements of the right and the left is a testament to their fundamental flexibility, and also their ambiguity. For the purposes of this book, I advance a set of cooperatives that are transformative and critical of existing capitalist practice in a variety of ways, from Mariposa's advocacy for food justice to POCA's critique of health care as we know it. I am a champion of cooperation that resists the status quo. That being said, if the goal is the enlargement of the cooperative economy, there must not be a simple ideological litmus test. The notion of a business owned by its members, one that distributes benefits accordingly, has no inherent ideological position. Some co-ops are avowedly anticapitalist, others are liberal but comfortable with an expression of compassionate capitalism. Other co-ops are merely trying to solve a market failure and make life better for their members, with no critique of the political economy whatsoever. Depending on how one turns the prism, co-ops can look like radical praxis or like a fundamentally conservative, communitarian response to a need. Rather than focusing on the political label, it is important to focus on enlarging democratic practice and shared wealth building. When co-ops are doing that work, transparently and effectively, they are advancing the practice of cooperation, though my own interest tends toward the more radical dimensions of the field.

At some level, cooperation needs to be rescued from its critics. All the critiques I have rehashed above are fundamentally limited by the view that capitalism is all-encompassing, natural, and unavoidable. Critics on both the right and the left are guilty of assuming that citizens have no role in deciding what kind of economy they want to have. Gibson-Graham lament society's reluctance to engage in economic experiments like cooperatives because we resign ourselves to their futility in advance. We are trapped under capitalism's thumb while we wait for the (eventual) revolution.[30] Ruccio advises: "We do cooperatives a disservice—we place too high a demand on them—when they are made the key to solving the problem of capitalist injustice."[31] Gibson-Graham find that problems like faulty economic analysis have hindered all forms of alternative economic experimentation, and this shortcoming needs to be addressed inside and outside of cooperative practice.[32] Instead of a game of economic *Waiting for Godot,* we should figure out where contemporary economic experimentation is taking place and determine how to strengthen and promote it.

In the spirit of promoting already existing economic experimentation, I will spend the rest of this chapter detailing cooperative practice around the world. Each of these examples responds to the critics of cooperation in different ways.

LEARNING FROM COOPERATIVE PRACTICE

Because cooperatives are so varied and take so many different forms around the world, it is beyond the scope of this book to catalog them all. Instead, I offer a curated collection of examples of inspiring cooperative practice to demonstrate the range of expression found in different places. I encourage readers who are curious about different cooperative movements to read up on them by looking at the work of the International Co-operative Alliance, the National Cooperative Business Association, the U.S. Federation of Worker Cooperatives, and other cooperative support organizations. Rather than attempting a comprehensive history of cooperation, I have chosen provocative and diverse examples in order to illustrate what cooperatives make possible rather than seeking to be exhaustive.[33] These examples will whet appetites for the rest of the book, where I focus on my own cooperative research.

In the next section, I will profile long-standing movements on different continents: the founding of the cooperative movement in Industrial Revolution-era England; the Mondragon cooperative economy in Spain; worker-controlled factories in Argentina; worker cooperatives in the United States; consumer cooperatives in Japan; and the history of Black cooperation. My intent here is to inspire, to show range and possibility, rather than to be comprehensive. Each of the following examples is meant to serve as a proof of the robustness of the concept of cooperation. In England, the Rochdale cooperatives offered an alternative to capitalism, even as capitalism itself was in its early stages. Next, I turn to Mondragon to see that cooperation can scale up. In Argentina, there exists a contemporary echo of the pushback against capitalism that occurred in England in the 1840s. Then I talk about how worker cooperatives are faring in the contemporary United States. Japan's consumer co-ops offer a powerful example of a women-led movement that is deeply committed to ecological sustainability and consumer empowerment. The history and present day efforts of Black cooperators demonstrate the power of Black communities in the United States and beyond to overcome racist exclusion to advance the cause of cooperation. Bringing it all back home, I profile the Philadelphia Area Cooperative Alliance, which has been a significant bolster to the advancement of case study co-ops Mariposa and Weavers Way.

The Industrial Revolution and the Cooperative Genesis

Cooperation—as a practice—seems to arise at various times throughout human history, particularly among Native and Indigenous peoples who aim to thrive collectively in the face of many hardships. Indeed, many traditional societies, past and present, value collectivity over the individual. Before the widespread colonization of the United States, Native American tribes practiced economic and social cooperation, much to the astonishment of new European arrivals.[34] The Haudenosaunee provide an example of cooperation and participatory democracy that is one of the most robust known to history, starting in the twelfth century until contact with the white settlers.[35] In 2016, protests at the Standing Rock Sioux Reservation against the expansion of the Dakota Access

Pipeline demonstrated the continuing power of tribal movements to organize and bring worldwide attention to issues of land sovereignty and climate change.

The cooperative spirit has been a rallying cry for advocates of mutual aid, from anarchist Peter Kropotkin in early twentieth-century Russia to evolutionary biologist Stephen Jay Gould writing in the 1980s.[36] There is no need for this book to attempt to summarize or synthesize the diversity of human cooperation—leave that work to the cultural anthropologists and historians. I focus on the cooperative movement that has taken place over the past two hundred years since the advent of the Industrial Revolution. It is through the framework of the cooperative movement that I examine the work of my contemporary cases. I argue that we should connect their guiding principles, implicitly or explicitly, to concepts framed and ground claimed by cooperators that fought back against the economic changes wrought by capitalism beginning in the nineteenth century.

Living conditions were extremely arduous during the first Industrial Revolution in England. Since 1760, powerful landowners had pushed the rules of enclosure through Parliament. The enclosures of the commons meant that peasants' customary rights to the land around them were gone, including the rights to graze animals, gather firewood, hunt, or even build a house. Seven million acres of agricultural land in England were enclosed between 1760 and 1843, the year before the creation of the first successful consumer cooperative.[37] In response to the enclosure of the commons, William King, an early cooperative pioneer, noted that the working man's "little perquisites, his right of common, his cow, his little piece of ground, fell off one by one: he was reduced to his mere wages, summer and winter."[38] Indeed, Karl Polanyi states, "Enclosures have appropriately been called a revolution of the rich against the poor."[39]

Work was precarious then, in ways that make today seem like an eerie echo. Around 1800, most of the population were agricultural workers: 80 percent of the people still lived in the countryside and worked as laborers.[40] Instead of managing their own work, laborers were hired on an as-needed basis, dependent on and at the mercy of a daily wage. From 1800 to 1834, the standard of life sank considerably: wages fell, hunger increased, child labor outside of the family became more widespread, and unsanitary and cramped housing conditions grew endemic. In England as a whole, the life expectancy was age twenty-seven, and lower in some districts. De-skilling of labor (and downward pressure on wages) was achieved partly through technological innovation but also through the exploitation of the labor of women and children in the production process.

Though the era of industrialization is often perceived as simply a time of mechanization, in fact it was a moment of an unheralded mobilization of labor as well. The capitalists of this era separated the traditional work of artisans into piecework. Instead of a single artisan making all pieces of the work, it would be divided in the factory or among pieceworkers—an early form of outsourcing, resulting in worker competition and stressful underemployment. Workers were thus integrated into the burgeoning market economy, and labor became reduced to an instrument of production. Labor had become a "fictitious commodity," according to Polanyi. People used to work in order to make something, and now they worked in order simply to trade their labor as a commodity in the marketplace in exchange for a wage.[41] Workers, in Marx's apt depiction, had become merely "an appendage of the machine."[42]

The cooperative movement in the United Kingdom did not begin among a demoralized cadre of agricultural workers. It came instead from the artisans, who had a higher level of education and income, from craftspeople proud of their craft, who worked at their own pace to their own standards. Through the late eighteenth century and early nineteenth century, there were early experiments in formal cooperation by the weavers of Fenwick, Scotland, and in the cooperatives started by the followers of utopian socialist Robert Owen in the 1830s. These experiments failed because they extended too much credit to members and sold products at below market value as part of a utopian scheme.[43] The first lasting example of formal economic cooperation began in industrialized northern England, in a small city called Rochdale. The weavers of Rochdale were "haunted by the legend of better days"—days when they were well compensated and lived in relative comfort.[44]

The weavers, and other members of the artisan class, had education, a sense of pride, and other communal traditions from their prior eras of success. They were inspired by the practical advice found in William King's publication *The Co-operator,* which advocated a gradual, rather than utopian, approach to building a cooperative democracy.[45] They wanted to do something productive with the small amount of capital they still possessed and controlled. Following King's advice, the Rochdale weavers took the money they had been setting aside to form a Weavers Union and put it into starting a cooperative store. This group included men and women as members, a progressive practice for the mid-nineteenth century. Thus England, the vanguard nation of the Industrial Revolution, was also the first to pioneer consumer cooperation.

The first Rochdale cooperative opened in 1844 in Toad Lane, in a store so simple that there were jeers from the local youth at the paucity of its provisions.[46] The co-op store grew quickly, though, and the members had goals beyond just selling cheap and unadulterated food. The Rochdale Pioneers (as they became known) also took on housing, wholesale manufacture, and the purchase of agricultural land that old or out of work members could cultivate. The quirky store soon birthed a movement, with 1,661 cooperatives counting a million members in their ranks thirty years later.[47]

The little Rochdale cooperative blossomed into something much larger that persists today. The Co-operative Group in the United Kingdom is the ultimate successor to the Rochdale Society and has 4.6 million member-owners. The Co-operative Group operates 2,500 retail stores and has annual sales of more than £9 billion in the fields of food, banking, insurance, and even funeral services.[48] In the next section, we look at a more recent cooperative innovation that defies critics who think cooperatives cannot scale up: the Mondragon Cooperative Corporation.

Cooperation Scales Up

It is nearly impossible to write about cooperative enterprise without including the Mondragon Cooperative Corporation in the Basque region of Spain. It is the largest and most comprehensive experiment in cooperative political economy in the world, and it is frequently held up as a paradigmatic model of cooperation by scholars and practitioners alike. Mondragon is symbolically important, freighted with the aspirations, disappointments, and axes to grind of numerous observers. Though there are other sources that cover Mondragon more fully, I will at least touch on the elements of Mondragon that make it worthy of scrutiny.

Mondragon is a multibillion-dollar network of cooperative businesses that includes industrial worker cooperatives, a retail grocery cooperative, a cooperative bank, agricultural production, and secondary co-ops that provide insurance and education.[49] In 2012, the Mondragon Cooperative Corporation consisted of 110 cooperatives, 147 subsidiary companies, and a number of related organizations.[50] Mondragon employs over eighty thousand people, mostly in Spain but with worldwide operations. The industrial cooperatives produce goods such as machine tools and hydraulic presses, as well as consumer goods such as bicycles and sporting goods. The group produces and sells its products all over the world, from Brazil to China to South Africa.

Geographer Stephen Healy finds worker cooperatives like Mondragon to be ethical economic spaces where participants make informed and deliberate choices about their future. Because workers are also owners, they decide for themselves how to manage profits.[51] In each of the Mondragon co-ops, workers are expected to become members of the cooperative. Co-ops send delegates to a general assembly of all worker-members, which elects a supervisory board that in turn appoints managers. These managers are advised by councils of workers who ensure accountability and adherence to the cooperative's principles.[52] There is a general council and cooperative congress that represents all of the cooperatives in the system.

Co-op historian Johnston Birchall attributes the success of Mondragon to three background factors: the Basque region of Spain was already highly industrialized before the Mondragon Group was founded; there was a sympathetic local labor movement; and the Basque region, with an identity distinct from the rest of Spain, possessed strong cultural and language ties.[53] The project began in the aftermath of the Spanish Civil War, when a Catholic priest named Father José Maria Arizmendi arrived in the town of Mondragon and founded a democratically governed technical school that taught cooperative principles alongside hands-on skills. Education, one of the core international cooperative principles, has been a cornerstone of Mondragon's activities since these early days. In 1955, some of Father Arizmendi's former students formed the first cooperative, Ulgor, to manufacture space heaters. Under Arizmendi's guidance, other cooperatives followed, as did cooperation among these Basque firms. They grew by mutual aid, with significant support from the surrounding community; thus, they were able to overcome the start-up difficulties that plague many businesses. These early co-ops collaborated in the founding of a bank, which was committed to reinvesting in the community, seeding yet more co-ops. The Mondragon Group experienced rapid growth over the ensuing decades, powered by a vocational school that trained workers, a bank that financed new cooperatives, and a policy of limiting the size of individual co-ops so that they did not become ungovernably large. This last decision helped grow the number and diversity of cooperative businesses rather than the size of any individual firm.

In the 1990s, the Mondragon Group decided to add internationalization as a strategic goal. This included serving more international customers, as well as expanding to seed and take over foreign firms. The goal was to remain competitive and create a stable business base for the enhancement of the Basque region above all. Most of the firms that Mondragon started abroad were capitalist, not cooperative, firms.[54] The internationalist or expansionist strategy was designed to lead Mondragon into overseas markets, but always with the goal of protecting and developing a Basque economy and culture. Though Mondragon has expanded overseas, the group seeks to bring manufacturing capacity back to the Basque region whenever possible.[55]

The employment of workers in noncooperative arrangements has led some observers to criticize Mondragon as ideologically impure and insufficiently alternative to the capitalist mainstream. Stephen Healy relates that such use of foreign direct investment to benefit the Basque cooperative economy has "led some to regard Mondragon not as a cooperative, but instead as a form of collective capitalism in which the justice experienced by the Mondragon 'cooperators' is underwritten by the same old injustice and exploitation elsewhere, particularly in the developing world."[56]

In response to such critiques, J. K. Gibson-Graham argue that we fail to see the importance of intentional economies like Mondragon when we are trapped in a framework that disregards the diversity and nuance in different forms of economic practice. Holding economic practices like Mondragon up to "a requirement of near-perfection" is an unnecessary admission of defeat.[57] Indeed, the Mondragon Group has had to make many difficult choices and negotiate changing economic conditions. Without discounting the ethical and practical dilemmas of Mondragon's business model, Gibson-Graham urge us to see the cooperators' ingenuity in the face of political and economic adversity, including the aftermath of war, ethnic discrimination, and limited economic opportunity. Mondragon has achieved real economic success, but we should also attend to the ways it counters skepticism about the viability of cooperative practice.

The Mondragon Group is clear about its goal of advancing quality of life for the Basque people. In this way, they resemble the Black cooperatives advocated by W. E. B. Du Bois and others, or any number of ethnic American cooperatives from the Finns to the Jews in the early twentieth century.[58] Co-ops can be an important self-help strategy for marginalized people, and the question of Mondragon's handling of internationalization must be understood in this light. Mondragon's leadership in international cooperative movement circles and its recent partnership with the United States' United Steelworkers union are evidence that it remains committed to expanding cooperation internationally.[59]

It is more productive to struggle with co-ops like Mondragon rather than holding them up to a standard of perfection. This active engagement provides an opportunity to repoliticize the economy, and consider all of the ethical implications and challenges, rather than accepting capitalism's dominance as a given.[60] Instead of armchair theory, I offer a cue from Father Arizmendi, who taught about ethical cooperation and practice but also encouraged experimentation and achieving transformation in the real world. In the next section, I demonstrate that worker control can prove a counterweight to capitalist excesses and abuses of power, as has occurred in Argentina over the past nearly twenty years.

Cooperation in Times of Capitalist Distress

One of the most inspiring developments in recent cooperative history is the uprising of Argentine workers that led to the creation of hundreds of cooperatively controlled factories throughout the country. Throughout the 1990s, Argentina undertook economic reforms pushed by the International Monetary Fund (IMF) that reduced the rights of workers and shredded social programs. Between 1999 and 2002, the country's GDP took a nosedive, unemployment soared, and Argentina defaulted on its sovereign debts.[61] Citizens took to the streets in protest, led by the unemployed workers movement known as the *piqueteros*.[62] During this crisis, thousands of factories were left idle as owners halted production and fled. For the workers left behind, cooperation seemed a way out of the quagmire. From Buenos Aires to the western province of Neuquén, workers seized control of factories and instituted cooperative management, sharply increasing production and revenues in some cases. Two decades later, the Argentine cooperatives, born out of necessity, continue to exist and to reckon with the challenges of organizational sustainability.

In 2015, there were 367 worker-recuperated enterprises, employing 16,000 workers. The most well-known is the Zanon ceramics factory in Neuquén, built with massive public subsidy by politically connected Italian immigrant Luigi Zanon. Opened in 1981, Zanon's factory became the largest in Argentina. Yet Zanon, like many factory owners, eagerly complied with the IMF's demand to reduce wages and worker protections. Workers found conditions exploitative and unbearable. The union was complicit with Zanon's schemes, so the factory's agitators organized a soccer league to facilitate clandestine organizing.[63] After a strike in 2000, Zanon abandoned the factory. In early 2002, the workers took over the factory and resumed production, under a new name: FaSinPat or "Factory without Bosses." Under worker ownership, accidents went down from three hundred per year to thirty-three, and there were no deaths, down from one a month on average.[64] In addition to successful ceramics production, FaSinPat demonstrated considerable generosity to its local region, embodying the seventh International Co-operative Alliance principle of concern for community. One significant contribution was the construction of a medical center for the local poor communities. The recovered factory workers became active in political organizing as well. As one leader put it: "Zanón moves on two legs—production and politics—they go together or they don't go at all."[65]

Argentina's cooperative tradition dates back to the early twentieth century, with co-ops in agriculture, credit, consumer, and other sectors. Many of these co-ops were informed by Italian and Jewish immigrants who brought cooperative and socialist ideas to the country.[66] Since 2006, the municipality of Buenos Aires has directed energy to the formation of small enterprises that begin in the informal economy, including cooperatives, as one major goal. Subsidies and technical assistance are vital for shoring up and scaling up these co-ops.[67] The worker-recuperated enterprises are a small fraction of a larger cooperative ecosystem. Their power lies in their influence on Argentinian politics and their worldwide visibility, and the alternative economic vision they promote.[68]

As inspiring as the model remains, there are still tensions and challenges to face. Other cooperative organizations have difficulty relating to the worker-recovered enterprises, as they had no previous relationship to the cooperative movement. In addition, some of the workers are not necessarily committed to cooperative, democratic organizing; it takes considerable effort to institute these practices over the long term. Next, I will turn to worker-cooperative organizing here in the United States.

U.S. Worker Cooperatives on the Rise

Of all the efforts to expand cooperatives in the United States, perhaps the most momentum is taking place among worker cooperatives. Long considered a marginal player in the overall capitalist economy, the past decade has seen a period of intense growth and transformation. There are now approximately four hundred worker co-ops in the United States, employing about seven thousand people.[69] Worker co-ops have a number of advantages, many of which are highlighted by planning scholar Stacey Sutton.[70] First, these co-ops embed participatory democracy in the workplace, as workers are both owners and managers of the enterprise. The workers break free from alienation, as they are the ones who set the value of their labor, decide on their wage, and make decisions about the distribution of the surplus.[71] This expansion of workplace democracy has a spillover effect, better setting up workers for civic participation. Second, worker co-ops create favorable conditions for workers, from higher wages to a much smaller gap in earnings between the lowest- and the highest-paid employees. (Large capitalist firms pay the highest earners several hundred times what the lowest earners make; at worker co-ops, that ratio is closer to six to one.) Workers also take home any of the firm's profits in the form of patronage that adds to their hourly wages. Third, workers often have better job security, since the direction of the firm is at their discretion, even in times of economic hardship. These qualities mean that worker cooperatives have better survivorship rates than many capitalist small businesses, as well as lower rates of employee turnover.

Despite their many benefits, worker cooperatives face an uphill battle compared to capitalist businesses. In a capitalocentric political economy, most people are not aware that they exist as an option. To remedy this lack of awareness, co-op advocates need to mount public awareness campaigns and educate public officials. Co-ops also require support in the form of legal frameworks that support cooperative formation, and capital for start-up and expansion. All of these kinds of resources are available to capitalist small businesses, which are the de facto type of firm but have somewhat different needs from worker co-ops.

Some cities have begun to create "enabling environments" for the development of worker co-ops.[72] New York City has established a multimillion-dollar fund to stimulate cooperative development. Cleveland has pursued an anchor-led strategy, where the Evergreen Cooperatives provide goods and services through contracts with anchor institutions. Austin leveraged federal funds for co-op development and supported technical assistance providers. There is still much to be done to convince finance capital to underwrite worker co-ops and to make democratic workplaces more mainstream. But these early steps pave the way to normalize cooperation as a practice in U.S. cities.

This is a moment of opportunity for cooperative start-up, expansion, and conversion of existing businesses. In times of economic upheaval, cooperatives fare well.[73] This latest wave of cooperative interest comes on the heels of the Great Recession of 2008 and its ramifications, including the political instability wrought by the Trump presidency. Add to that the "silver tsunami" of baby boomer retirement, and the need is clear for a serious look at cooperatives as a model for community wealth and resilience. Next, I move beyond worker cooperation to see that consumer-owned co-ops can influence policy and the market, as well as satisfying their members' needs.

Women-Led Co-ops Stand Up for Sustainability

Worker cooperatives attract a lot of attention in the cooperative literature, perhaps because transforming labor is such a radical departure from the capitalist norm. But globally, consumer cooperatives are more widespread and are able to achieve massive community control of assets, as well as influence the quality of consumer products through education and advocacy. In most cases, the transformation of consumption is an easier first step than the transformation of work, though both are necessary elements of a cooperative democracy.

One of the most active consumer cooperative cultures exists in Japan, where co-ops dominate the landscape. In Japan, the largest confederation of consumer cooperatives boasts 28 million members and gross sales of 3.4 trillion Japanese yen (over $30 billion in U.S. dollars).[74] Cooperatives are particularly crucial to Japan's rural economy, where they are the backbone of the agriculture, fishery, and forestry industries.[75]

The Japanese government encouraged the development of cooperatives beginning in the early twentieth century. At times, the state closely controlled cooperatives, particularly in agriculture, in order to ensure food supplies during wartime. Even today, questions remain about the autonomy of the cooperative sector at large, given the direct involvement of the state in the economy and many civil society activities. Nevertheless, the organizing and advocacy of the cooperative societies themselves has given them influence over public policy.[76]

Though formal cooperation has a long history in Japan, the rise of today's consumer cooperatives commenced in the aftermath of World War II. Their focus on peacebuilding and quality of life set Japanese cooperatives apart from those in other national contexts, drawing on a legacy of collectivism with deep roots in Japanese culture.[77] Cooperatives' role in food security after the war led to their ongoing concern for fair prices and high-quality goods, echoing the concerns of the Rochdale Pioneers during the Industrial Revolution. The culture of cooperation in the 1950s and beyond was based on a unique cultural concept: the *han*, or small group buying club. Originally composed of women homeworkers, the han provided social strength and unity at a local level. Each han makes group orders for consumer products and pays as a group, garnering lower prices. But the han is more than just a group purchasing scheme. Each han elects a representative to send to a regional council and, ultimately, a national body that guides decisions about products and works directly with producers.[78] The heyday of the han occurred from the 1960s to the 1990s, before delivery of products to individual members' homes and many women entering the workforce. Nevertheless, the system persists and continues to affect food prices and quality through democratic participation.

The most provocative example of Japanese consumer cooperation is the Seikatsu or "livelihood" cooperative. Started in 1965, the Seikatsu Club has continued to focus on women's empowerment and political voice. Today it has over 340,000 members across twenty-one Japanese prefectures. In addition to its consumer activities, the Seikatsu Club operates worker cooperatives, milk factories, and elder- and childcare facilities. The club operates its own stores with a limited number of products deemed to be safe and of the highest quality. Unlike the broader consumer cooperative organizations in Japan, they do not seek to compete with commercial supermarkets but depend instead on the loyalty of their members to purchase previously vetted products.[79] The Seikatsu Club maintains a political analysis that undergirds its cooperative vision, stating: "We demonstrate an alternative life and society, being against mass production, mass consumption, and mass disposal, and by developing consumer materials highly necessary for life, and trying to solve problems of health, environment and safety, as well as members purchasing goods."[80]

The Seikatsu Club is involved in organizing against genetically modified food and unsafe or unsustainable food practices within Japan and internationally. Such advocacy work has led to the mobilization of co-op members to run as political candidates. These cooperators, mostly women, have succeeded in getting elected to municipal councils throughout Japan. The cooperative movement maintains political neutrality by not backing a particular party, but the presence of its members in official decision-making roles means that the Seikatsu Club can manifest its commitment to food security, social welfare, and environmental protection.[81] In the final example, we look at the history and present-day conditions of Black cooperation in the United States, taking inspiration from this community's ongoing embrace of cooperation as a tool of self-determination.

Cooperation against Racial Oppression

One of the most pernicious myths about cooperation in the United States is that Black Americans do not, or cannot, sustain cooperative businesses. In my research, more than one person blamed the failure of cooperative ventures set in Black neighborhoods on the inability of the population to understand or support cooperatives. Contradicting this view are inspiring examples around the country of Black cooperation, including the worker-owned grocery Mandela Foods in Oakland, California, the regional Federation of Southern Cooperatives, and the determination of the people of Jackson, Mississippi, to build a comprehensive cooperative economy. Each of these contemporary beacons of Black cooperation owes a debt to the history of cooperative organizing in America dating back to before the Civil War. Some of this activity originally derives from communal forms of business among the Bantu tribes in southern Africa, inspiring similar behavior throughout the Black diaspora.[82]

Until recently, the history of Black cooperation was fragmentary and largely hidden from view. The determined scholarship of Jessica Gordon Nembhard systematically assembles this history and documents how Black cooperative thought and practice developed over America's history.[83] Her work demonstrates how cooperation worked even in the era of slavery, including mutual aid societies among enslaved peoples, communes of runaways from enslavement, and cooperation with abolitionists to support the development of communes for freed Black Americans.

Over time, Black cooperation grew and diversified. Much of the growth was fueled by study circles and community training courses in which Black cooperatives imbibed the history, philosophy, and methods of the pioneers of cooperation. This focus on education led to the creation of Black housing cooperatives, credit unions, consumer cooperatives, and worker-owned businesses from Harlem to Gary, Indiana. In the case of consumer cooperation, organizers insisted on the primacy of race, rather than class, in their analysis; this led them to create separate structures outside of mainstream white organizations and unions.[84]

Some of the greatest thinkers in Black history advocated cooperation as a means of economic and racial uplift. The American movement was guided for a time by W. E. B. Du Bois, who used the pages of *The Crisis,* the monthly journal of the National Association for the Advancement of Colored People, to challenge the prevailing economic system through cooperation. Black women organizers, including Ella Jo Baker and Fannie Lou Hamer, were responsible for vital work in the cooperative movement.[85]

Black cooperation also plays a vital role in the economy of the Americas more broadly. Extending beyond the United States, Caroline Shenaz Hossein's work documents how Black people have reoriented the economy to be inclusive of their needs, even at tremendous risk to themselves. She argues that anti-Black oppression is particularly egregious in the Americas because of the legacy of slavery, colonialism, and persistent racism. And yet, Black social economies in the Americas have thrived since before European cooperative development. The work of Hossein and her colleagues works to redress the lack of Black voices in the community and social economies literature.[86]

One example of Black social cooperation is the use of the *susu,* or rotating savings and credit association. These money pools consist of people, usually women, who get together and contribute an equal amount of money into a fund on a weekly or monthly basis. The total pool of money, or "hand," is paid to one member at a time on a previously determined schedule. The pool rotates until all the money is paid out, at which point it may begin again. Susus are based on trust, mutual respect, and mutual aid. They are a response to mistrust or outright exclusion from the formal banking sector. The concept originated in West Africa and is known by many names throughout African and Caribbean countries. It is used in North America today by women who seek to practice grassroots economic cooperation to achieve their personal and community goals.[87]

Black cooperation often confronts white racism and white supremacy, whether arising from being shut out of the nascent organized labor movement or explicitly violent attempts to shut down Black economic self-determination. These outside forces, coupled with a desire to encourage racial solidarity, led the Black cooperative movement to sometimes operate out of sight of the white cooperative world and thus seem less than visible. This focus on self-determination may partly explain why non-Black cooperators in the 2010s scoffed at the suggestion that Black consumers or organizers lacked the capacity to succeed.

The many examples of contemporary cooperation among Black communities and other communities of color constitute convincing empirical evidence to offset those misguided assumptions. Indeed, people of color and women are responsible for much of the recent growth in the cooperative economy.[88] The Black Lives Matter movement recommends cooperative development as a core plank of its economic justice policy platform. National political figures like Bernie Sanders and Kirsten Gillibrand of New York support worker co-ops and have proposed legislation that increases worker control of companies.

Communities of color are not waiting for a national sea change; they are building the cooperative economy themselves in real time. In Oakland, California, the worker-owned Mandela Grocery Cooperative recently celebrated ten years in business and announced plans to expand to a second location. The Black-led cooperative is thinking carefully about how to navigate expansion amid the gentrification of the Bay Area while remaining true to its politics. In Jackson, Mississippi, activists from the New Afrikan People's Organization and Malcolm X Grassroots Movement work alongside Mayor Chokwe Antar Lumumba to remake the city along cooperative lines in a project called Cooperation Jackson. Their goal is the creation of a federation of cooperatives, a cooperative incubator, school and training center, and a cooperative bank.[89]

But the work of creating a people-of-color-led cooperative system is as difficult as it is ambitious. The activists behind Cooperation Jackson have tempered their goals with a dose of reality, admitting that it will take up to ten years to create the cooperatives they envision. Other cooperatives have not been able to fully realize their vision. Renaissance Community Cooperative was a community-led solution to the problem of lack of fresh food availability in downtown Greensboro, North Carolina. Despite national attention and strong early sales, it closed after just three years in business. Nevertheless, all of these businesses help change the narrative of the current United States cooperative movement, which is dominated by white voices.[90] Their examples strengthen the cooperative movement, as people of color and low income take charge in organizing the cooperative economy.

Philadelphia, a Cooperative City

Philadelphia, where I live, has long been a hub for cooperative development, dating back to Indigenous practices that predate the colonial period. The cooperative tradition in Philadelphia is still going strong. Today, the Philadelphia Area Cooperative Alliance (PACA) is a co-op that supports the ongoing development of the cooperative economy in the Philadelphia region. PACA was started in 2011 by a grassroots coalition of members from a range of local co-ops. Today, PACA has about a dozen cooperative organizations as members, while several new start-up co-ops are in the process of coming onboard. PACA offers its members networking opportunities, educational programs, and technical assistance with business plans, governance issues, and fundraising. As a result of their membership in the same organization, co-ops have started to collaborate, including making loans and donations to one another, producing promotional material for one another, and more, all on the basis of the established principle of cooperation among co-ops. In addition to serving the needs of existing co-ops, PACA runs a Cooperative Leadership Institute, which teaches the core values, principles, and skills found in cooperative practices to leaders from nonprofit and for-profit businesses, as well as co-ops. By pooling resources to invest in the cooperative economy, the members of PACA make thoughtful use of their social surplus.

In its most inventive program, PACA obtained philanthropic funding to run a program in 2016 called 20 Book Clubs → 20 Cooperative Businesses. This program was inspired by the co-op study circles that form the basis of considerable organizing throughout co-op history, particularly among Black groups.[91] For 20 Book Clubs, PACA worked intensively for a year with aspiring cooperators, derived mostly from historically exploited communities of color. Members of the book clubs included the Black- and Brown-led radical gardening coalition called Soil Generation, an aspiring worker cooperative of Mexican immigrant construction workers, and the Refugee Women's Textile Cooperative. After six months of study, groups that were prepared to move forward with starting a business received training, technical assistance, and seed funding. At the program's conclusion, 185 people had participated, and seven new cooperative businesses were operating because of their participation in PACA's study circles.

PACA partners with the City of Philadelphia's Commerce Department as part of its ongoing quest to raise resources to strengthen the local co-op sector. Commerce supports PACA's mission to cultivate start-ups, as well as convert existing businesses to cooperatives. The latter issue presents a unique opportunity. In Philadelphia and elsewhere in the United States, many small businesses are sole proprietorships, run by aging entrepreneurs. This state of affairs has led to concern that when these entrepreneurs are no longer able to run the business—they do not often get to retire—the business will shut down, stranding the employees and leaving a gap in the city's retail fabric. This wave of baby boomer business retirement has been termed the "silver tsunami."[92] In 2018, the National League of Cities (an advocacy organization) and the Democracy at Work Institute (an organization that promotes worker-owned cooperatives) established the Shared Equity in Economic Development (SEED) Fellowship. PACA and the Commerce Department—along with similar partnerships in Miami, Atlanta, and Durham—work together to research and target opportunities on commercial corridors for co-op conversion. This project (in which I served on the Philadelphia advisory board) forms part of a broader equitable economic development strategy, promoting worker agency, job creation, and local economic development.

PACA is the latest addition to a rich history of support for cooperative development in Philadelphia. From 1939 to 1952, there was a local federation of food cooperatives called the Philadelphia Area Cooperative Federation. Like PACA, it supported new co-op development, provided training and bookkeeping services, and fostered collaboration among its members. This pioneering organization was led for a time by the fascinating historical figure Mary Ellicott Arnold. In addition to co-op organizing in Philadelphia, Arnold served as the treasurer for the Cooperative League of the USA and organized cooperative housing and credit unions among miners and fisherman in Nova Scotia in the 1930s.[93] In the 1980s, there was another effort at co-op organizing in Philadelphia: the Philadelphia Association for Cooperative Enterprise, which focused on worker cooperatives. This group helped convert two former A&P grocery stores into O&O (Owned and Operated) Supermarkets. Finally, since 2010, the Mid-Atlantic Food Cooperative

Alliance has coordinated the efforts of thirty-nine food co-ops, buying clubs, and start-ups across six states.

These efforts are not limited to Philadelphia. Since 1979, the Northwest Cooperative Development Center has organized co-ops in Oregon, Washington, and Idaho. In the Northeast, the Cooperative Development Institute has developed new co-ops and supported existing ones since 1994. Similar to PACA, the Cooperative Economics Alliance of New York City seeks to close the racial and gender wealth gap through peer education, training, technical assistance, and antiracism and antigentrification training. These are some but not all of the examples of organizations working to scale up and federate the cooperative economy in the United States.

RECONSTRUCTING THE ECONOMY

Over the course of this chapter, I have outlined some foundational concepts about cooperatives, as well as the ways they are made manifest in different parts of the world and at different times. Before transitioning to the rest of the book, in which specific Philadelphia and United States case studies will take center stage, I want to make four observations about cooperatives that will help contextualize the rest of what is to come. First, cooperation is a tradition with histories of its own. From the Iroquois and Benjamin Franklin in the land now called the United States, to the emergence of cooperation in Western Europe in the mid-nineteenth century, to the African and Caribbean diasporic traditions of cooperation, there is a plethora of historical reference points that demonstrate the long-standing popularity of cooperation. Tradition can serve as an inspiration and a guide, as well as a place from which to depart, as I will show in the upcoming chapters. Cooperative traditions have much to offer today's practitioners. Second, cooperation is a global project that can emerge and thrive in any region or economic set of conditions. From the Basque region of Spain to the cities of Japan, cooperation thrives in diverse geographic contexts. There are rural and urban cooperatives, serving farmers, rural utility customers, urban grocery shoppers, and childcare workers. This model is able to thrive in a variety of locales, adapting for circumstance. Third, cooperation is more than marginal. There are places and times when it emerges with more force and visibility, but cooperatives claim a large share of the planet's inhabitants in their projects. Finally, cooperation is flexible. There is more than one way to effect social and economic change through cooperative methods. I have showcased just a minute sampling of the range of cooperatives in the world, and their diversity of approaches is part of their strength.

Nevertheless, looking around at the mainstream of the United States' political economy, times can seem rather rough. Hopefully, a more just economic future lies ahead. But there is no time to sit back and wait for it; a future of economic empowerment is everyone's collective responsibility. Even in the precarious sharing economy, cooperators are making their stand. In response to the failures of the sharing economy to advance collective liberation, some have turned to making the sharing economy a more cooperative space. The movement behind platform cooperativism is an innovative international consortium set up to harness the technological innovations made possible by internet and smartphone connectivity in service of a fairer economy. The Platform Cooperativism Consortium (platform.coop) connects and promotes projects such as taxicab cooperatives that design their own apps or task services where users buy labor from worker cooperatives. (Though the corporate sharing economy behemoths like Uber have the backing of Silicon Valley and hedge funds, the internet was built on the back of open source code and other forms of real sharing.) The platform cooperative movement seeks to return the internet to a place of liberation. Cooperation of this kind draws from a long history, an international reputation, and growing momentum among young progressive groups like the Movement for Black Lives and the Democratic Socialists of America, who cite support for cooperatives as a key plank of their policy platforms.

One way to address the growing dearth of democracy and equality is to first admit that something went fundamentally wrong a long time ago in the guise of modern liberal individualism. As I will show in the next chapter, the reconstruction of society begins with the reconstruction of the self.[94] American pragmatist philosopher George Herbert Mead explains that "social reconstruction and self or personality reconstruction are the two sides of a single process—the process of human social evolution."[95] To fix something so thoroughly broken, we need to move to a cooperative paradigm. Cooperation, a dominant activity extending back to the Enlightenment and forward to the diverse economies program championed by Gibson-Graham, must be thought of as an ongoing social practice. This book offers an ethical and practical guide to cooperative practice, undertaken through scrutiny and careful reflection. It attempts to seize David Ruccio's utopian moment and offer a critique of existing practice and pragmatic solutions to the challenges of cooperation.

Such a move requires a fundamental reorientation to our reality at a variety of scales where neoliberal capitalism has pulled the wool over our eyes. It is beneficial to think at the scale of the body and the importance of embodied emotion in governing our lives. It is urgent to think about labor as a cooperative practice, as this chapter's discussion of the sharing economy makes plain. It is necessary to think about how cooperation scales up in the economy, from the way retail co-ops can anchor neighborhood commercial corridors to the way co-ops like Mondragon transform whole regions. And finally, it is possible to think about our cooperative democracy in an era where individualism reigns supreme in political life and polarization is the norm. The rest of this book is organized along these four scales, tracing a critical path through the practice of cooperation, in pursuit of a focused understanding of what it takes to empower a cooperative future. But in order to undertake that journey, there are some helpful conceptual tools that I will present in the next chapter. These include a social conception of the self, a focus on practices, and an awareness of the diversity of economic possibility to undergird cooperative practice.

TOOLS FOR THE JOURNEY

The chapters that follow examine the practice of cooperation at a variety of scales through a deep dive into several examples of cooperative projects in the United States. In order to make sense of these cases, I will set forth some tools to help frame an understanding of what is to come. These conceptual tools are meant to inspire a more expansive awareness of what the cases represent. Armed in this way, it becomes possible to see the cases not as disparate and eclectic examples of practice, but as united by several core qualities. This chapter serves as an entryway into these ideas, which will reappear throughout the book. (In particular, I will elaborate on discussions of practice in chapter 4 and on diverse economies in chapter 5.)

The first conceptual tool is a critique of modern liberal individualism. All of the projects in this book proceed from a critical awareness that individualism pervades modern social and economic life, encouraging competitiveness and discouraging thoroughgoing cooperation. As I maintain below, one can live as an individual, with hard-won rights and responsibilities, without subscribing to a doctrine of individualism. This leads to the second conceptual tool: the notion of a social self. The idea of the social self is a different way of understanding individuality and collectivity. There is no standpoint from which people are truly separate, atomistic beings. The social self is an alternate conception of human existence that asserts that identity itself is socially constituted. As beings who possess a social self, we are mutually interdependent, and it is incumbent upon us to build relationships, institutions, and systems that proceed from that understanding.

The third conceptual tool proceeds from this assumption and holds that ethical economies can be built within and beyond capitalism. The projects profiled in this book fall under such a notion of diverse economic practices, giving the lie to the assumption that capitalist logic is all-encompassing and that there is no other way to organize ourselves as social beings. The final conceptual tool, the practice perspective, maintains that ethical community life is based on sustained, complex forms of association known as practices. Practices are specific to a given time and place, derived from traditions, and based in shared narratives. Through practices, it is possible to pursue democratic, just, and inclusive ends.

A cardinal goal of this chapter is to inspire reflection and introspection. How do these ideas help reframe received understandings about the way things are, the way things have to be? Where do they offer opportunities for a revised, enhanced understanding of social and economic life that holds out more hope and possibility for productive change? In what ways do they inspire? These are the tools I set forth to power the journey of ethical cooperation across a variety of scales that forms the basis of the rest of the book.

RUGGED (RAGGED?) INDIVIDUALISM

For hundreds of years, the United States been in thrall to an ideal of rugged individualism. Individualism elevates the self-as-atom, someone who engages in social relationships in a self-interested and transactional way. This concept of the world leaves little room for real cooperation. Individualism has seeped into our politics and the culture at large, and it has gained legitimacy partly through its promotion by mainstream economists, who are often highly influential in policymaking.[1] The only kind of cooperation they promote is the kind of self-interested cooperation demonstrated by famous simulations like the prisoner's dilemma.

In the classic formulation of the prisoner's dilemma, two players are pitted against one another in an imaginary jailhouse interrogation and have to determine whether it is in their rational self-interest to cooperate or betray one another. The classic formulation of this game tacks on theoretical punishments that get more severe if the two players opt for betrayal.[2] The whole framework of the prisoner's dilemma is based on uncertainty, fear, silence, and retribution. While provocative as a game theory version of human behavior, critics of the prisoner's dilemma have pointed out that the real world does not rest on narrowly rationalistic foundations.

Once such critic, political theorist Michael Taylor (a reformed practitioner of this kind of rational choice economics), came to see the inaccuracy, even the danger, of seeing the world like a game of prisoner's dilemma. His work opens a window into the work of rational choice thinkers, explaining, "The economists don't just use the standard model of Rational Choice to explain behavior; they idealize a world . . . in which there is no normativity and no moral motivation . . . no framing or structuring ideals, and whose inhabitants therefore lack identities."[3] In this ideal world, rugged, rational individuals think only like consumers, making a constant cost-benefit analysis that values everything based on the utility it offers. Individuals are only motivated by incentives or sanctions on their behavior, not morality or care. Every kind of decision is subject to a calculus of utility, whether marriage, crime, immigration, education, or any other aspect of social life.[4] The idealization of a world without moral motivations has distressing consequences for the care of people and animals, as well as the environment. According to Taylor, educating individuals to believe they are merely rational and autonomous maximizers of utility encourages them to live their lives this way and fosters a world where the "integrity or coherence of people's lives, communities, and ecosystems would be lost or gravely weakened."[5]

Another term for this rational individual is *Homo economicus*, literally "economic man." We are surrounded by narratives of this economic man, whether it is the supposed job creator at the top of the economic pyramid who deserves massive tax breaks (whether or not they created any jobs) or the idealized gig economy worker, who is pleased as punch to be driving for Uber to add spending money to their retirement years. To many of us, these depictions of economic life appear false. But where do these ideas originate?

According to moral philosopher Alasdair MacIntyre, modern political and social disconnection is symptomatic of a long-term decline in our society that began as far back as the eighteenth-century Enlightenment, when modern liberal individualism was born. European and American society became wedded to individual achievement, to looking out for ourselves and our own, and not to any sort of communal project steeped in a moral tradition.[6] Political economist Karl Polanyi traces the problem even further back in history, to the enclosures of common lands in sixteenth-century England, when landowners privatized the common lands, leading to mass physical and economic displacement.[7] From this first "great abdication" of social responsibility, as John Dewey puts it, to the dystopian present, a disconnect between individual and social responsibility is at the center.[8]

Such a critique of individualism does not mean that individual identity or achievement is unimportant. Humans exist in social settings and respond to them, but have freedom of choice in how to respond and which course of action to select as individuals. Both community and individual autonomy are necessary to staking out identity. The development of the concept of the individual led to breakthroughs like universal suffrage and liberation from a feudal economic system. Indeed, the value of individual liberty as freedom from tyranny cannot be overstated. But individualism as freedom from oppression falls short of figuring out the kind of social and economic organization society needs to thrive. It leads toward the valorization of wealth acquisition and a politics of the personal above all else. It leads to the push of a button on a smartphone app by a consumer who sees no connection to the consequences free same-day delivery may have on a real human worker. The point I am making is that one can still be an individual without being individualist. A cooperative politics understands the individual differently—as a social self.

ORIGINS OF THE SOCIAL SELF

The notion of the social self can be traced to the work of pragmatist philosopher George Herbert Mead. The social self represents a fundamental reorientation to identity, which is a necessary precursor to an understanding of the practice of cooperation. Mead argues that the human self is not initially present at birth but arises through social experience. During systematic interactions with others, an individual begins to emerge, learning to view herself from the perspective of others. This creates a self-awareness that is fundamental to functioning in the world. Language, games, and play are all forms of symbolic interaction that teach the individual how to relate to others and themselves. When they are sufficiently socialized, they can engage in social projects and goals in appropriate and productive ways.[9]

Feminist theorists like Marilyn Friedman and Jane Mansbridge have also endorsed the social self as a counterpoint to individualism. They observe that individualism seems to ignore dependence in favor of self-sufficiency and separation from others, instead of prizing connection and care. For women, who have often held positions of caretaking, identity configured this way rings both false and irresponsible. Such an individualism denigrates the work that women often do and suppresses the values of love and solidarity that undergird such labor.[10] Rather than repudiating the possibilities inherent in autonomy, some feminists call for a form of relational autonomy that recognizes the social complexity of identity while still calling for self-determination and an end to oppression on gender or racial grounds.[11]

The social self participates in a web of relationships that structure experience in a variety of areas. Economic geographers J. K. Gibson-Graham ask us to consider the individual as an interdependent economic subject, capable of contributing to a new understanding and configuration of economy. In this type of public, shared activity, we must recover a sense of being-together and "proper plural singular co-essence."[12] This requires, as Jean-Luc Nancy explains, a totally new beginning for philosophy and practice, because being-together has been so thoroughly suppressed as a way of understanding experience.[13] Yet how can we refocus on sociality when the language of individualism has become dominant? One requirement is to tell stories to one another and begin to solve the problem of empathy and connection. Being-in-common has a manifestly narrative dimension, as living together requires language to shape social interactions. A concern with narrative has frequently traveled alongside a concern for shaking off the shackles of individualism and embracing cooperation.

Back in the 1930s, John Dewey lamented the tragedy of the "lost individual," who participates in many social arrangements and associations but lacks "harmonious and coherent reflection of the import of these connections into the imaginative and emotional outlook on life."[14] In short, the lost individual lacks narrative coherence. Such individuals act as selves with no history and no context. The possession of a historical identity and the possession of a social identity coincide.[15] Our origins and our relationships are important shapers of our narratives. A sense of history and tradition is paramount. Rather than paying unthinking homage to the families, faiths, and communities from which we arise, we should remain aware and integrate our origins into our present self-understanding. That does not mean we have to remain on the same trajectory, or around the same people, from which we started. Authoring new narratives as a means of rebelling against an identity is a perfectly valid mode of self-expression. As James Baldwin observes, "To accept one's past—one's history—is not the same thing as drowning in it; it is learning how to use it."[16]

Michael Taylor found out the importance of narrative the hard way—in the economics lab. He relates that when players of the prisoner's dilemma are allowed to discuss the dilemma before making their choices, cooperation significantly increases.[17] He concludes that any understanding of behavior must pay attention to stories about real life. Indeed, we tell ourselves stories in order to live, as Joan Didion famously said.[18] A life well lived is a life rich in narrative, embedded in social practice. The practice of cooperation offers a renewed economic and societal narrative, one built with a deep embrace of the social self. Rather than an individualist war of all against all, cooperation challenges and points toward the highest human potential. This potential, in all its manifestations, can be seen in the diversity of social and economic relationships that challenge the domination of an individualist, capitalist view of human activity. In the next section, I turn to the work of the diverse economies body of scholarship to elaborate the contours of that potential.

DIVERSE ECONOMIES AND THE ROLE OF COOPERATION

Diverse economies research makes visible the myriad ways in which economic relationships occur. Around and in-between the spaces of contemporary capitalism, there are solidarity economies, gift economies, cooperative economies, and so on. The diverse economies project aims to catalog, advance, and critique these different social and economic arrangements. This approach offers an opportunity to debate, contest, and ultimately experiment with the form our economy takes. Otherwise, we are forced to accept the domination of capitalism as given and immutable. As Gibson-Graham explain, the diverse economies framework "refuses to pose economic power as already distributed to capitalist interests and opens up the possibility for non-capitalist practices to be the focus for an invigorated economic politics."[19] This is a radical project seeking to uproot settled ways of thinking and doing economy. The diverse economies effort grew from Marxist and feminist traditions, but it is not content to wait for a political revolution. Instead, diverse economies researchers seek to advance the many small ways practitioners revolutionize their worlds each day. By promoting this work, even in a critical way, it is possible to manifest a very different future.

There is a large and growing literature on diverse economies, and though I will not try to summarize it all here, I will go into greater depth on diverse economies later in the book. But there are a number of elements I find especially useful. These elements include a focus on possibilities rather than limits; thoughtful discussions on the multiple scales on which economy takes place; the importance of collective action; and a vision of the individual self that emphasizes its social nature. As a way of grounding this project in such important work, I will talk about each of these in turn and how it speaks to the practice of cooperation.

A key element of the diverse economies project is its focus on possibilities rather than limits. For instance, when talking about the work of slum dwellers in India (who face enormous obstacles to alleviating poverty), Gibson-Graham explain, "While they expect to confront obstacles, difficulties, threats of annihilation, and co-optation, they treat these as everyday political challenges rather than as limits to politics."[20] There is no doubt that our actions are constrained by circumstance; the goal is to recognize which of these limits can be overcome by determined and sustained practice. The work of building community economy is not a settled project. It is ongoing and unfinished. Along the way, there will be stumbles, even failures.

In light of the constant barrage of distressing news available on any given cable channel or internet portal, Gibson-Graham offer an invigorating counternarrative. Diverse economies research is avowedly hopeful in the face of the increased scope and velocity of oppressive and exploitative activity. Jeff Popke sees it as a new way of seeing what was already there and giving it new value: "We are perhaps just learning to see differently, to be more attuned to the ways in which the in-common is always already a collective performance, brimming with affect, care and hidden potentialities."[21] This hope is not born of ignorance of the challenges, but it refuses to ignore the practices that inspire hope. It is this quality of caring and mutual aid that this book seeks to foster. In this way, diverse economies research represents a project deeply concerned with ethics, a relationship that I explore in more depth in chapter 4.

The diverse economies approach has faced its share of criticism, partly because of a perception of reflexive optimism. Diverse economies scholar Peter North draws a distinction between an ethics of hope versus uncritical optimism. He argues that postcapitalist politics looks at conditions of possibility, focusing on the "perhaps" not the "probable," in order to encourage more hopeful developments in the future.[22] A related criticism charges that diverse economies research attempts to merely think itself out of the dominance and materiality of capitalism. Changing thought and discourse are important steps in manifesting a more just and sustainable future, but thought alone is not enough. In recent years, diverse economies researchers have devoted considerable attention to exploring the strengths and weaknesses of actual material practices in the world.[23]

Many researchers who study political economy see any research that is not framed in terms of totalizing narratives like globalization and capitalism as theoretically weak and politically unserious.[24] Gibson-Graham push back on such concerns, citing the importance of examining the diversity of existing practices, which provide very real sources of material support to communities around the world. Instead of falling into the trap of looking for a totalizing theory of economic behavior, Gibson-Graham emphasize diverse economies as "weak theory." Weak theory draws explanatory power by questioning the naturalness and dominance of capitalism through attention to specific geographies and histories, rather than looking for a grand unified theory of everything.[25]

Despite Gibson-Graham's call for focus on specific geography and history, some critics take diverse economies research to task for lacking such a focus. Lack of attention to historical-geographic contexts can produce ahistorical narratives that portray such practices as (merely) contemporary phenomena.[26] I have demonstrated in the preceding chapter that cooperative practice stems from a number of cultural traditions and spans centuries. As with most forms of nonmainstream economic practice, cooperative subjects can draw from various examples and trajectories to inspire contemporary movements.

In the same vein, there are concerns about a dearth of attention to power relations and gendered positions within diverse economies research.[27] Just as capitalist structures should be subject to critique, so should diverse economic practices. Indeed, any catalog of diverse economies will turn up examples of coercion, oppression, and disadvantage alongside examples that inspire. With my focus on the paradox of exclusivity in the cooperative spaces I profile, I contribute positively to a politically robust analysis of cooperative practice.

Gibson-Graham's work has been seen as uncritical praise of the local, small-scale, and noncapitalist practices they encounter. But there is a difference between reflexively valuing anything that is local and postcapitalist versus looking for hopeful examples and subjecting them to critical evaluation. Negative conditions exist and they are deserving of attention; this alone is not cause for skepticism of the diverse economies project. This book tries to walk that fine line, searching for the value in the practice of cooperation, while looking for ways to make the cooperation more just and more effective through careful analysis. One way to begin that journey toward justice is to start with a cooperative vision of the self that values interdependence and mutuality.

The diverse economies framework offers a vision of the human self that is thoroughly compatible with a cooperative vision. An understanding of the self as fundamentally social is an important precursor for understanding the ways in which cooperation ought to be thought about and put into practice. Gibson-Graham emphasize a "being-in-common" as opposed to a solitary individual essence. Being together in the world ought to be a "ground for thought or politics" rather than a challenge to be overcome on the road to building political coalitions.[28] This effort toward being-in-common should not be confused with localism or tribalism. There is nothing inherently just about any given manifestation of collectivity. Rather, the goal is to find common ground through social and economic projects that unite us collectively in a variety of ways. It is possible to live together differently, with more empathy, if we cultivate a collective body, infused with feeling, derived from relationships in the world.[29]

Building on this notion of collectivity, diverse economy scholars elaborate the notion of "cooperative subjects"—subjects who move beyond the binary constraints of either making a fortune or rejecting capitalism outright.[30] Instead, these cooperative subjects are pragmatists, seeking strategies and tactics that sustain the cooperative project, independent of their ideological origins. Cooperative subjects seek autonomy and freedom in their workplaces rather than looking to capitalist owners for direction. They determine how any surplus is allocated and open up collaborative spaces of governance. The radicalism of their approach lies in its nondogmatic pursuit of economic democracy in the here and now. Working together as cooperative subjects can take a variety of forms and is fundamentally flexible. The work of developing cooperative subjects also aids in the development of cooperative firms and movements. Therefore, cooperation in the community economy ought to be seen as "the praxis of coexistence and interdependence."[31]

Over the past twenty-five years, Gibson-Graham and other diverse economies researchers have counted cooperatives as one of the most prominent ways in which to practice an alternative to capitalism. Much of this work has focused on worker cooperatives, notably through case studies of worker-ownership in Mondragon in the Basque region of Spain. This book examines a variety of cooperative projects, from consumer-owned grocers in Philadelphia, to a large federation of community-based acupuncture clinics, to an arts collective that uses principles shared with cooperatives but operates outside the cooperative business form. My goal in exploring cooperation is to apply diverse economies thinking to a broad range of practices in order to provoke and inspire cooperators and those who think carefully about cooperation.

In addition to this dialogue with diverse economies, there is another perspective that I want to offer: the theory of practices as outlined by moral philosopher Alasdair MacIntyre, which I discuss in the next section. One of the best ways I know to give more power to the work of Gibson-Graham is to place it in provocative conversation with other ideas. The practice perspective shares with diverse economies the desire to recognize both the shortcomings of our current set of social arrangements and the potential transformation that lies in rethinking them.

THE PRACTICE PERSPECTIVE

A cornerstone of this book is that social and economic cooperation is a practice. The cooperative impulse needs to be fostered through repetition over time, like a muscle that gets strengthened by exercise. When it comes to noncooperative social and economic activities, these are too often governed (at least in the United States) by a drive toward individual achievement, a jockeying for position and recognition, and hoarding of its spoils. Cooperation, at its best, stands opposed to all that. It does not negate the importance of individual contributions, nor does it ignore the importance of achieving success. Yet it frames success as a collective enterprise, something that cannot be garnered alone. In order to fully explore the notion of cooperation as a practice, it is important to have a thorough sense of what practices are. The work of practice theorists is helpful in generating a deep awareness of the meaning and urgency of socially responsible cooperative practices.

It is difficult to articulate which shared social activities constitute a practice. A baseline definition suggests: "Let practices be socially recognized forms of activity, done on the basis of what members learn from others, and capable of being done well or badly, correctly or incorrectly."[32] A central aspect of this definition is the project of mutual learning that a practice engenders. A secondary characteristic is the notion that a practice can be executed well or poorly. The performance of a practice depends on embodied knowledge (as I will demonstrate in chapter 3), skill, and material resources that become inscribed in bodies, artifacts, and things.[33] Certainly, cooperation fails when it is plagued by exclusivity, poor management, or pursues socially unjust ends (such as economic cartels or organized crime). To succeed as a virtuous practice, it needs to be the product of shared, ongoing learning that takes into account the ways in which it inevitably falls short of its ideal. (I talk more about virtue and organization in chapter 4.) This book is very interested in the gaps between cooperative practice and cooperative ideals.

There has been a call to juxtapose practice theory with diverse economies research into a "diverse practices" framework. Each has the potential to complement the other and address its conceptual shortcomings. Practice theory adds to the diverse economies framework a focus on the importance of everyday practices and how those routines are built into institutions and movements. Diverse economy research adds to the practice framework by exposing the ethical and political entanglements of routinized practices.[34] By bringing power into the equation, diverse economies counterbalances one of the main critiques of a focus on practices. The benefit of combining these two approaches is the ability to speak to a politics of transformation. Both the diverse economies and practice approaches focus on the prefiguration of a more equitable future while "sticking close to the phenomena under study and avoiding overwhelming theoretical foreshadowing."[35]

While there are a number of theoretical avenues to explore regarding practices, one of the most generative is the work of Scottish American moral philosopher Alasdair MacIntyre. Unlike some of the more utilitarian strains of practice scholarship discussed above, which evade critical discussions of capitalism, MacIntyre situates his whole project as a reaction to the problems created by a capitalist (and individualist) political economy. MacIntyre's attention to narrative as a key tool for both understanding and transformation closely aligns his approach with Gibson-Graham's work on discourse. In MacIntyre's work, practices must be situated in a tradition and a narrative, allowing for ample critique of those ideas and constructs that have been received from prior eras and discursive tropes.

In his wide-ranging critique of individualism in his landmark book *After Virtue* and other works, MacIntyre arrives at practices as a solution to the problems of that individualist worldview. Practices, when executed well, also bring into being a more just society. Along with a broader incorporation of practice theory, it is useful for the diverse economies framework to incorporate the provocation of MacIntyre's thought as a means of scrutinizing the kinds of activities that animate a more just economy and society.

Writing forty years ago, MacIntyre recognized the same sorts of political, economic, and social dysfunction that we see today. At the time, he traced the root of much of our turmoil to our society's inability to communicate. He said contemporary discourse was marred by intense disagreements. He found these disagreements "interminable," meaning both that they go on and on and that they can find no resolution. Our failure to communicate can be traced to the incommensurable nature of our discussions. We are not even in the same book, much less on the same page. Yet we all insist that we are being perfectly rational, while it is the other side that has the problem. We use force and rancor to convey our ideas, ideas that we believe to be totally natural and self-evidently justified.

This trouble seeing eye to eye is symptomatic of a long-term decline in our society that began as far back as the eighteenth-century Enlightenment, a time when modern liberal individualism was born. European and American societies became wedded to individual achievement, to looking out for ourselves and our own, and not to any sort of communal project steeped in a moral tradition.

But this is fixable—and projects like the ones profiled in this book are part of the solution. What will it take to fix these issues? There needs to be some sort of reinvestment in sustained, complex communal projects, or what MacIntyre calls "practices." The goal of practices is to cultivate virtue, a word that may be off-putting to some. But this vision of virtue is not the same as what many of us have been taught, which is to behave in ways that go against the grain of our being and our desires, because of something that traditional morality dictates us to do. This is not necessary according to MacIntyre, who emphasizes the importance of engaging in a communal search for the good life, for what is virtuous, by working "to achieve a common project, to bring about some good recognized as [the] shared good by all those engaging in the project."[36] For this transformation to occur, for virtue to be reinstated, three things need to happen: the building up of practices, the embedding of these practices in socially enacted narratives, and the connecting of all of this to relevant traditions.

For MacIntyre, a practice is a "coherent and complex form of socially established cooperative human activity."[37] These activities provide both internal and external benefits. The internal benefits are the ones that you derive simply from doing the thing itself, for its own sake. You learn chess to become good at chess, to train your mind, not to become rich and famous. The external benefits sometimes come—maybe you are really good at chess and win competitions all over the world. But the pursuit of virtue is all about achieving excellence for its own sake in these cooperative practices. These kinds of projects, undertaken in community, are the foundation of the good life.

To me, cooperative projects like the ones in this book are the ultimate form of practice. These projects form a critical "third way," one that is neither fundamentally capitalist nor socialist.[38] Cooperatives spur new narratives that propel us out of the conundrum of modern liberal individualism, out of our capitalocentric worldview; they guide us into emancipatory territory. Cooperatives have proven resilient in times of economic crisis.[39] Though cooperatives are not necessarily anticapitalist, diverse economies scholars have recognized that co-ops are able to contribute to critiques of capitalism by offering real world examples of sustainable organizations.

All human actions occur in narrative settings; humans are essentially storytelling animals. Any practice we undertake is part of the narrative of our life story. MacIntyre's key insight about narrative is this: "I can only answer the question 'What am I to do?' if I can answer the prior question 'Of what story or stories do I find myself a part?'"[40] The importance of storytelling and narrative to a project like this one cannot be overstated. As Gibson-Graham state: "Narratives and social representations of existing and potential alternatives to capitalism may begin to resonate, to generate affect, to interpolate subjects, to ignite desire."[41] The power of narrative is not passive; it is a tool for activating new ways of being in common.

The work of securing the place of practices in the transformation of society is to emphasize that nothing is done in isolation from anything else or anyone else. That work requires acknowledging our history and our accumulated debts. Traditions constitute the given of our lives and give us our moral particularity. This can be challenging in a society like America, where we want to believe we are all self-made and transcend where we came from. MacIntyre gives a few examples, like the white southerner who rejects reparations because she was not a slaveholder or the young German who feels no responsibility for the Holocaust because it occurred before his lifetime.

Individuals thus act as selves with no history. In a way, they are playing into the myth of individualism. Instead, MacIntyre urges us to own up to the connection between the story of our lives and broader stories, saying:

> For the story of my life is always embedded in the story of those communities from which I derive my identity. I am born with a past; and to try to cut myself off from the past, in the individualist mode, is to deform my present relationships. The possession of an historical identity and the possession of a social identity coincide.[42]

It is entirely possible, perhaps desirable, to rebel against tradition with all of its moral limitations. Traditions embody continuities of conflict, not forced, oppressive agreements that bound their participants against their will.[43] Tradition informs the way to conduct a life, as a jumping-off point. We are not bound to our traditions, we must only acknowledge their shaping power.

In sum, the effect of practices is self-transformation. Changing one's circumstance through changing the self is nothing short of transformative practice. But this change cannot occur simply through a change of heart. Transformative change can only come through new ways of getting things done, through an acquisition and deployment of particular skills.[44]

CONCLUSION

In this short chapter, I have offered a set of tools to guide readers through the rest of the journey of the book. By understanding the shortcomings of an individualist identity and worldview, I open space for possibility and hope that the world can work differently. An acknowledgment of a social ontology of self is a first step in the direction of recognizing the virtue of interdependence. A diverse economies approach offers a way of conceiving social and economic relations that moves beyond an individualistic, exploitative, capitalocentric worldview, in search of already existing examples of transformative practice taking place in the economy around us. The benefit of practice theory is a focus on everyday routines that are then built into bodies, institutions, and systems. By paying attention to the everyday sites of transformation, it is possible to encourage the expansion of equitable and sustainable practices. Combining the diverse economies and practice perspectives allows each to control for the possible shortcomings of the other and expands the power of the analysis.

Having laid out these useful tools, it is time to move to the core offerings of this book. Looking back to when I first got interested in cooperative practice, I had little idea of the rich history, the thorny practical challenges, or the dilemmas inherent in making them succeed. The rest of the book will delve into the complexities that each of the cases represent and follow them across scales as they seek to achieve their visions of a more equitable world.

PRACTICES OF THE BODY

It may not be a traditional co-op, but Headlong Dance Theater is a deeply cooperative enterprise. For twenty years, Headlong was managed collectively by three founding codirectors, who shared the administrative and the artistic work of sustaining the company. Headlong believed in building a cooperative community for dance in Philadelphia; a number of related artists and arts groups found their footing as a result of Headlong's mentorship and support. Headlong's story offers an example of grounding cooperation in the body as a foundational component of the making of cooperative subjects. Throughout this chapter, I rely on Headlong's and the other cases' experiences to demonstrate the power and pitfalls of the practice of embodied cooperation. Such bodily cooperation is intensely relational and serves as a form of proof that a social self undergirds cooperation, rather than the rational autonomous individuality of so much contemporary discourse and practice.

Headlong's story begins with emotions of hope, joy, and a sense of utopian possibility. The company was formed in 1993. Founding codirectors Andrew Simonet, Amy Smith, and David Brick met during college at Wesleyan University in rural Connecticut. Once they moved to Philly, their collaboration expressed itself through bodies in constant proximity: living, working, and dancing together. David recalled: "In the early days there was such an intensity to the dancing. We would have these parties sometimes three or four times a week in Old City that would go on until the wee hours of the morning. There would be hours of throwing yourself against the wall dancing."[1]

At first, the three Headlong codirectors made pieces with themselves as the principal dancers. Early work included *Permit,* in which dancers needed to receive permission from one another to make the next move. It was based on the sexual assault/consent policy at Wesleyan, an issue they tackled before such campus policies were a topic of widespread public conversation. *Take 3* featured the three codirectors dancing to music on Walkmans that only the dancers could hear and describing their contradictory interpretations and resulting movements. The work was inventive, provocative, and sometimes quite funny. Over the years, the company grew, becoming a nonprofit corporation, obtaining grant funding, and building a company of dancers.

Impressed by these qualities, I began to volunteer at Headlong in 2008 as a board member, before I thought of conducting systematic research on the practice of cooperation. As I started to think more broadly about the way cooperation works, I found myself wanting to add Headlong to the mix. It was an intuitive decision; though Headlong is not a co-op in the sense of collective ownership, it is a nonprofit that operates collectively. The participants pool their labor and the funds and make decisions collaboratively. That was certainly part of the appeal. But as I got to know Headlong better, there was something more that spoke to me, something that went beyond how Headlong is organized. I began to think about the nature of dance itself as cooperative enterprise. I wondered how Headlong embodied cooperation—as dancers, so much of their work celebrates and interrogates bodies. I began to wonder, what is the connection between cooperation and the body?

At first, it may seem contradictory. After all, bodies bound and delimit us from others. They are the containers we inhabit as individuals, while cooperation thrives on what is shared. Yet individual bodies do not operate in isolation from one another. Bodies come into intimate contact. Bodies are birthed from other bodies, bodies nurture other bodies to health, and bodies inflict violence on one another. This dialectical relationship between the individual body and cooperative practice intrigued me, and I wanted to ask Headlong about it.

In 2014, as I prepared to interview Headlong's codirectors, dancers, administrators, students, and supporters, I brought a tool with me: I printed an outline of a nongendered human body, seen from front and back, on a piece of paper. At the end of each interview, I asked the Headlong interviewees to draw how Headlong worked as a bodily phenomenon. I did not give them much guidance beyond that (and I felt like I was going out on a limb as a researcher), but I had an intuitive sense that this activity would speak to them. Without hesitation, each of the interviewees grabbed a pen and began drawing on the bodies, excitedly narrating as they went. Here are three of those participant drawings, with condensed excerpts from the narration. These reflections serve as an entrée into thinking about how cooperation works as a practice at the most intimate scale. Here I begin to make the case, elaborated in the rest of this chapter, that understanding cooperation begins by locating it in the body.

Hana's Headlong Body

Hana[2] is a theater artist and director, having trained in France and the United States. She has created pieces with Headlong and teaches in their Headlong Performance Institute (a training course for young creators, accredited for many years through Bryn Mawr College). When we spoke, Hana reflected as she drew on the body diagram (Figure 6):

> There is a lot of generosity and presence [in Headlong]. I do think they have an effect on the space around them [drawing outward directed lines around the left-hand figure]. There's this idea of really working with the back and seeing, "where is the back?" [indicating the eye drawn on the back of the right-hand figure's head]. Also

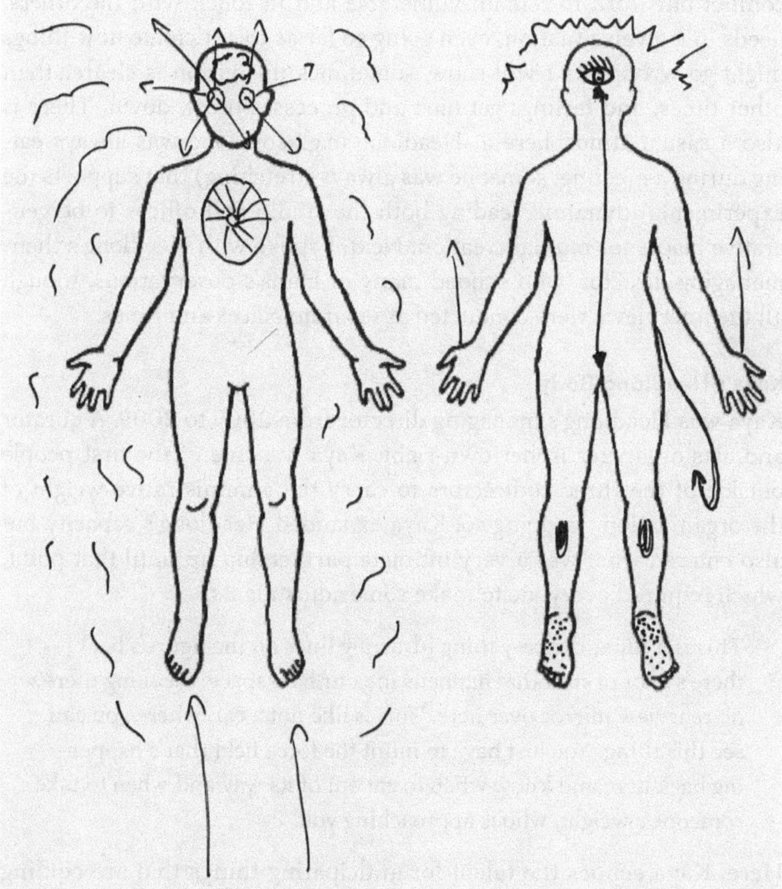

FIGURE 6. Hana's Headlong body illustration.

> [they are] really alert, this alertness in the whole body and then the whole dimension. The connection to something higher and also to the earth. Then there's also something super casual in their bodies, but it's always open and that's what I really get excited about. And then also sometimes it's very intellectual [drawing a little brain inside the left-hand figure].

Hana captured several key ideas about Headlong as an embodied phenomenon. The people involved in Headlong have a heightened awareness of, and sensitivity to, their surroundings—a kind of alertness to seeing around corners, even seeing behind their backs. In organizational practice, this translates to a strong commitment to emotional intelligence and sensitivity to group process. They do not shy away from conflict but work to remain vulnerable and in touch with the others' needs in a given situation, even going so far as to anticipate how things might go wrong. As I will show, sometimes this vision is clearer than other times, and feelings get hurt and processes break down. There is also a casual atmosphere at Headlong (e.g., someone was always eating during a meeting, someone was always stretching) that supports the experimental dynamic, leading both the studio and offices to be generative places for mutual creation. Next, I spoke with Headlong's then-managing director, who echoed many of Hana's observations, though all the interviews were conducted at separate places and times.

Kaya's Headlong Body

Kaya was Headlong's managing director from 2005 to 2009. A curator and arts organizer in her own right, Kaya was one of the first people outside of the three codirectors to carry the administrative weight of the organization. In doing so, Kaya expanded Headlong's capacity but also entered what was a very intimate partnership up until that point, which required everyone to make some adjustments.

> This is a super dance-y thing [drawing lines on the figure's back]—there's a lot of stuff that happens in your backspace, meaning there's no rearview mirror over here. This is like not a car, where you can see this thing. You just have to intuit the force field that's happening back here and know when to get out of its way and when to take someone's weight, who is approaching you.

Here, Kaya echoes the talent for anticipating things that are coming from other collaborators and to occasionally "take someone's weight" (in a dance context) or meet their needs in another way. She notes the challenge of not being able to see but needing to intuit what is happening all around. Kaya also drew a ground for the figures to relate to, noting that Headlong was not always the most grounded organization:

> The ground is over here [draws line at bottom of diagram to illustrate]. Some people are jumping away from it. Some people are hovering above it. The relationship to the ground is different depending on who the person is. I think that at different times, motivated by various factors that are more often emotional and occasionally really fear-based . . . people are hovering above it, making assumptions about things that were completely unrealistic or having a hard time rectifying the facts in front of us. That was because they were holding onto something that they desperately were interested in and that maybe was not possible.
>
> [Headlong is in an] intense period of growth. We're going to figure out how to remain on the ground but increase a lot of activity which is about this jumping away from the spot they were at for the sake of growth. We didn't just do this [indicating a straight line]. No organization does that. We kind of did *this*—that's my weird mountain system [stepped lines on the bottom left].
>
> So, yeah, figuring out how to both remain grounded then also want[ing] to experience something beyond that, and rectifying those two things with the—here I'll do it over here—the amount of work and time and just energy that is needed toward realizing something that's kind of a big, audacious goal. That's the difference between the jumping and the hovering.

Finally, Kaya noted that Headlong was suffused with love and care for the people involved, which had an influence on the place it occupied in the Philadelphia arts ecosystem:

> Around all of this, today and even then, and even when it was hard, especially when it was hard, there's just this huge sense of real care and consideration [draws lines toward heart and head] and love both of the community and the people who are there, and the city and their place that really, I think, influences, positive or negative, the ways in which business is conducted and the ways in which Headlong conducts itself in the city and within their company.

Like Hana, Kaya brought up the idea of seeing behind oneself. Investing in cooperative relationships requires both empathy and a bit of intuition. The second aspect of Kaya's drawing is the distance from the ground that characterized Headlong in those years. This "hovering" signaled both exuberance, being lighter than air, and also a failure to be grounded in reality. This metaphor holds for many cooperative projects.

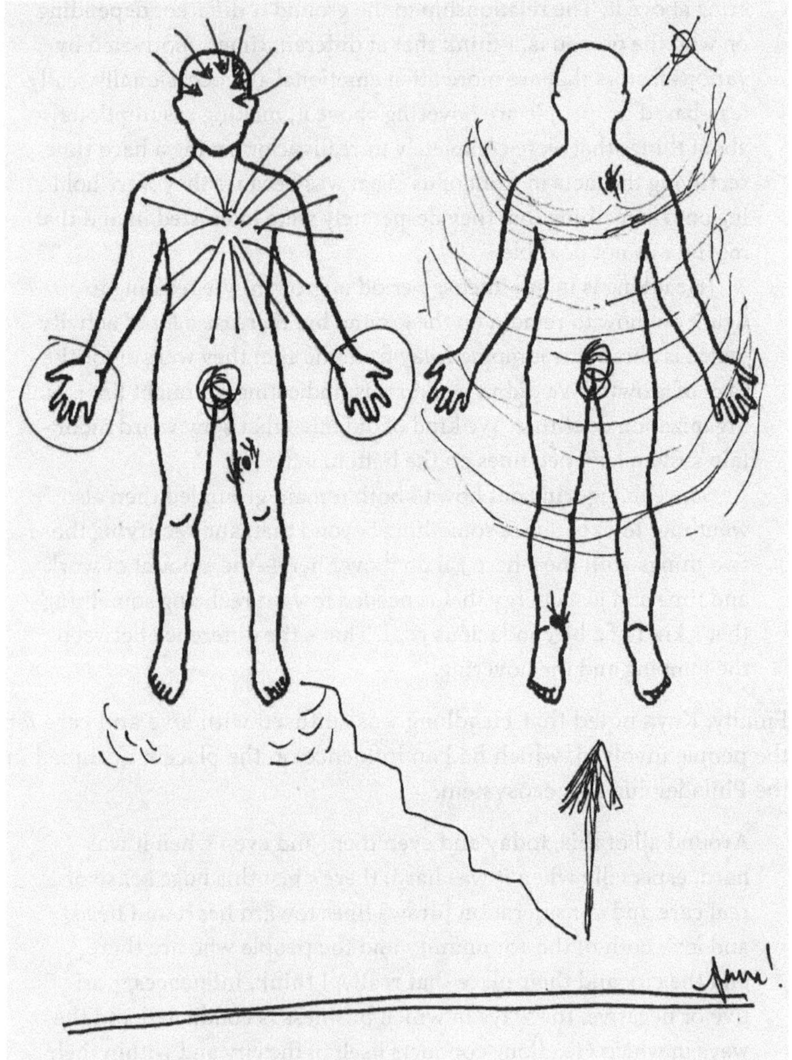

FIGURE 7. Kaya's Headlong body illustration.

They possess utopian impulses ("jumping" in Kaya's depiction) and are driven by passion for advancing social and economic practice. But they are always struggling to keep their feet on the ground and operate in the real world. Finally, Kaya noted the heartfulness and love present in Headlong, which partly explains the longevity of the Headlong collaboration. Many of the same themes are present in the final Headlong body diagram by Amy Smith, founding codirector of Headlong.

Amy's Headlong Body

Amy Smith is a cofounder and codirector of Headlong Dance Theater, active from 1993 to 2019. She has choreographed, performed, toured, and taught extensively, inside and outside Headlong. She also maintains an active business as a tax preparer for artists, and she is an advocate for artists building sustainable lives through sound financial planning.

> [Amy starts to write on the diagram while narrating.] Being a dancer is awesome because you get to be in your body. You get to be in your body with other people who are in their bodies doing things. Because most of us don't really live in our bodies at all, or only live in our bodies when we're taking a shower or having sex or really hurt or in the hospital.

Here, Amy articulates the core reason I wanted to lead this discussion of bodies with Headlong's work. She is correct in asserting that many people do not think about or feel their bodies in the course of the day, until something extraordinarily pleasurable or painful occurs. But we exist in bodies all of the time; reckoning with our physicality is an important precursor to understanding how bodies cooperate. Amy went on, moving from the head to the toes of the abstract figure:

> In a funny way we're very intellectual [draws brain on diagram]. We've been called brainy by other writers, but we're also anti-intellectual, in that we disdain a really intellectual language or things that are only for the dance literate, which is most dances. They are really not for everybody. They're for the dance literate audience. So, [there is] this kind of—I don't know—brain-gut dichotomy. I do think we follow our guts. We have followed our guts a lot. Like George W. Bush!
>
> [Moving to the feet and ground in the diagram.] In a Headlong practice there'd often be some weight-sharing going on, some sort of leaning or counterbalancing. It's funny—these feet are not on the

floor. I definitely think of us as always trying to be grounded, feet grounded, literally pressing into the floor, spreading out on the floor. This is spreading [indicates toes spreading]. Physically your feet are really relaxed and softening into the floor. You're not tense or lifting up out of the floor, a kind of yoga idea of feet.

I'm often thinking about teaching this idea of up and down happening at the same time. The skull's lifting up towards the space and the tailbone is dropping down between the heels. That feels like a metaphor. Just like being grounded in the center, being strong in the center so that you can be fluid in your limbs. [Drawing on the shoulders of the left-hand figure] This is the tension I feel when we're having tension [in Headlong], a trapezoidal tension monster.

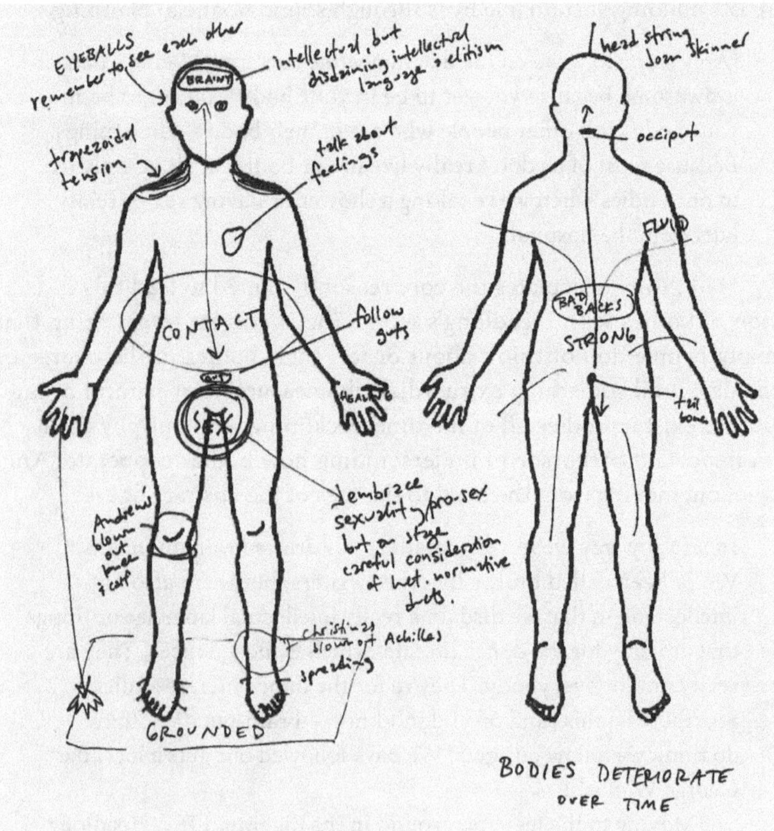

FIGURE 8. Amy's Headlong body illustration.

> [Drawing and writing on the figure's back.] Andrew and David both had back problems too. Their backs had been a thing. Bodies deteriorating have been a thing. Deteriorate over time, as we all head towards death. We're dying. We're always dying. Living and dying at the same time.

Amy picks up on some of the same themes as the others who did the exercise. Most of the interviewees mentioned the heart-centeredness and love that has been a feature or at least a strongly articulated value of Headlong's practice over time. Amy also mentions the notion of being grounded but constantly, simultaneously, reaching out for something more. But she surprises us with the darker and necessary observation that bodies struggle, experience pain and decay—so do creative partnerships and collaborations.

Headlong, an experimental dance company, may be an extreme way to make the case for the body's importance in cooperation, but extreme cases are frequently the best way to illustrate a broader point.[3] I begin with Headlong in this chapter because I want to make a strong argument for the body as the initial and fundamental site of cooperation. By understanding how unexamined assumptions about the body cloud our thinking about this issue, it is easier to understand how to put cooperation into practice.

LOCATING COOPERATION IN THE BODY

Poring over Headlong's annotated figures, I opened myself up to the body: the body that takes another's weight, the body that sees behind itself, the body that leaps at chance and lands on solid ground. This awareness serves as preparation to examine the relationship of the body to the social self, discussed in the previous chapters. The self operates in social context, but it is housed in a body with its own dependencies, needs, and resources. For cooperation to reproduce itself throughout society, it is vital to start at the most intimate scale. That creates an opening to undertake a fundamental reorientation of practice at all scales, putting bodies in service of a more cooperative workplace, economy, and democracy. This is a recursive process; beginning with the body does not denigrate other scales but places everything else in relationship to it and allows departure from the body with an ever-present possibility of the body's return.

This project is partly corrective; bodies are often sidelined when thinking about how work gets done, how democracy gets stronger. A rationalist, individualistic society is dominated by attempts to ignore or overcome physicality. Consumers are encouraged to hack their lives, finding ways to get around their bodies' needs with energy drinks, fad diets, and one-minute meditation apps for their phones. They are part of an economic system where these tools for better living are packed and shipped to their doors by low-wage workers at fulfillment centers. These workers have to race through the aisles of massive warehouses to meet their hourly quotas, risking termination if they sit down.[4] Some have it even worse than that—in a number of poultry plants, workers wear adult diapers because they are not given sufficient bathroom breaks.[5] Examples abound of precarious labor that is either physically punishing or outright dangerous.

In addition to the cruel and oppressive conditions of certain workplaces, bodies are also punished at the hands of civil and political institutions. The United States has seen an epidemic of police shootings of Black people, sparking responses like the Movement for Black Lives. Many (but by no means all) of the victims of police shootings live in neighborhoods where formal work has all but disappeared, rendering part of a population as a sort of surplus labor force, whose bodies are fodder for the nation's extensive and profitable prison system.[6] Economic and political migrants are dubbed "illegals" as elected officeholders seek to turn them back to their countries of origin to face violent deaths.

At the same time as bodies are subject to physical punishment, they also serve as props to provoke outrage and political posturing. The fight to restrict women's reproductive rights is well-documented and unrelenting. Recent right-wing activism in the United States seeks to ban people who are transgender from bathrooms that align with their gender identity. Many politicians support allowing businesses to discriminate against the LGBTQ population on religious grounds.

Whether it is a question of gender, race, age, or ability, bodies are on the line. To build a robust practice of cooperation, we need to start by embracing a diversity of bodies (including our own) and situating them in the cooperative project. This is the aim of the organizations I profile in this book, yet it is also an area where there is a lot of potential for growth.

Making embodiment central to cooperative practices requires an exploration of what is lacking in the way we currently think about bodies.

Much of that thinking is subconscious, but it is held in place by history and considerable inertia. For hundreds of years, from Descartes to Kant and beyond, the dominant view in Western thought has considered man (always *man*) a "rational, autonomous, disembodied, and constituting subject."[7] Earlier, I critiqued the notion of a rational and autonomous self. The rendering of that self as disembodied is hardly a coincidence. Denying bodies makes them peripheral and distracting, so that considerations that come along with bodies—race, gender, age, emotion—can be readily ignored in favor of the rational subject.[8] What is left is an impoverished self—devoid of physicality and context, yet ostensibly objective and free to maximize its material satisfaction.

Troubled by the consequences of this disembodied individualism, feminist and queer theory scholars have begun a radical rethinking of the role of human bodies in society.[9] Much of this critique emphasizes that the politics and practicalities presented by bodies cannot be ignored when conceiving a just society. Many feminist thinkers are concerned with the oppression and subjugation of women, whether through violence in the home or discriminatory treatment in the workplace. Certainly, women around the world face considerable barriers to the fullest expression of their human potential.[10] But women's concerns are linked to the banishment of oppression for all people, regardless of gender. Gibson-Graham explore the way masculine bodies achieve a kind of emancipation in the 1997 film *The Full Monty*. They trace the transformation of the unemployed steelworkers from a position of economic exploitation to a new freedom based in a reclaiming of their bodies through dance.[11] For Gibson-Graham, the human body and the economic body are connected and the struggle to transform our political economy is fundamentally a struggle that invokes our bodies.

Our very morality is predicated on the fact that we possess a body—an animal body at that. The human struggle for a life of virtue through practices is connected to our status as a vulnerable and dependent species. Feminist scholars have overturned a tendency to see humans as "continuously rational, healthy, and untroubled."[12] Rather, we are often deeply troubled, and thus deeply dependent on those around us. Vulnerability and disability pervade human life, from early childhood to old age, and acknowledging it requires the rejection of a solitary individual consciousness that floats outside of our very embodied, very contingent lives. In the place of an ethics of rational detachment, we possess a "virtue of acknowledged dependence" as a necessary counterpart to any notion we possess of our own independence.[13] In a framework of acknowledged dependence, we organize our relationships around giving and receiving generously, for we know that we are all, at one time or another, both the giver and receiver of aid. Virtue calls us to rise to the level of our best inclinations and to participate in affectionate, reciprocal relationships with those around us.

SUSTAINING AN ETHIC OF CARE

Embodied cooperation is not unfeeling; affect is a critical part of sustaining cooperative relationships. Another way of describing such supportive, reciprocal relationships is an ethic of care. Care ethics can be seen in contrast to the individualist nature of liberalism and a different way to think about social relationships.[14] This framework was pioneered by psychologist Carol Gilligan in the early 1980s and elaborated by others over the past few decades. Among her many insights, Gilligan draws a distinction between a feminine ethic of care, which is characterized by a selfless suppression of personal development, and a feminist ethic, which carries demands for self-actualization and resists the suppression of a patriarchal system. A feminist ethic of care refutes the notion of an autonomous, rational (male) figure determined to live in isolation. The alternative is a relational, connected, feminist voice calling out for social change.[15] This feminist ethic of care comprehends bodies and selves as fundamentally relational. The ethical dimension requires that care not be exploited and that caregivers not be marginalized.

Though care has always been thought of as a relation, initially that relation was conceptualized as between a mother and child; caring relationships were seen as a dyad between caregiver and care-receiver. The caregiver was usually marked as a woman in this arrangement. Yet this approach is severely limited, because it fails to encompass the variety of caregivers that exist, that care is often a two-way practice, and that care can exist at a distance, not merely between two people in physical, intimate contact.[16]

Recently, scholars have attempted to update care ethics as an intersectional practice that encompasses all of the identities people hold and accounts for their complex interaction.[17] Intersectionality has its roots in Black feminism, Indigenous, queer, and postcolonial theory.[18] This approach adds to care ethics an intersectional view, demonstrating how gender, race, class, ability, immigration status, and more are co-constituted, interacting, and different than the sum of their parts. An intersectional view rejects the prioritizing of any particular social category, even gender. It attempts to portray individuals in a holistic and contextual manner. Most importantly, it recognizes that there are differences within groups. For example, women of color working as domestic laborers do not have the same needs or face the same power dynamics as professional class white women.[19] Social work scholar Nicki Ward warns, "When we fail to understand and engage with people in all of their complexity, we compromise their ability to be a whole person in all of the activities of their life."[20]

In the diverse economies context, Gibson-Graham see care as a political and economic project, envisioning a turn toward care in human relationships as subjects of the economy, finding illustrative power from their own field research. In one passage, they relate the story of a supervisor of a power station that was shut down in Australia in the 1990s. The supervisor tearfully urged that care be taken with the economic fortunes of his colleagues who lost their jobs. For him, the received corporate logic of restructuring and economic competitiveness was ethically and morally insufficient when it comes to the lives and livelihoods of his colleagues. The social and economic spheres of care are merged here, showing through this worker's example that there is an opening for the reconfiguring of economic relationships around an ethic of care for others' well-being.[21]

Diverse economies researcher Stephen Healy elaborates on the caring economy in his study of informal caregivers in Western Massachusetts.[22] The work these caregivers provide is largely uncompensated and virtually invisible to outsiders. In making their work visible, Healy highlights "the richness of individual subjects' economic lives" without shrinking from their complexity.[23] Caregiving is depicted by Healy as an ethical act, with transgressive and transformative aspects. The work is transformative, as caregivers uncover new capacities and forms of self-realization in the process of caring for others. And, like other forms of cooperation, caregiving is transgressive because it undermines the norms of long-standing individualist, utility-maximizing behavior. Individualism and autonomy here are impossible, as such caregiving often involves a transgression of the norms of bodily autonomy, since one person actively supports another in the bodily functions that make possible the continuation of life. This finding clearly underscores that humans must reckon with our vulnerability, our animality, and our dependence on others.

Care work can be soul-satisfying. But Healy admits that an uncritical acceptance of the notions of care and community can be detrimental.[24] There is a danger of romanticizing this challenging cooperation as a care practice. There is also danger in calling for commodifying care for loved ones, turning it into just another market transaction. And there is risk in promoting it as a replacement for state-sponsored health and welfare policies. Nevertheless, Healy searches for ways to unite the ethical aspects of caregiving with its political possibilities. These possibilities include both policy change and also change of the exploitative dynamics that occur within households. We learn from Healy's caregivers, who manage to find the grace and transformative potential of caring labor while nevertheless advocating for greater support and remuneration for their efforts.

EMBODYING EMOTION IN PRACTICE

Care work is grounded in emotion, which is deeply implicated in embodied practice. In recent decades, scholars have uncovered emotion as a subject of concern. These developments reverse a history in which academics, like other workers, have "often had trouble expressing feelings."[25] Not being able to express feelings is a liability, in scholarship and in everyday life. Emotions occur in a social, transpersonal context, beyond the experience of just one person. Yet, while the power of emotion is acknowledged in private contexts, the challenge of uncovering the emotional terrain undergirding everyday life leads to emotions getting suppressed or denied in a variety of everyday interactions, including organizations. Emotions are lived experiences that play out on the body, in expressions like tears or laughter and feelings like ecstasy or shame. But emotions are more than mere attributes of the body or static things. It is helpful to think of emotions existing socially and spatially. They function more as "relational flows, fluxes or currents, in between people and places."[26]

Though emotions are experienced through the body, they are not limited to it (think of the social contagion of anger in a lovers' quarrel). Emotions pass among bodies and do not "belong exclusively to any individual—even though they are experienced and expressed this way—but are part of what we might call a psychodynamics connected to space and place."[27] Embodied emotions connect to specific sites and contexts.[28] In sum, our bodies experience emotion socially and in space. Cooperative workplaces are no exception, whether it is the dance studio, the community acupuncture clinic, the food co-op checkout line, or any other setting.

IF YOU WANT MY BODY; OR, THE PARADOX OF EXCLUSIVITY

Social action emanates from everyday embodied practices.[29] Humans (and other beings) collectively organize and orient their bodies to achieve their goals: childcare, factory work, park cleanups. There is inspiration in Simone de Beauvoir's notion of the body as a "situation."[30] Bodies are situated not only in time and space but also in terms of race, class, nationality, and more. Each body is unique because of these differentiating characteristics but can align with other bodies in similar situations.[31] As Headlong's body diagrams demonstrate, cooperation is inscribed on each body differently, even when they are part of the same cooperative project. Whether it is Hana and Kaya thinking about what is approaching from behind their backs, or Amy's concern with eyes and seeing, the body is an essential tool for manifesting cooperative practice. These lessons about cooperation, bodies, and care also inhere in the other cases in the book.

To align different sorts of bodies, it is vital to reckon with the paradox of exclusivity. Many ostensibly cooperative spaces exclude bodies based on race, gender, age, and ability—often without realizing it. Recall the story of Weavers Way, which turned away from the store young people of color whose parents were not members. Co-op staff did not intend to discriminate based on race—they were just following membership policy—but they discriminated nonetheless. Consumer-owned co-ops like Weavers Way face a paradoxical imperative: they need to create a feeling that co-op membership is special and not for everyone. They have to engage their customers as vital parts of the co-op's existence, otherwise they risk losing them to the competition. But closing ranks around an exclusive notion of membership (which, at one time, required members to work a few hours per month at the store) limits the number, and the kind, of people who can participate. It creates a condition of exclusivity that makes many people wary of the cooperative structure and associate negatively with it. Most grocery co-ops, Weavers Way included, have moved away from a mandatory membership that requires in-store labor (Brooklyn's Park Slope Food Coop is a notable exception), yet now they struggle with member engagement and loyalty. This is a particular quandary for consumer cooperatives, which are owned by their customers, but worker cooperatives face similar challenges in achieving social integration and total buy-in from worker owners.[32]

Other cooperative projects share this struggle. POCA is the cooperative outlier in a very competitive acupuncture industry. It tries to overcome the training most acupuncturists receive from conventional acupuncture schools. This training regimen is built around excluding bodies that do not fit the ideal acupuncture patient.

One POCA clinic owner in Philadelphia explained to me how acupuncture school encouraged her to build a clientele that matched her demographic profile:

> You're taught in acupuncture school that you are going to attract people that are like you and that the people who are going to see you the most often are the people that resonate with you like a friend, that have things in common with you. I was told that I should court people who are Jewish, who look the same, like the same things I do, read the same books, play the same sports. . . . So you do have to kind of shake that off so you can come outside of it and treat more people.[33]

She had to work to overcome the idea that her patient base would be people just like her. POCA has developed training for its acupunks that helps them overcome their biases against bodies that differ from them in skin color, in gender, in size and shape, in hygiene. The movement's goal is radical inclusion and what POCA calls liberation acupuncture, which can only happen when the practice and the acupunk can care for all the bodies in the clinic's neighborhood.

A POCA clinic volunteer from Portland told me that the objective of acupuncture was to treat bodies different from her own: "You park yourself with the right attitude in the right place and wait, and when people who look different from you and who eat badly, or vote for God-knows-who, or carry guns or whatever, you're delighted to see them—and you treat them exactly the way you treat the organic-food-eating hippies." This kind of active engagement of people from outside the acupuncturists' own subcultures marks the POCA co-op as striving to be different from other cooperatives, which can be homogeneous and exclusive. This is not to say that POCA fully succeeds in this aim, as one study found economic diversity but not significant racial diversity in the Working Class Acupuncture clinics in Portland.[34] (The racial homogeneity of Portland itself likely influenced the findings, but the question deserves investigation.)

Bodies that represent the healthy, able-bodied, white, middle class standard of many alternative food cooperatives and alternative health practices are often the standard by which other bodies are judged as deficient or deviant. These normate bodies hold significant power in those domains and in the culture more broadly.[35] Ultimately, different bodies possess different quantities and qualities of power. Philosopher Iris Marion Young finds that power relations affect bodies differently: "When the dominant culture defines some groups as 'other' . . . the members of those groups are imprisoned in their bodies. They are defined in terms of bodily characteristics and constructed as ugly, dirty, defiled, impure, contaminated, or sick."[36] It is possible, even for well-meaning cooperators, to mark bodies of those around them as other and to thereby exclude them from cooperative practices. In many contemporary settings, this exclusion means that cooperators fail to make room for other bodies in their projects. The standard for thin, able, cisgender bodies is communicated by alternative food and health businesses through their advertising, their products, and the visual evidence of who is already present in these spaces.

A Weavers Way board member explained to me how Black members had a tenuous relationship with the co-op in prior years. She said: "Back in those days, in the African American community, we psychologically said, we're not going to beg anybody to take our money. If for one split second we felt we're unwelcome, you'll never see us there again. We can go someplace else." One of the signs that Black shoppers were unwelcome was the lack of inventory that met their culinary needs. She explained:

> Some of the product line we tout—we buy or subscribe or try and obtain things that members want—but some things that [Black members] wanted were totally ignored. One of the things was collard greens, to give you a good example. They just didn't stock it. So [while] I managed to—not *manage*—I *enjoyed* the coop, I also knew that this is a role our generation played, my generation played. As we moved into the corporate environment, into new neighborhoods, into new schools, we knew that we were the ones that had to have to set the example. We were the ones that would have to teach the white community that we're just like you. . . . But some people

didn't care to go that direction, "Why should I bother? Why should I go through that kind of, you know, aggravation of not being sure of being wanted?"

Cultural signifiers like food alienate people who do not see their bodily needs and desires represented. The way people respond to the bodies of others considered transgressive reveals their own internalized preferences and prejudices.[37] This makes it all the more vital that everyone be aware and reflective about their relationship to a variety of different bodies. Crafting a cooperative practice that is inclusive of all bodies requires a commitment to unpacking fears and strong feelings, as well as prejudices and preferences.

LET'S DANCE: INTEGRATING BODIES AND EMOTIONS INTO THE SPACE OF PRACTICE

I started this discussion with dancing bodies, and I want to spend the rest of the chapter in that world. The link with emotional bodies at work in the world is most clearly visible in dance. Also rampant in dance is the exclusion of bodies that do not conform to idealized pictures of health, athleticism, virtuosity, and beauty. Dance has the potential to be exclusive of possible attendees as well—just look at the complexion of the audience at most experimental dance performances.

There are, however, forms and settings for dance that are radically inclusive, as they are part of the folkloric practice and ritual life of entire communities. Dance, at its most powerful, is an embodied practice connected to ritual, the rhythms of manual labor, the construction of community, and leisure. Since dance lives beyond the rational auspices of Western societies, it is often rendered invisible in serious scholarship.[38] In part, geographer Nigel Thrift explains, dance's invisibility is a consequence of its "as-ifness"—dance is not "for real" but a commentary on reality. Therefore, we should endorse dance for its political possibilities to model a different future. By embracing the "as-ifness," the character of dance-as-play, we allow dance to be immediate and resistant to control from outside. Dance possesses "the grounds for configuring an alternative way of being that eludes the grasp of power."[39] It has a transgressive power derived from its historical linkage with desire, degeneracy, and resistance to socially approved forms of movement.[40] Simply put, dance has the potential to reconfigure body and space.

This dialectic of dance—rarefied and elite on one hand, deeply democratic on the other—is one that Headlong has explored throughout its creative life. I am focusing on Headlong, then, first by talking about Headlong as an organization and then by briefly profiling two of its pieces, *Cell* (2006) and *More* (2009). To begin, Headlong sees itself as a caring organization, putting care at the center of its organizational culture. Many of my interviewees volunteered this observation early in our conversations, and my own volunteer work with the company bore it out. As codirector Amy Smith related while she made her drawing, Headlong is very "heart-centered." As she drew a heart on her figure, she went on: "I think we really care about our hearts; we talk about our feelings a lot. Especially David [Brick, codirector], I think David is the most emotionally intelligent person I've ever known."

What does that mean in practice? Part of it consists in the way Headlong runs rehearsals. According to David: "There's a high premium on conscious emotional exchange, a lot of checking in where people are at, how you're feeling, how you're doing, more so than [in Headlong's] early years. I do think it's like a support group aspect to rehearsal." The intimacy of dance must be easier to achieve when dancers obtain some sense of how other dancers are feeling.

Making space in the studio to talk about dancers' lives and needs creates an atmosphere of trust. This can make for better, more meaningful performances. One Headlong dancer told me, "They [the codirectors] were completely reliant on the 360 degrees of being a human being." That contrasts significantly with many workplaces; those who have spent much of their dancing lives in Headlong could not imagine forsaking it. David marveled at how people who work in other settings must manage without this kind of space to be fully themselves. He related, "Some of my friends who don't have social artistic practices, I'm like, 'You don't have money for therapy—where do you do all of that kind of opening it up?'"

Indeed, I have felt, working in higher education, that opportunities to be emotionally honest with coworkers are lacking, and my work is sometimes compromised by not having an opportunity to be more fully emotionally present. The bias against emotions at work is evident when searching online for research on emotions in the workplace. The initial results run along the lines of articles such as "How to Control Your Emotions at Work." Of course, whether they are encouraged or suppressed, emotions permeate our lives at work.[41] This can be a particularly acute issue for women and people of color, who are often deemed overly emotional, leading to the marginalization of their voices.[42] Oftentimes, these workers are called upon to perform emotional and caring labor while their own needs are sidelined. Imagine a future that opens up space, and builds maturity, toward a workplace where feelings are validated. David summed up the feeling: "There's a value to just saying how you're feeling in the world." Sometimes, I wish I had a Headlong dance rehearsal in my work life to process my experiences in a comprehensive way.

My praise of emotion at work is tempered by the acknowledgment that sometimes emotion can be exhausting or even manipulative or damaging. Sociologist Elizabeth A. Hoffmann writes about the forcing or feigning of emotion that sometimes happens in worker cooperatives.[43] She found that cooperators appreciated the flexibility to emote in the workplace but realized that certain emotions were required by the workplace dynamics, whether or not the cooperator felt them in the moment. Sometimes cooperators merely feigned the requisite emotion, like enthusiasm for an endless committee meeting or a distended decision-making process; other times they were able to internalize the emotion and feel it enough to portray it authentically. This high bar for emotional labor might not work for everyone, especially if we have not been accustomed to it. And even when cooperators are prepared to emote at work, one person's emotions may not sync with another's needs, leading to moments of disappointment or hurt. David related the hurt that sometimes came from a lack of validation by the other members of Headlong in the early days and how emotional maturity took time to grow, on everyone's part. This suggests that operationalizing emotion is perhaps more difficult than it looks, and as I will show later in this chapter, it may be dangerous to embrace without adequate training and procedures in place.

In addition to a positive affective stance as an organization, Headlong operationalized its interest in emotion through bodily proximity. In contrast to many workplaces, touching bodies was a necessary part of the workday. Dancers recalled the many hours spent warming up before rehearsals in the studio. Dancer Eve explained, "One thing people don't understand about dancers is we're always touching each other and massaging each other and snuggling." There was a lot of physical contact in those moments, and it serves as an extension of the building of trust. That kind of physical trust and space of safety is an astonishing contrast with the culture of misogyny and sexual abuse that we find around us in the broader culture. As far-fetched as this picture of a sweaty studio full of dancers massaging each other is from our conventional, modestly clad workplaces, I personally wish for the esprit de corps, if not the leggings. What do we give up when our workplaces are places of mistrust, possessing a latent threat of harassment (or worse) based on gendered power imbalances? (I am not saying that there is no sexual misconduct in the dance world—it just was not part of the Headlong story, to my knowledge.) Indeed, when trust and connection are available in an organizational context, it changes the parameters of what you can gain from the experience. Eve went on to explain this to me, saying, "You're getting something from that relationship that you don't get from, you know, your relationships with your friends in life or your partner or whatever." There is an intimacy in these work relationships that allows the dances to be rendered much more powerfully.

A part of this power is the kind of spatial intuition it fosters. Wendy, one of the company dancers, related: "I was so used to being in close contact with my fellow performers, in terms of the way we would see each other when we would perform together. If we were seeing with our peripheral-sensorial body, I would know if Eve was behind me, because I could sense her with the eyes in my back that we had worked on opening up." This conjures the drawings that I highlighted at the beginning of this chapter: Headlong clearly got the message of seeing and sensing through to its members.

In Amy Smith's drawing, she described the importance of using one's eyes:

> [Amy draws eyeballs on the diagram.] David [Brick] always says, "I see you seeing me." Eyeballs are super important. Where are we looking? Are we seeing each other? A lot of times before we would start an improvisational dance, we would just go like this [points two fingers toward her eyes], just like reminding ourselves to look, to remember to see each other.

Like other interviewees, Amy believes that seeing and awareness of others' needs is a cardinal Headlong cooperative practice. It builds trust and bolsters the work. Amy, seemingly inspired while making her drawing, moved from questions of seeing to questions of gender:

> What's funny is that these bodies [the diagrams] aren't gendered. . . . In a way we also really embraced gender politics or something in the company, tried to have a pretty broad idea about gender. There were

romantic things in our work, not a lot of like unexamined heterosexual normative duets.

She picks up on the dynamics of love, romance, and gender that are foundational in any relationship as intimate as a long-term collaborative partnership. Headlong endorses intimacy without falling back on patriarchal tropes or gendered power imbalance. In a moment when gender-based violence is finally getting the attention it deserves, I am all too aware of how far we have to go in building safe spaces for emotional exchange in the workplace. The qualities Amy champions are present but flawed in most working relationships, though they impact the participants whether they are acknowledged or not.

Throughout this discussion of the role of embodied emotion and care in Headlong, I have related their practices generally. Now I want to briefly talk about two of the dances they created that addressed these issues in very different ways. I want to emphasize that along with the positive potential for nurturing and sensing bodies, the kind of bodily intimacy Headlong promoted has a related danger. This danger is injury, both physical and emotional, and it is always present when bodies are on the line.

"WE'RE SUPPORTING EACH OTHER, EVEN WHEN THE SUPPORTING IS ACTUALLY LIKE COLLIDING"

The quote that serves as this section's title was related to me by Autumn, an alum of Headlong Performance Institute who went on to form her own successful partnership (with dancer Libby) that tried to embody many of the same values as Headlong. In one early piece, Autumn and Libby ran toward one another as fast as they could, to the point of colliding. The kinetic energy of these collisions stands in for the explosive positive and destructively negative energy that coexist in any cooperative relationship.

In 2006, Headlong premiered *Cell*, a performance built for only one audience member at a time. Headlong worked with artists Jennifer and Kevin McCoy to craft a journey through the streets of Philadelphia, the audience member guided via phone by a hidden dispatcher. As the audience member moved through the piece, it was not always clear who else was part of the dance and who was a passerby. *Cell* culminates when a whole group of dancers comes together for a private, customized dance created on the spot, just for that one audience member. This work shows the way Headlong made bodies welcome in their artistic space, not just

FIGURE 9. Audience member receives instructions from Headlong via cell phone as part of Headlong's *Cell*. Photograph copyright Jacques-Jean Tiziou / www.jjtiziou.net.

FIGURE 10. Dancers accompany an audience member in the streets of Philadelphia's Old City as part of Headlong's *Cell*. Photograph copyright Jacques-Jean Tiziou / www.jjtiziou.net.

those of the dancing inner circle but by opening that circle to make the audience part of the cooperative practice.

I had an extended conversation with dancer Wendy about performing in *Cell* and what it meant to her about cooperating deeply with a member of the audience:

> We were just stunned by everyone's differences and how much we gave. I felt like I was doing a service. [It was about] really seeing a person. We reveal so much in the way that we move or approach the situation, approach a room, and I think some of the brilliance of that piece was that the person had the sense of being watched the whole time, and then to be released. . . . This was a private moment for them and we were there, their caretakers in that private moment.

Here, Wendy recalls the capacity of seeing that she and others generated as part of Headlong, and that everyone mentioned in their drawing sessions. Their ability to see and to care for others in the group allowed them to extend that empathy out to the audience members and create a dance based on the perceived needs of those temporary cooperators in the artistic process.

Wendy went on to explain that the dancers were so enthralled by the experience that they dared not take a break between performances. She begins with an admission:

> WENDY: It was a *lot* of dances. . . . [Laughter.] You know sometimes we'd be so tired and feel like, "Do you want to take a break?" And we'd be like, "No." We can't miss somebody, we can't miss what happens. Something great happens every single time.
>
> ANDREW: No two times are alike.
>
> WENDY: Never, oh, never. Like radically different every single time, which was challenging too, especially when—if we were getting tired sometimes it was hard to give that much, to be true to the task of really being like: What is the dance that this body is asking for? And what is this person bringing? And how can we really answer it and support it versus, like, you know, getting lazy and riding the wave of the music or something?

The embodied practice of dancers combined in *Cell* with an empathetic and reflective collaboration with the audience, making a statement about the potential of dance to break down and reconstruct the situation of bodies in our culture. This is a powerfully emancipatory gesture for art to make, especially when much modern dance is very difficult to penetrate as an audience member. And because so many of us are deeply alienated from the kind of healthy risk-taking demanded by participating in such a performance. Of course, audience members did not know they would be put in this position of power to direct the dance, and interviewees told me that some audience members did not fully engage with the dancers. Ironically, it was often people from the institutional dance world who were more reluctant to let go and get in the spirit of *Cell*.

Wendy spoke eloquently to the way this work transcended performance for her and became a uniting of personal and professional qualities that she had never before been given a chance to integrate:

> It wasn't about performance to me. It was about a personal experience for someone that was facilitated by all these skills that we have. And as a dancer, I never felt so truly at home in a performance. I really felt like I have all these weird physical empathetic skills and ways to read people that are subtle and below the radar and this is my job, and I'm doing it and it's actually making people feel good.
>
> That's kind of how I operate in the world, but to have it brought into my professional life in such a clear way was profound, it was the perfect wrapping up of everything for me.

Echoes of *Cell* and its democratic and caring engagement with audience members can be found in later Headlong pieces, including *This Town Is a Mystery* (2013), where dances were set all over Philadelphia in audience members' homes, with the audience members serving as the dancers, and *W*LM*RT Nature Trail,* where audience members were taken, one at a time, on a dancer-led tour through a Philadelphia Walmart and out to a hidden nature trail. Though Headlong continued on this inclusive exploration of bodily practices, a work undertaken a few years after *Cell* yielded very different experiences for the company. That work, *More* (2009), is just as crucial for understanding the power of the cooperative body, since the bodies involved were sometimes pushed too far for their own comfort.

BODIES INJURED AND ISOLATED, PUSHING AWAY

After *Cell,* things began to change in Headlong. The codirectors grew older, people got married, had kids—they stopped living in a communal utopia. There were grant deadlines and employees to fund. And with each production, the creative ambition of each codirector grew, and not always in unison. Company members began to notice the wear and tear of emotional wounds that built up over Headlong's intense, long-term collaboration. Recalling a later piece called *Explanatorium* (2007), Jasmine described the "heartbreak" of watching Andrew, Amy, and David fighting to be heard:

> Something seemed to be breaking down. . . . None of them felt like they could be whole. These little fights for small sections or small decisions really represented a lot for them. They would come to the table with a desperation of "We have to do this," and it was almost like when other people disagreed or had a different view, it represented something bigger than the moment. You think, we're fundamentally different in a way that's not pieces of a puzzle fitting together well. The shapes of each puzzle have changed so much that they kind of poke and irritate and rub instead of sliding in.

It demonstrated the frustration of a puzzle that will not come together, bodies whose situations no longer align. When cooperative relationships start to unravel, small disagreements ricochet off of hurts and regrets that may have been suppressed. And "little fights" can signal bigger rifts. A dancer contrasted the struggle to make *Explanatorium* with the ease of doing *Cell* a year or two before: "Maybe that was a bit of a hangover from *Cell* or trying to re-envision that generosity toward an audience, and how to keep that being the focus of the work." These dynamics only became more pronounced as time passed.

Headlong's next major work permanently altered the way their collaboration worked and fundamentally changed the organization. In 2007, Headlong invited celebrated New York choreographer Tere O'Connor to come to Philadelphia to create a piece. O'Connor asked each codirector to meditate on Headlong's next move and found that each person wanted something different. O'Connor proposed a process he called "unbraiding," in which each codirector would create a separate work, with the same dancers, without collaborating or sharing information. Though prior pieces were led by an individual codirector, all of them had input on the collective work. That was about to change.

O'Connor's provocation had ramifications for the way Headlong collaborated, as he exiled the bodies of the other codirectors from the studio while he sought to excavate each individual sensibility. Initially, unbraiding liberated Andrew, Amy, and David. One dancer recalled the free play of "space and generosity" that flowed from Andrew as he attempted to rediscover his own choreographic voice. Another recalled how Amy, the codirector most devoted to collaboration, turned to the dancers as creative partners in this phase. Dancers enjoyed knowing what each codirector was plotting, while the other codirectors had no idea; they felt as if they were part of a secret club, coming together in a new way as a company. But underneath all these aesthetic excursions was a dark uncertainty about the state of Headlong's collaboration. While the unbraiding process seemed a radical break from their earlier work, Headlong's collaborative spirit had been under strain for some time.

The codirectors witnessed one another's individual pieces for the first time in front of an audience in spring 2008. Instead of leaving those individual creative statements as stand-alone works, Headlong decided to craft a fourth, collaborative piece out of the many strands. They planned to "rebraid" the individual sections into a larger work, eventually called *More*. From talking to both company dancers and the codirectors, it is clear that this phase of creation was deeply challenging to the hearts, minds, and bodies that composed Headlong. Jasmine recalled, "They just didn't have a system that they could rely on. All their past instincts and the past system just didn't work anymore." Wendy lamented, "We were islands unto ourselves."

Dancers felt that they had gone from being embraced as coconspirators and collaborators with the separate codirectors to being mere bodies working at the directors' whims. Their situation was being completely reconfigured in unprecedented ways. Eve recalled:

> I think what was really heartbreaking for the dancers [was that] we replaced [the codirectors] in the first part ["unbraiding"]; we became the collaborators that they were so good at embracing. And they basically turned their backs on us and went behind closed doors for all the discussions after that. So then they would just show up with the piece of paper and give us lists and it just felt cold and traditional.
>
> In order to generate all of this juicy material, we had to have a certain kind of process. We have a certain kind of energy in the room and love [and] openness. Honestly, so much was asked of us, we were asked to be so open and so much a part of something. And then that door shut—and the focus was on them trying to figure out how to be together. The focus was then on their marriage and no one knew how or what the piece was, what its details were.

Eve contrasts the warmth of the "embrace" of the unbraiding period with the "cold" feeling of having the codirectors turn their backs on the dancers in the stressful rebraiding period that followed. The consequences of the apparent emotional strain in the "marriage" were clear to the dancers. Without the love, the generosity that flowed in the earlier moment, dancers felt unmoored and disconnected from the process. The dances themselves were hard to do. One dancer explained that *More* was about doing the impossible, and not in a good way. The work was a manifestation of that struggle. During the development of the piece, Wendy injured her Achilles tendon. Instead of replacing her in the piece with an uninjured dancer, Headlong decided to feature her in *More,* dancing in her brace and wheelchair. It made the metaphor explicit, a representation of dancing through pain.

Company dancers told me how the piece challenged them, sometimes in ways that felt painful. That pain may have come from physical exertion, but it was also a product of emotional exposure. In one poignant section of *More,* Andrew Simonet had the dancers write about what they do to nourish their bodies each day. These instructions for the body were idiosyncratic and very personal; they were read aloud in voiceover during the performance. Eve related the dancers' experience with this process: "It wasn't particularly jarring for me, but it was really hard for some other people in the room who felt like they were exposing themselves and have many more sort of less ordinary or unusual things that they do to maintain themselves." For Eve, this was intimate, difficult, and profound.

But not all the dancers agreed. Carrie explained that asking for that kind of radical openness required more caretaking than Headlong as a dance organization was set up to provide. She spoke to her frustration, saying:

> You don't have the professional experience to deal with the ramifications of what happens when you ask a group of people to open up at that level. I don't trust you to have the skill set to manage that. . . . It ended up feeling emotionally manipulative to me because I'm like, "You're just doing this to make some exponential deliverance," and that felt very unsafe.

Another dancer linked the emotional toll the piece took on the dancers and their bodies to the codirectors' uncertainty about how to proceed creatively:

FIGURE 11. Headlong dancers perform a scene from *More*. Photograph by Cylla von Tiedemann.

> I think what was so hard is that it felt like a violation, but . . . it wasn't intended to be. These people that we love, they were hurting so much that they didn't have the space to take care of us, and how dare I asked to be taken care of? We wanted to be our best selves for them; we wanted to help them get through this.
>
> How to really help them became mysterious because they didn't really know what they needed, you know, aside from us letting them try things, try things that might hurt our bodies, hurt our psyche. The piece turned into a piece about loneliness, physical exhaustion, doing things that were impossible. The things we were drawing on [were] things that are hard to look at, so to embody all of them [was hard].

What dancers are asked to do is intimate and extraordinary. It seems almost unfair to ask them to use their bodies to serve someone else's objective and agenda, yet this is the job. The dancers in Headlong experienced a different bodily situation, one in which they were cocreators, being held and felt and valued. This dynamic is unique in dance because of the hierarchical nature of a lot of it. To have that taken away and then to be asked to move again in a sort of forced way could easily feel like a violation. The shift in emotional dynamics would have consequences for Headlong's cooperative project.

After *More*, the collaboration radically changed. Andrew Simonet, after twenty years in Headlong, announced that he was quitting the company and planning to make a career outside the arts, or at least not as a dancer. (He is currently writing novels for young adults and running an artist professional development program called Artists U.) This move forced Headlong to decide whether or not to continue without Andrew. The split with Andrew meant the end of the "marriage"; it was a painful and complicated time.

Part of what Andrew highlighted in our interview was the relief he felt at leaving something that no longer felt emotionally tenable. He remembers people reacting to the news of his departure: "You're like 'You're leaving the Headlong community'—I'm like, 'Yeah, leaving those awful meetings? And those stressful rehearsals?' It didn't feel like leaving a community, it felt like leaving a tense workplace." For Andrew, and for other people I interviewed, the very process of running an arts organization held inherent tension between creativity and the stress of running a successful nonprofit. Yet, Andrew felt that the collaboration could perhaps have been sustained through a set of embodied practices instead of the practices that ended up preoccupying the codirectors in the later years:

> One thing that we didn't do, that I think would have helped, is that if we danced together . . . as a prelude to every meeting—I think it would be really different. And why we couldn't, though I think we even knew at the time we needed to, is very interesting to me. It's a weird gearshift thing. People come in, armored for a meeting—it's really hard to soften into a body that dances and responds. It is stupid and profound. . . . It feels almost cruel, like I suited up for battle and now you're asking me to have sex? I can't! I'm ready to fight. Why didn't we just dance in the middle of the meeting?

Andrew continued, further drawing the distinction between an embodied organization and one that is just governed by administrative tasks:

> It's so funny to run a dance organization because there's bodily shame about organization. An organization is documents and [sitting] in meetings. . . . We kind of professionalized and became what people are, which is that they sit in front of computers. . . . We're "knowledge workers." But it's not inevitable. . . . There's a body, there's a smell, there's atoms, not just bits. But weirdly, in a dance

> company, it's like tons of bits being moved around and then occasionally you get to dance. But why? Why is that true? We had a chance. We could have totally overcome that, but we didn't.

If the professional, emotionally suppressed dimensions of administering a dance company had been let go, even for a few minutes a day, perhaps the collaboration would have survived. Perhaps not. In the end, after a lot of soul searching, Amy and David decided to continue to work together (through 2019, when Amy also left to pursue other opportunities) under a new plan to bring in other artists and companies to be incubated under the Headlong organizational banner.

In one of our conversations in 2013, Amy offered a kind of tribute to Headlong's first twenty years, taking care to emphasize the evolution that it has undergone, rather than emphasizing loss. She explained:

> I don't want to romanticize Headlong too much, nor do I want to overemphasize the difficulties or imply that we went from utopia to sad reality. I still feel very hopeful. I feel really happy about what we're doing, and that David and I are still doing it. I'm so glad that this is the life I have. I'm not mournful that what we had is no longer there. It's just evolved. It's changed.

Certainly, evolution and change are inevitable and to be praised. Practices evolve along with the people who bring them into the world, and progress is never linear or certain. Headlong should be celebrated, both before and after *More,* for the collaboration it sustained, for the loving attachments it fostered, for the dancers and students it mentored, and for the mark it has left on the artistic community of Philadelphia. It continues to sponsor and develop the work of emerging artists, as well as produce work led by Amy or David. It is no longer the collective it once was, but it has grown up, remaining vital for over two decades while many other small arts organizations have come and gone. And the work lives on, in the hearts and minds of the audiences who were touched, provoked, and uplifted by Headlong's cultural practice.

GROUNDEDNESS AND THE UTOPIAN AIR

In the drawings at the start of the chapter, bodies were always drawn in relationship to the ground. Sometimes they hovered above it, as if gravity had no purchase. Sometimes they seemed ready to crash (headlong) into the floor. These bodies convey a contradiction of cooperative practice. For transformative cooperation to work, it needs to be utopian and pragmatic at once. It needs to assert, following Gibson-Graham, that other worlds, other economies, are already here! And it needs to keep the lights on, the dancers limber, the co-op shelves stocked with food.

In the spirit of remaining grounded, in the utopian air, I offer the following three takeaways for cooperative practice as this chapter comes to a close.

Demand Respect for Bodies, Building Spaces of Care

All social action springs from embodied practice. Denying the body its rightful place in cooperative work denies an essential part of the self. Whether we acknowledge it or not, we live our lives in collective situations, and we are vulnerable beings in need of validation and support. The rigors of cooperation require that emotions are taken into account—they will show up whether we plan for them or not—and we ought to have direct and honest conversations about how to make this possible.

It seems unlikely that many workplaces are ready to handle emotion. We live in a world where toxic masculinity exerts power, and workplaces are more likely to be soaked in innuendo or outright misogyny than suffused with care for vulnerable selves. But that is changing because of a radical confrontation with the gendered power dynamics playing out in societies around the world. This risky work—often led by women, trans, and gender nonconforming workers and people of color—inspires us to liberate all organizational practices from the tyranny of body-based violence and humiliation. We are witnessing a moment of radical critique that opens toward future possibility. This critique itself constitutes utopian work![44] At the same time as our critique points toward utopia, we do not have to wait for some future-perfect condition. We need to inventory the sustaining, nonoppressive practices of the body that exist now and spread the message widely. This was evident in Headlong's praxis. It was evident by the community acupunks who refused to treat only bodies that look just like them. This is present in all contemporary movements for positive self-expression around race, body size, gender, sexual orientation, ability, and more. An intersectional cooperative movement needs to lean on the organizing work that is being done in these areas and ask: How can we help make this work more cooperative? How can we build links to our existing practices and let them be nourished by the prophecy of our utopian critique?

In 2016 and 2017, the Philadelphia Area Cooperative Alliance led an initiative called 20 Book Clubs → 20 Cooperative Businesses. Using study circles, staff worked with community stakeholders to incubate cooperative businesses that arose from local needs. The diversity of these study circles was thrilling, both in terms of business proposals and demographics of the groups. These included plans for a Mexican-owned worker cooperative construction company, a Black healers' collective, and a refugee women's textile cooperative. By recognizing these startups as the future of cooperation, the Philadelphia Area Cooperative Alliance is breaking barriers of exclusivity and access.

All Bodies Are Welcome

Recent events have only reinforced how unwelcome many bodies are in the spaces of our economy and our society. Xenophobic rhetoric has turned into reactionary policy, as immigrant families are seized and separated at the U.S. border. For Black Americans, even a Philadelphia Starbucks is not safe, as two young men found out in the spring of 2018 when the police came to arrest them two minutes after they arrived, following a white manager's phone call. For cooperation to exist, we must start by welcoming all bodies and pushing back against the tendency to violently exile those who make us uncomfortable. The examples in this chapter offer a tantalizing glimpse of a future condition where all bodies are welcome.

Headlong admits a diverse array of bodies into its project, from dancers of different shapes, sizes, and genders to audiences that included homeowners and neighbors in far-flung Philly neighborhoods in pieces like *This Town Is a Mystery*. Over the past several years, Headlong has dedicated itself to antiracist advocacy in the arts and has also begun a program of offering administrative and financial oversight to small arts organizations. These incubated artists represent a broad demographic and aesthetic swath of the local and national arts scenes and provide mentorship and stability to artists who might not find it elsewhere. All these bodies and more are welcome in Headlong's tent now that Headlong is no longer solely about expressing the creative vision of its three founding codirectors.

Mariposa and Weavers Way have also made inroads toward welcoming all bodies. Mariposa has a revolving fund that helps low-income members pay for their equity investments and receives regular staff training to prevent racism, gender discrimination, and Islamophobia. Weavers Way has a food justice committee that thinks carefully about the pricing and sourcing of its food to make sure it is accessible to all member and nonmember shoppers. These co-ops are slowly raising awareness that they are community owned and offer an opportunity for local control and local hiring in the hands of the neighbors who feel comfortable enough to take part.

Finally, POCA has devoted its energy and attention to a trauma-informed model of care and trains its student acupunks in the tools they need to embrace all bodies in POCA clinics. These examples stand in stark contrast to spaces that are usually encoded as white and affluent.[45] In order to make these inclusive practices catch on, we have to admit emotion and care into our social practices. But this has to be done with delicacy and forethought.

Nurture the Body, Do No Harm

It is not acceptable to include diverse bodies if we push them too far. In this chapter, I demonstrated the consequences of physical and emotional strain on the dancers in Headlong. But this kind of strain exists throughout our working worlds, from the discreet (repetitive stress injuries arising from office work) to the dangerous (workers at poultry plants who risk their health in unsanitary conditions). All jobs can be made safe if proper precautions are taken. Truly cooperative projects see their employees and members as humans, and equals, and strive to nurture everyone's well-being. Even in Headlong, the experience of *More* was an aberration that caused no permanent harm; everyone I spoke to from the organization felt that it changed their lives for the better in profound ways.

In order to protect the bodies in a cooperative practice, we need to become aware of each other's physical and emotional needs. For many workplaces, ongoing training in active listening, dispute resolution, and antibias are an important start. At many food co-ops, this training occurs during compensated time rather than being optional or extra. Democratic systems of management also cultivate a feeling of nurture, in that everyone has permission to raise a voice and be heard when something needs to change.[46]

As we move to the next chapter, we will explore the body at work. In order for cooperation to scale up from the level of individual bodies interacting and sharing weight, we have to examine practices of work and labor. Labor, even knowledge work, involves and implicates the body. From the sprung floors that dancers require to the ergonomics of co-op managers' computers, cooperation at work requires caring for bodies. While we travel along in our bodies, we will move in the next chapter to thinking about the way shared labor brings us closer to the ideal of a more cooperative practice.

PRACTICES OF WORK AND ORGANIZATION

A few years ago, I sat at a café table on a leafy northwest Philadelphia sidewalk outside Weavers Way Co-op. On that sunny June afternoon, the streets swelled with pedestrians, dipping in and out of the co-op, the café, the bookstore, and the dry cleaner. I was there to meet Gary, Weavers Way's general manager. Settling in, Gary and I spoke about the co-op's mission and operations, though our conversation was punctuated by hearty greetings from many of the passersby. After each person finished schmoozing with Gary and moved on, he would lean in and explain each person's connection to the co-op, the contributions each had made. Every person seemed to be an integral piece of the process. It was clear that Gary was the mayor of the corner of Greene and Carpenter, the person who managed a co-op that formed an essential part of the everyday life of the neighborhood.

Our conversation turned to the co-op's use of member labor. For most of its history, Weavers Way required shoppers to hold memberships in order to purchase goods from the store. Membership, which constituted a partial ownership stake in the co-op, also came with a work requirement. Members worked a few hours a month in order to keep prices down through reduced labor costs. But member work was about more than the bottom line. It allowed the co-op's thousands of members to labor in common, stocking shelves, staffing committees, serving as cashiers. Their shared contribution brought the lofty idea of the co-op back down to the level of bricks and mortar, reminding everyone each month what they collectively owned.

Once Gary finished greeting the last of the passing neighbors, he related an anecdote about a young Weavers Way staffer. He had recently asked her what she liked about working at the co-op. The staff member, who had been with the co-op about a year, was happy about the competitive salary and benefits. It was a good job for someone of her age and experience. "That was one reason." Gary went on:

> But the other thing she likes about this place, [what] is really unique from anywhere else she has worked, is that one day she's in grocery, stocking shelves with an architect. Another day, it's an artist. Another day, it's a housekeeper, someone who's at home. And another day, it's a very famous civil rights lawyer. She said the conversations are just fantastic. And so that's what she likes about it. What was interesting was the relationship between the worker and the shopper is structurally different than anywhere else I've ever worked.[1]

This young worker felt connected to the co-op's member-owners through the experience of shared labor. Together, staff and members made the work of the store happen. Members returned, month after month, to do the tasks they learned from years of covering that particular shift. Over time, they began to feel an affiliation with their department (deli, cashier, produce) and got to know the co-op inside and out. The workers, far from existing at a remove from the co-op's customers, got to know many of them, spending hours at a time working side by side.

That summer day, Gary related a vision of empowered, meaningful labor sustained by an institution that was based on social and economic foundations beyond the profit motive. By encouraging member labor, Weavers Way is guided by internationally codified cooperative values of equality, democracy, and solidarity.[2] These values establish an ideal—a lodestar—to which co-ops align their institutional practices. Member involvement is a cornerstone of co-op identity, for without robust engagement, members might fall away, in search of another place to devote their time and money.

The use of member labor is not without its issues, which I will explore below. In fact, by the time of our conversation, Weavers Way had transitioned from a mandatory to a voluntary member labor system. Yet the co-op continues to promote member involvement as a cardinal value, endorsing a vision of shared labor that stands in sharp relief to the prevailing conditions of work and organization in the contemporary United States that foster pervasive alienation from work.

Gary's story makes a case for the importance of bodies performing meaningful work, sustained by ethical organizations. The previous chapter explored the role of the body in cooperative practice. Indeed, the body is cooperation's foundation; it is a necessary component. But cooperation cannot rely on individual bodies laboring alone. Cooperation is sustained by bodies in situation, aligned, and integrated, laboring together toward a common goal. In turn, this embodied work is supported by organizations that struggle to uphold their ethical objectives while doing business effectively.

This chapter takes place at the scale of work and organization. It discusses issues of labor, management, and governance across the case studies, painting them as a counterweight to business as usual in the competitive, individualistic political economy. I take a grounded approach, designed to illuminate what happens inside an organization, from the way tasks get done all the way to the running of an enterprise. In the rest of the chapter, I will examine the relationship between alienated and meaningful labor and between practices and the institutions that are designed to sustain them. Then I will catalog several examples of cooperative projects striving to advance a vision of work and organization that is empowering and effective. This chapter makes clear that there are tensions regarding race, class, membership status, and other factors. These can be linked to the tensions I highlighted in the previous chapter around bodies, emotions, vulnerability, and the potential for burnout. When bodies are aligned into institutional arrangements, there are additional factors to consider in sustaining the integrity of the cooperative project.

ALIENATION AND ALIENATED LABOR

Too few workers in the contemporary United States economy find their work truly satisfying. Unlike the young Weavers Way employee who treasured working alongside the member owners of the co-op, workers often find their labor a source of alienation. Alienation from one's labor, and therefore from a vital aspect of the self, is pervasive and damaging. The term *alienation* is used colloquially to refer to a sense of distance from things one values, with an attendant sense of powerlessness. German philosopher Rahel Jaeggi traces an intellectual legacy of alienation, from the Enlightenment through to contemporary thought.[3] Alienation is a condition of internal division, a sense of relationlessness and dislocation. The alienated person is "a stranger in the world he himself has made."[4] There are a variety of ways people experience alienation. But particularly salient for this project is the alienation that separates workers from their labor. The distance imposed by alienation stunts human potential and limits workers' ability to fully live up to their capacities. In MacIntyrean terms, it curtails the ability to pursue excellence and virtue.

Alienated labor was an ongoing concern for Karl Marx. The concept first appeared in his *Economic and Philosophical Manuscripts of 1844.* Marx argues that capitalism changes the relationship between the worker and his labor—conditions of exploitation lead to the laborer being denied the fruits of his labor. These spoils are enjoyed by the capitalist instead, leaving the worker with an impoverished relationship to work and to himself. Since the conditions of his work are out of the worker's control, the product of his labor is a foreign object: "It becomes a power of its own, confronting him . . . as something hostile and alien."[5] This objectified labor produces the kind of alienation that Jaeggi and others see as endemic to modern life. In Marx's analysis, alienation infects a worker's relationship with the self, with the products of his labor, with work itself, and with his fellow humans.

Marxist geographer David Harvey explains that seemingly individual and localized alienations are connected to processes of globalization, dispossession, and exploitation that have been made possible by capitalism running rampant.[6] Under capitalism, alienation can be found in all places, at all scales. It is a near-universal condition, though it is unevenly distributed by class and race. It can be found among members of the professional class, in service of administrative bloat that anthropologist David Graeber calls "bullshit jobs."[7] It can also be found among workers in a service economy whose services bring no satisfaction or meaning to them. Harvey recognizes that, in the past, work has often been exploitative (like the production of goods in a factory) while remaining meaningful. Now, he argues, the exploitation remains, while the jobs (for example, a shopping mall security guard) appear to have little purpose or meaning.[8] Some work appears to have no intrinsic purpose; it is not performed for its own sake.[9]

Alienation distorts relationships between people, who begin to judge one another based on the work they do rather than on their character. We readily recognize this condition today in the ubiquitous small-talk conversation starter, "What do you do?" Such a question stratifies us according to the objectified labor we produce and marginalizes those who do not have high-status jobs or even reliable paid employment. As we compare the work we do, we ought to ask ourselves, "For whom and what do we really work?" Poignantly, Marx decries a state in which "life itself appears only as a means to life" because only the "life-engendering life" of productive, nonalienated labor relates one adequately to the human species.[10]

Jaeggi suggests that there is a way to overcome alienation that does not rely on outmoded philosophical concepts like the perfection of some essential self or a restoration to a previous ideal from an era that we have simply forgotten. Instead, overcoming alienation is a pragmatic, forward-looking process of reappropriation. It is a means for enabling people to do and will that which serves our individual and collective human capacities. When we reappropriate our labor, we rediscover ourselves.

It is one matter to theorize about the reappropriation of our labor and ourselves. But how can we achieve these goals in practice? Does contemporary capitalism present opportunities for overcoming alienation? Predictably, for a Marxist like David Harvey, nothing less than a political revolution in class relations will suffice. He decries "anarchist" strategies such as alternative economic practices and social movements.[11] With deference to Harvey's aspiration, and not wanting to deny the allure of a political economic revolution, I argue that meaningful, nonalienated work occurs in many places within, around, and beyond a capitalist framework.

Diverse economy research explores a range of forms of labor, finding that capitalist societies contain a great variety of types of work, from unpaid labor like volunteering and caring for family members, to unionized wage labor, to alternative paid labor schemes including cooperatives. Gibson-Graham remind us that "difference within the category of capitalist enterprise is as important to recognize as the difference between enterprise forms and class processes."[12] Much of this labor is deeply meaningful and satisfying to the laborers, whether or not it adequately answers the small-talk staple, "So, what do you do?" This economic diversity needs greater visibility, since workers can better pursue possibilities that they know exist, and policymakers can shift resources toward supporting the variety of forms of labor undertaken by their constituents. It is the work of diverse economies researchers to generate this visibility within and beyond the academy. They are joined by a vanguard of practitioners helping to bring these economic options into being. When it comes to cooperation, pathbreaking work is being done by grassroots local groups like the Cooperative Economics Alliance of New York City, across the United States by the Democracy at Work Institute, and globally by entities such as the International Labour Organization.

Despite my celebration of the diversity of labor available under current economic conditions, it is important to remember that diversity does not always equal freedom. Many modern labors are not voluntary, including the continued existence of indentured servitude, human trafficking, and prison labor. Even unpaid work like taking care of a sick family member may be more a matter of economic necessity (because of lack of adequate health insurance) than a matter of choice. Nonalienated labor is too often a privilege of the few. And those few are often highly educated, with class privilege and mobility.

One aim of cooperative practice is to massively extend the opportunity for meaningful work. This is as true of small worker cooperatives in the United States as it is of consumer-owned cooperatives like Weavers Way that employ nearly 150 people and as it is of massive producer cooperatives that aggregate the labor of hundreds of producers to compete in a capitalist market. Any economic project can be organized cooperatively; any institution can be run in a manner that prizes and advances the humanity of all who participate. In Jaeggi's words, a human is "capable of consciously forming herself and her world through social cooperation; moreover, she realizes herself in this process and also produces herself in the very concrete sense that she develops her own capacities, her senses, and her needs to the degree that she labors on and forms the world."[13] Overcoming alienation does not occur through a sudden flash of awareness that leads workers toward a permanent state of enlightenment. For the worker to realize herself in the process of work requires ongoing practice. As MacIntyre scholar Kelvin Knight explains, "Capital is not a power separate from humanity. Rather, it is accumulated, alienated labour."[14] Breaking capital's powerful spell requires a fight for structural change at every scale. Institutions, as one manifestation of capitalism's power, need to be transformed into carriers of virtuous, democratic practice.

THE DILEMMA OF VIRTUE IN ORGANIZATIONS

Alienation is not caused by labor itself (teaching, driving a truck, caring for the sick), but it is inherent in the conditions created by organizations. It is organizations that turn avocations into vocations. Alienation occurs when organizations fail to support their members in pursuing the practices that are at the heart of their institutional project.[15] Oftentimes, capitalist and bureaucratic organizations fall short of the imperative to create suitable conditions for the goods internal to a practice to adequately flourish.[16] These organizations suffer from a "partitioned morality," in which the goals of the organization are in direct conflict with the virtuous aspects of the underlying practice.[17] One need only think of the Silicon Valley company that touts its environmentally sustainable manufacturing processes and the liberating potential of its technological offerings. All the while, the same company is hard at work exploiting labor, monetizing users' personal data, and creating short-lived products that will end up in landfills in a couple of years. The drive to amass market share and build value stands in contrast to the techno-utopian goals that drive the organization's rhetoric.

This shortcoming is equally present in bureaucratic NGOs and nonprofit organizations, where the demands of raising funds to operate or demonstrating impact through outcomes analysis can sometimes trump the fulfillment of the organization's core mandate.[18] External goods like philanthropic funding or corporate donations are unavoidable; they provide a financial bulwark, sustaining fragile, cause-driven organizations. For all the good they make possible, these funding sources are often not accountable to a public and are often inequitable in how they distribute funds. At the very least, nonprofit organizations need to wrestle with the tensions inherent in maintaining a virtuous organization in the face of the partitioned morality encouraged by the broader political economy.

These tensions can be addressed through careful attention to the relationship between organizations and practices. As a reminder, practices are defined by MacIntyre as "any coherent and complex form of socially established cooperative human activity" that strives to achieve standards of excellence through goods internal to the practice.[19] As a primary goal, humans pursue practices in order to perfect them, make them effective; these are the internal goods. External goods like wealth, fame, glory, and the like should be subordinate to the pursuit of internal goods.

Just like human beings, an organization pursues practices. In addition to its primary goals, every organization has a secondary practice: the practice of making and sustaining the institution.[20] Institutions serve as the carriers of practices, and organizations can be thought of as practice-institution combinations. Practices need to be thoughtfully inscribed into institutions or else they will not be able to thrive. Despite the importance of practices on their own, they require a structure of support to achieve their transformative potential. This is certainly true of organizations built around the complex, sustained social practices of cooperation.

Practices thrive on the pursuit of internal goods, while organizations are sustained through external goods like revenue, brand recognition, and market share. At the same time as practices need institutions to thrive, institutions and organizations have the potential to corrupt practices. As organizations gather external resources, they distribute these goods in the form of compensation such as money, benefits, and organizational status. These external goods sit in tension with the pursuit of internal goods. Indeed, practitioners face conditions "in which the cooperative care for common goods of the practice is always vulnerable to the competitiveness of the institution."[21]

Given these concerns, practices themselves need to be fortified so that they are not eviscerated by the organization's mandate to succeed organizationally in the political economy. This fortification comes through attention to virtuous practice. MacIntyre warns of the attrition of virtue in a society dominated by the pursuit of external goods, especially because we might be confused by the proliferation of "simulacra" of virtue.[22] We need only to regard the public pronouncements of major companies to find examples of such simulacra, like the aforementioned Silicon Valley tech venture. It is only through maintaining focus on the virtues of practice that the institution can be held back from being dominated by its own institutional self-justification.

So how does one construct a virtuous institution? There are three preconditions. The first is the presence of virtuous agents at the levels of both the practice and the organization. The virtues must have representation at both the worker and managerial levels. Under any structure, the decision makers in the organization need to have a grasp of and a commitment to virtuous practice. Second, decision-making authority and criteria should be distributed throughout the organization. In the case of cooperative projects, this requires a form of organizational democracy, since the practice itself is grounded in mutuality. The third precondition of the virtuous organization is an environment that is suitable to the reproduction of the relevant practice.[23] It is difficult to maintain a virtuous organization in political economic conditions that work to subvert or deny the virtues that undergird the relevant practice. For this reason, it is important that cooperative practices band together in alliance and federation so that they can create a broader context in which cooperation can thrive. One example of co-ops' response to a difficult business environment is the Mid-Atlantic Food Cooperative Alliance, an association of food co-ops in several U.S. states who come together quarterly to offer support and business assistance amid changing conditions in the retail grocery sector. This federation of cooperatives helps to keep the member food co-ops on the right track as both business enterprises and associations of like-minded, virtue-driven cooperators.

Formal cooperatives, by dint of their commitment to the international cooperative principles and values, are supposedly bound to adhere to virtuous conduct. Beyond formal members of the cooperative movement, all mission-driven organizations ostensibly pursue a set of values commensurate with the goals of their practice. But this work is easier said than done. Cooperative projects face tough competition from normatively capitalist firms; firms with human services, community health, or cultural agendas face austerity and paucity of funding for their work. All such projects risk the burnout of key individuals so aligned with the project that they put their physical and mental health on the line.

Cooperatives have a dual role to play in order to succeed as virtuous institutions that adequately achieve the external goods necessary for their survival. They must exist as both enterprises and associations. Indeed, the ICA definition of a co-op includes both terms. They have both an ameliorative social purpose and a business purpose. The social purpose they serve can be compared to their pursuit of internal goods; the business purpose is a venue for the pursuit of goods external to the practices. This dual character lets co-ops act in markets, take risks, have successes and failures, and have some kind of a financial bottom line that they have to meet. Conversely, co-ops also have to engage members, be transparent, and have a social bottom line rooted in cooperative values.[24] This also makes co-ops tremendously difficult to operate, as these two logics are often in competition. Consumer food co-ops struggle with needing to stay in business and make money when some of them want to "give away the store." In 2013, Weavers Way was able to lower prices on more than two hundred items because of its financial success and good management. But general manager Gary wishes he could go further, saying, "If it were up to me, I would give away food for those who needed it at no cost, or sell everything at a sliding scale."

Co-ops that turn too much toward the market logic risk becoming co-ops in name only and pursuing economic success above all else. If co-ops focus too much on the community logic, they risk failing at businesses and being unable to operate at all. Zamagni and Zamagni call co-ops a "genuine, two-faced Janus," quipping that: "If conventional economics has trouble explaining the conduct of an agent who does not pursue only self-interested ends, social sciences also has trouble understanding how an agent like the cooperative can successfully act through the market to forge strong ties of solidarity and advanced forms of participatory democracy."[25] It is the challenge of cooperative organization to balance these multiple logics.

As enterprises, cooperatives must function as businesses concerned with external goods, with financial sustainability, market share, and robust compensation for stakeholders. As associations, they must act as democratic, accountable, and transparent entities that engage and involve members who share a common sense of identity through the cooperative. Co-ops that succeed as both enterprise and association ensure the balance of internal and external goods and the maintenance of virtuous conduct. These qualities need to be present not just in formal cooperatives but in any project that sees itself as an embodiment of collectivism, cooperativism, or mutual aid.

Ultimately, these institutional mandates are carried out through a process of inquiry and constant refinement. Cooperative projects are not simply set in motion, with their initial goodwill carrying them through indefinitely. Rather, it is through "participative enquiry [that] we learn how to give, receive and question accounts in ways that extend our understanding of the goods at which we aim and thereby enable us to take better decisions."[26] In the remainder of the chapter, I will discuss how the case study organizations pursued virtue through processes of reflection and inquiry, some of the decisions these projects faced, and how they struggled to maintain their practices through the institutions they fostered.

In what ways does each cooperative project in this book carry its practice forward? What are the sites of struggle? What needs to change over time to continue to advance the practice? Each of the projects has its own telos, or ultimate purpose, animating its practice. For Mariposa and Weavers Way, the telos is nourishment of the body through healthy food access. For POCA, it is the empowering, and shame-free, provision of community health. For Headlong, the telos is artistic experimentation and the projection of unique voices. I am determined to highlight not only instances of success in these practices but also times when projects fell short of their goals. Sometimes these shortcomings took place when the organizations prioritized external goods. But it is not just the pursuit of external goods that corrupts institutions. It can be the corruption of its practice through exclusivity and erasure. What are some ways each of these organizations have managed to sustain their practices while building a robust institution? Because they handle these challenges so differently, I will discuss each project in turn.

LABORING IN COMMON

I want to revisit member engagement in consumer food co-ops in order to demonstrate how these institutions struggle to uphold their practice of cooperation. Food co-ops engage in a practice in the MacIntyrean sense because of their focus on selling quality food, but only in part; their practice also models collective ownership and stewardship of a needed community function. Collective ownership of a grocery store allows for self-determination through locally relevant food offerings, the creation of jobs, and the retention of profits in the local economy. Consumer co-ops participate in a community economy that demonstrates that not only capitalist firms can succeed at meeting people's needs. In addition, consumer ownership requires a form of participatory democracy, with collective deliberation about means and ends as part of the program of sustaining the cooperative as both enterprise and association.

In fact, if consumer food co-ops mistake their purpose for simply selling expensive organic food, rather than promoting collective ownership and stewardship (as some do), they close off the potential for people of all backgrounds to shop there. The same exclusivity occurs when they choose products to sell that are not representative of the diversity of the neighborhood's foodways. It is even more apparent when cooperatives embrace a culture of racism, ableism, classism, and the like.[27] In the fall of 2017, CDS Consulting Co-op (a cooperative development service) released a report exploring personal narratives about race and food co-ops. The report detailed the racial misinformation that led white-led cooperatives to think that people of color were unable to manage co-ops or were simply uninterested in them. The report found a number of reasons driving exclusivity, from unacknowledged racism, to types of food sold, to the idea that just saying "Everyone's welcome here" would be enough to truly invite participation by people of color.[28] The pursuit of white or wealthy customers, whether by design or by failure to consider who is being excluded, is a violation of the virtue of justice and an endorsement of external goods—profit and status—at the expense of broad inclusion.

Therefore, these institutions need to engage a diverse membership and encourage participation to fulfill their organizational raison d'être. If people merely shop at the co-ops because they are good-enough organic grocers, as soon as a large capitalist organic grocer like Whole Foods comes along, their loyalty to the co-op will disappear—and the co-op might fail. When construed thoughtfully, member engagement is the positive side of the paradox of exclusivity: shoppers feel a sense of deep affiliation and an urge to participate in the co-op. This leads to the fulfillment of the association function of the co-op.

At the same time, co-ops need to have a large enough customer base to support the co-op's enterprise function. A few deeply engaged members alone may support a buying club, but to serve an entire neighborhood's needs, the co-ops need to attract thousands of customers per week. The larger and more robust the sales are at co-ops, the more power they have to bring in a wide variety of goods, to negotiate fair prices from vendors and distributors, and to provide more employment for local workers. In this way, they successfully manage the external goods necessary for their practice.

Member engagement is therefore critical to the success of a consumer-owned cooperative. During the time of my research, both Mariposa and Weavers Way were engaged in a deliberative process to redefine themselves in relationship to their membership structure. In these cases, the immediate context was store expansion. Both stores recognized an opportunity to grow their operations, after decades in the same small stores. The drive for expansion was based on a number of factors, including increasing demand for organic food, population growth, gentrification (particularly in the case of Mariposa's West Philadelphia neighborhood), and interest in supporting local businesses on a walkable commercial corridor. But with expansion came massive risk. These small co-ops would have to raise millions of dollars to purchase and renovate new buildings, secure a larger inventory, and hire additional workers. The whole notion of expansion carried with it the possibility of failure. Member engagement was key to making the transition to a larger store and a larger impact.

HORIZONS OF PARTICIPATION

When I began my research, both Weavers Way and Mariposa required members to work in the store each month in order to maintain good standing and retain shopping privileges. Both co-ops also required a financial investment in the co-op in order to secure membership (this equity investment was refundable with the termination of membership and also entitled the member to a share of the co-op's profits at the end of each year). A small number of co-ops around the United States still require member labor, in service of stimulating member engagement (one notable example is New York City's Park Slope Food Coop, which has more than seventeen thousand members and 75 percent of the labor is performed by members instead of paid staff). Member labor can help keep prices down, since the cost of labor as a percentage of sales can be minimized. Of course, this requires that the co-op be efficiently managed and that people consistently show up for their work shifts. Co-ops with member labor often struggle with these issues, finding that staff management of working members can be time-consuming and frustrating.[29] Nevertheless, member labor has the potential for fostering bonds among members, as well as lowering cost.

During the course of my fieldwork, both Weavers Way and Mariposa removed the requirement to be a member to shop in the co-op and abandoned mandatory member labor.[30] In its place, both co-ops offered member labor as an option that provided a discount. Both continue to push member ownership as a core value, with labor as an option. Given the organizational growth needed to power the expansion, co-op leaders worried about the horizons for depending on mandatory membership in these enlarged organizations. In my time at the co-ops, members disagreed about the wisdom of abandoning mandatory membership and member labor. Some were concerned that the larger the co-op became, the less involved people would be, reducing the association function of the cooperative.

Gary, Weavers Way's general manager, found the working member co-op to be an empowering model:

> What I see is a strong brand built upon the working membership and that if you don't have the working membership as part of it, then you have to do a little bit more work to get that message across about the principles of the co-op and the mission, and it's harder.

Nevertheless, shopping at a member-only co-op can alienate new members, who are unfamiliar with the culture of the stores. Since Weavers Way and Mariposa historically did not serve the general public, they developed shopping norms that differed from conventional grocers: weighing and pricing one's own bulk items; packing one's groceries into the store's spare cardboard boxes instead of the store supplying paper or plastic bags; and in the case of Mariposa, being able to let oneself into the store after hours to shop on credit.

Former Mariposa staff member Sam explained the complicated relationship between workers and other shoppers in the co-op in its original location. He explained that shopping at Mariposa required a lot of self-confidence. There was a very small staff, and the working members were not trained to do customer service. They were there simply to stock the shelves or ring up purchases. Other shoppers had to fend for themselves:

> [Mariposa] required an active shopper. If you wanted your groceries to be on the shelf and you didn't want to have to look for stuff or ask for stuff or go to the basement and get it yourself, I could see that being an obstacle. It excludes whatever portion of the population that wants to get soymilk and get out quickly.

Using member labor is certainly more complex than having a store operated exclusively by paid professionals. It asks the members to be trained as grocers, which is outside the skill set of most people. Mariposa's store culture, into the late 2000s, was a legacy of its original 1970s radical organizational politics, which eschewed the building of traditional forms of expertise and encouraged a mistrust of any kind of hierarchy or specialization. According to Sam, "[Mariposa had a] system that relied on nonexperts to do expert work in store functions. No one cleaned; no one wanted to yell at their friends for not doing work shifts." Clearly, these conditions could not sustain a significantly expanded store. The dynamics of member labor and paid staffing would have to change somehow.

MORE ACCESS AND LESS ENGAGEMENT?

Weavers Way and Mariposa depended on member labor so heavily and for so long, and were such small, tight-knit co-ops, that an influx of new people was seen by some as a challenge to the organization's identity. One Mariposa staff member lamented, "There is something about the larger the co-op has gotten, the less a sense of ownership, connectedness, community happens for people." Another staff member, Siobhan, elaborated on this point, speaking to me on the eve of the expansion, when work shifts were still mandatory:

> I think if our membership grows and the popularity of shopping in the store grows, the number of people that are deeply involved will either stay the same as it is in this space or get even smaller because there is a diffusement [*sic*] of responsibility and people will be less aware of, "Oh, I am shopping at a co-op." I think that a lot of people join because of the food and not because it's a cooperative.

Quantity of participation and intensity of participation are both important for a cooperative project. But not everyone agreed that each shopper needs to participate at the same level. Member Jenny was troubled by the idea among some on the Mariposa board that everyone needed to have a participatory relationship with the co-op. She just did not think it was possible, nor should it be expected:

> I really don't think we can buy this gigantic store and require everyone to participate. There aren't enough people. I think we've already kind of tapped out our participatory community. We bought a huge building, like ten times bigger than our current building, but we are not going to find ten times more people that want to go to four-hour [membership] meetings without food, and vote with thumbs in the air [referencing the very specific hand signals Mariposa used in its consensus decision-making process].

A response to this reality, as Jenny saw it, was to allow people to participate simply by doing the baseline thing that makes people stakeholders in a co-op: consume its goods and services through purchases. But this suggestion offended some of the people in the co-op:

> I recently brought up that spending money at the co-op is a form of participation and some people were super like, "That's not what we want! We want more than their dollars! We would just be a grocery store if we just wanted their money." I mean, I walk out of my way sometimes to go spend more for something at the co-op that I could get elsewhere because I love the co-op. But I feel like different types of participation aren't validated.

Yet, over time, the desire to open the co-op to more people won out, while the co-ops looked for ways to encourage member ownership. One staff member told me, "Just looking at the diversity of folks in the neighborhood . . . the proper response to that is to respond with a diversity of options. It's time to stop being gatekeepers."

DEFENDING MANDATORY MEMBER LABOR

In light of the changes at Weavers Way and Mariposa, I checked in with Jacob, a staff member at the Park Slope Food Coop in New York City. He remains strongly in favor of the use of member labor to address the paradox of exclusivity. At Park Slope, mandatory member labor keeps the prices down, which makes the co-op more inclusive to people of all incomes. For Jacob, the higher priced food co-ops, even the ones that have open membership policies, are discriminatory:

> You are from that co-op that excludes people that don't want to work—you are one of those people who excludes people that don't have the money for the good food. Every model has exclusion. We take this exclusive stuff called healthy food and make it cheaper or the same as the less healthy food—and we are doing it through people's self-help.

Jacob recognizes the paradox of exclusivity that co-ops face. If they attempt to include everyone by leaving membership open, then prices will rise. If they have membership and work requirements, prices can be lower (if the co-op is efficiently run), but the co-op excludes people who cannot do the work shifts.[31] I followed up by asking him what the co-op thinks about people who have to work more than one job and do not have the time to work at the co-op. He did not think there were enough people in this category to warrant concern, which is surprising considering the high cost of living in Brooklyn, where the co-op is located:

> You could exclude the 1 percent that has two jobs. [But it's] not even 1 or 2 percent. [It's a] nice theory. There are people who are too busy—tell people to shop at a grocery store! Why should the co-op water down its system of connectivity and strength?
>
> No one's telling you, you are not a good person if you can't join the Park Slope Food Coop. You don't have time? You could be saving the world. Save the world and don't shop here. Don't expect us to change the rules of something that brought people together—don't make it the only store in town.

During my fieldwork, I learned that Park Slope Food Coop had forged a strong partnership with a startup co-op, Chester's Community Grocery Co-op, and its founder, Candace. Chester is a majority Black city in southeastern Pennsylvania that had no other grocers at the time, having been long abandoned by any other food markets. In talking to Candace, I learned that she feels strongly that the members-only model is the only one appropriate for co-ops, as she relates below. Candace contrasted her member-only model with the open model recently instituted at Weavers Way and Mariposa, feeling that these co-ops' prices would rise when member labor became optional, causing exclusion of shoppers with low incomes:

> The model that Weavers Way is doing and the model that Mariposa is doing are for the rich. That's pretty much what they are saying. [Chester] didn't choose this model because it is the poor man's model! We chose it because it had all of these wonderful layers to it. Empowerment, and all of the things that the co-op model suggests you have to have: self-reliance, independence, this educational component of it, you can share with other co-ops. All of this stuff that meant community. I mean the core of a co-op is community and suddenly we have been relegated to a poor man's model and a rich man's model. . . . And that's really, for me, problematic.

Unfortunately, while the Park Slope Food Coop remains strong, the Chester startup closed after only a couple of years. It is impossible to say that the requirement of member labor was the issue, since the city of Chester had been unable to sustain a grocer of its own for many years. There is now another grocer operating in Chester, so perhaps the co-op was able to pave the way for the residents of the city to have more fresh food options.

Even though Weavers Way made member labor optional, that did not mean that it was no longer a priority. After the switch, the co-op's board issued a directive to its general manager to try and raise the number of working members: "Forget about getting new members. We love new members, as I said, but we really don't want to be just new members. We want cooperators." Since our conversations, Weavers Way has pushed the importance of member ownership and particularly working membership through gestures like member appreciation days and a section on their website called "Why I Am a Working Member."

Consumer food cooperatives like the ones I have discussed in this section have a duty to focus on member engagement in order to sustain the practice of food justice and collective ownership. The particular struggle in these cases was the decision to do away with member labor in order to make the co-ops more accessible, while continuing to engage members in the life of the co-op. That work continues to happen at Mariposa and Weavers Way through members who work in the store, serve on boards and committees, and generally aid in the running of the co-op. In addition, a broader base of shoppers has yielded more revenue and more paid staff at the co-ops. They continue to struggle with the paradox of exclusivity, as they always will.

More important than the decision of whether to open up shopping privileges was the deliberative process and soul searching regarding the identity of the co-op that took place in the co-ops during their time of expansion. This process of inquiry, of searching for the goods that will sustain practices, is the work of building ethical and accountable institutions.

SOLIDARITY ACROSS SPACE

As an institution, the People's Organization of Community Acupuncture focuses to the greatest possible extent on the goods internal to the provision of low-cost alternative health care. With a decentralized network that contains so many nodes across the country, POCA sustains the community acupuncture movement by producing solidarity across space through shared governance and mutual business support. POCA has had to develop structures that help individual clinic owners thrive. The organization also strives to create a unified experience of community acupuncture in clinics that have very different geographical and economic contexts. In the rest of this section, I will explore the many ways POCA cultivates this sense of solidarity across space.

In MacIntyre's framework, community acupuncture functions as a practice: it has its own complex modalities and knowledge transmission; it is a social collaboration with patients as well as other practitioners in the co-op; and its goal is excellence through a set of goods internal to the practice of acupuncture—namely, the increase of health and well-being. Though (noncommunity) acupuncture may also constitute a practice, the community organizing and democratic empowerment framework utilized by POCA marks it as distinct and different from mainstream health care in the United States. Mainstream health care, with its pursuit of profit, focuses on goods (like wealth and prestige) that are external to the practice of enhancing health. The health-care industry in the United States is dominated by large corporate institutions, which MacIntyre warns possess a "partitioned morality" that stands in contrast to "the integrated morality of practice-based communities" like POCA.[32] Despite the rhetoric of U.S. health-care management organizations, the political and financial structure of that industry at present all but ensures that the institutions will be corrupted by the pursuit of external goods.

POCA, by contrast, nests its practice of community acupuncture in a narrative of empowerment that it traces back to the Black Panthers and Young Lords. (Both groups provided free public acupuncture in the 1970s as a tool to treat drug addiction.) Rather than aspiring to business success through cultivating wealthy clients and a spa-like setting, acupunks aspire to emulate the Young Lords and have spartan, though comfortable, clinics that emphasize practicality and thrift (down to the donated chairs). They attempt to live out an integrated morality informed by a tradition of organizing and empowerment, which is the focusing narrative of their own acupuncture training school, POCA Tech. POCA holds itself accountable by offering an intelligible narrative of its practices that places them within a tradition of accumulated moral debt to POCA's radical forebears.

The multistakeholder co-op model that POCA employs allows the flexibility of small working communities (one feature of MacIntyre's idealized organizational structure) with the advantages of a national network. Lisa Rohleder writes that the community acupuncture movement stumbled on traditions of cooperation as a result of trying to comprehend what was already happening in the clinics:

> By 2010, we recognized that there was a name for this phenomenon. It's called the principle of mutual aid, or the spirit of mutualism, and it is the cornerstone of the cooperative movement. Because none of us knew much about business, let alone cooperatives, it didn't dawn on us that what we were doing was more like a cooperative than it was like anything else.[33]

POCA is unlike most cooperative businesses: it does not own or operate any clinics itself; it provides no direct income to practitioners or benefits to consumers. There are no dividends or rebates offered to members who participate financially. Indeed, Daniel, a cooperative development specialist I spoke to, stated that the defining feature of POCA is its commitment to democratic governance and building a mutualistic platform for transforming acupuncture. In the co-op's own words, "POCA's dividends are affordable acupuncture treatments, living wage jobs, and stable community clinics. . . . The return on your investment is not financial but social."[34]

POCA hosts popular online forums and a series of videos where practitioners share information on everything from acupuncture practice to clinic administration to dealing with challenging patients. In this sense, it functions as something of a peer-to-peer support network, a kind of knowledge commons.[35] Carol, an acupuncturist from Providence who had experience starting her own clinic, expressed gratitude for these shared resources:

> I knew I was going to start a clinic, but luckily, I have all of the templates and models. [POCA] was my beginning of experiencing what it was like to have an open source refuge to be able to get in there and ask a million questions and have people offer you all of their things that they had done.

In addition, POCA offers microloans for clinics to start up or expand. It hosts a job board where clinics seek acupuncturists or new owners. It offers minicourses that provide continuing education credits to licensed acupuncturists. Videos and posts are geared toward patients as well, with a section devoted to patient testimonials. The goal is to attract a diverse group of members, not erect an intellectual and political monolith. Sara, an acupuncturist from California, compared recruiting POCA members to community organizing:

> You've got people in the treatment room who are pretty different from yourself and each other. Different in lots of ways, including political. Emphatically, we don't just treat folks who eat organic and think like us. I like treating people who I couldn't have had a political conversation with before I began working at a high-volume CA clinic. Divisions, real and imagined, potential conflicts and political differences become blurred in the treatment room. We're all in this together and that's the huge lesson.

POCA is governed by a series of committees devoted to counseling clinics on achieving success, supporting acupuncturists in the professional difficulties they encounter, running the school, and making small loans to establish new clinics. POCA maintains an online directory of clinics so that patients in one geographic location can find a clinic if they relocate or want to refer friends and family to a POCA facility. POCA offers member clinics discounts on supplies like needles. POCA membership for patients allows them to volunteer at clinics without violating labor regulations. Finally, POCA offers leadership and guidance as clinics struggle to articulate, uphold, and advance the mission of the cooperative.

POCA founder Lisa Rohleder advocates for a federated model of growth rather than having any one clinic achieve massive scale. Most clinics operate one or two branches in a given city. Like many co-ops, POCA distributes its activities across a range of firms rather than seeking the creation of a behemoth. Rohleder calls this model the Big Damn Clinic. The Big Damn Clinic is a collection of small, independent entities that needed to find a way to partner for growth and sustainability. In the Big Damn Clinic model, acupunks are supposed to focus less on ego and individual achievement, cultivating a group of patients that are loyal to only them. Instead, acupunks should replicate the model and encourage patients to go to any POCA practitioner or clinic that is convenient for them. One of POCA's leaders explained to me how she advises clinic owners:

> Do you think of this business as your business? Or do you think of it as this entity outside yourself that you steward and that you're a part of, but that your goal is to bring more people into it? It's not *your* practice.

This insistence on fealty to the movement's goals has drawn fire from conventional acupuncturists who are interested in providing lower-cost acupuncture in groups but do not subscribe to the radical narrative and tradition that has been championed by Rohleder and other leaders. In their public pronouncements, POCA adherents are not shy about calling out conventional acupuncturists for the way they have mishandled the practice of acupuncture. Rohleder, in particular, struggled with the gulf she perceived in the acupuncture world between boutique practices for the upper and middle classes and public health acupuncture for poor patients. As she puts it:

> People who had functional lives and modest resources did not exist as potential patients. They were completely invisible. . . . If acupuncture clinics were restaurants, there would be only soup kitchens and four-star bistros, with nothing in between.[36]

According to POCA, private acupuncturists have hoarded treatment through high prices and cultural insensitivity to people of color, trans people, fat people, and working-class people (the first POCA clinic is called Working Class Acupuncture).

POCA's acupunks emphasize their solidarity with patients. In interviews, acupuncturists often represented themselves as working class and saw themselves as part of the same struggle patients faced. (The non-POCA acupuncturists I interviewed also felt connected with their patients but often referenced a middle- or upper-class clientele that could afford their services.) Emma, an acupuncturist from a small clinic in California's Bay Area, described her frustration with trying to treat people with disposable income, when she herself had little money:

> It was just frustrating. It was just incongruent being really poor and always struggling and not having access, and then coming out of that to set up a practice where no one like me would have access to it.

When she discovered Lisa Rohleder's work, she set up a practice that could treat people like her. In one of the most intensely emotional exchanges of these interviews, Angela, a leader of POCA, made it clear why treating working-class people meant so much to her: "By staking my life on this, I prove to myself that people like me are valuable. So, God, was it worth it."

Another POCA value is solidarity among acupuncturists. Many interviewees spoke about the commitment to working together as a community of practitioners instead of competing against one another. Tamara, who runs a practice by herself in the rural Midwest, described a diverse economies vision of how POCA helps her overcome isolation:

> No matter whether you're successful or not as an acupuncturist, it sucks to be isolated. Most acupuncturists work by themselves. It's incredible having colleagues and friends that are supportive, that are trying to build something beautiful together, and it's inspirational . . . having that sense of being a co-op and doing cooperative work. . . . It helps with the isolation of capitalism.

Carol emphasized the interconnection of all the POCA clinics: "I don't have a financial interest in Carly's clinic in Philly, but I have a tremendous passion for her to be successful there because I know that it's going to be amazing for the community, and the community really needs it—and it's also selfishly creating a place for my patients when they move to Philly or have family [who live there]." One of the defining features of each POCA clinic is the presence of a large United States wall map with hundreds of pins in it, each one representing a clinic. The map is surrounded by business cards from other POCA clinics for patients to take in case of travel, relocation, or to send to family and friends in distant cities who need acupuncture.

POCA's work is not without risk. In addition to figuring out how to sustain acupunks on wages often less than $50,000 per year, POCA and its school are mostly run on volunteer labor. Like other social movement organizations, it risks burning out key personnel. And conventional acupuncture is nipping at its heels, opening competing community clinics in an effort to capitalize on the high-volume model without any of POCA's ideological commitments. The practice of community acupuncture needs the institution of POCA to sustain it. As MacIntyre explains: "The ability of a practice to retain its integrity will depend on the way in which the virtues can be and are exercised in sustaining the institutional forms which are the social bearers of the practice."[37] If POCA is able to sustain its unique form of cooperation, punks, and patients, the alternative health field will benefit.

SUSTAINING COLLABORATION OVER TIME

The practice of Headlong Dance Theater advances a series of artistic questions. For the first two decades of their history, those questions could only be answered with a multivocal, collective yes. The three founding codirectors each served as choreographer, performer, and arts administrator. Collaboration, while never easy, was an essential element in their organizational design. During my years of working with Headlong, I witnessed an act of continual creation to determine how the organization should run, an evolving process of negotiation. To this day, Headlong continues to revisit the questions at the core of its artistic inquiry, seeking the organizational form that best fits the tasks at hand. Headlong exhibits the features of a MacIntyrean practice through its complex, social examination of cultural questions, with an emphasis on excellence in artistic production rather than on seeking mass appeal and approval.

As I related in the previous chapter, founding codirector Andrew Simonet departed in 2013, after twenty years. In 2019, another founding codirector, Amy Smith, exited the organization, leaving the future of Headlong in the hands of David Brick. The company is no longer the three-headed collaborative that it was in the 1990s and 2000s. But one thing I have learned through this research is that not every cooperative project needs to last forever to be meaningful. Permanence is not a requirement of success. At the time of his departure, Andrew Simonet reflected on the challenge required of sustaining institutions: "An organization is a set of agreements. . . . It's full of compromises, and despite every attempt to counteract it, it becomes an entity outside of individuals. You can counteract that to some extent, but you can't eliminate it." Headlong was the creation of three very different individuals who came together and built an institution, an ongoing creative improvisation.

At its formation, the founders pushed back against the egotism they found rampant in contemporary dance. Amy Smith explained that, from the outset, they rejected individual ownership of the work or individual credit-taking. That collaborative ethos played into the decision to take Headlong Dance Theater as the company name, back in the early 1990s. According to David Brick, they were fighting their own egos. As he explained: "We wanted to erase the problem of individual authorship. . . . I thought that the most flamboyant thing we could do is to erase our names and be like 'It's all Headlong.'" Amy Smith remembered they wanted to name the company something bigger than or inclusive of the three of them. She explained, "We knew very clearly it wasn't like 'Amy Smith Dance Company' or even 'Amy Smith–David Brick–Andrew Simonet Dance Company.'"

Headlong was designed to be a collaborative, not a collective, as David Brick saw it. A collective might share a name, a space, or an evening-length bill at a festival. But a collaborative was based in the cocreation of work from the idea phase to its ultimate execution. David joked that starting Headlong as a collaborative would be the purest expression of the founders' "communist communitarian values," the ones they first explored during their dance training at Wesleyan University. These values derived from a shared distaste for top-down hierarchy, while recognizing the importance of strong leadership:

> All of us have a little bit of loathing of the hierarchy of leadership. Not leadership [itself]. I remember thinking, "I finally separated leadership as a thing that happens from hierarchy." That was the big moment in my thinking because I don't like hierarchy. I feel like I work best from a place of mutuality. [Yet] I really believe in leadership.

David's observation draws a distinction between the value of leadership as a feature of organization and the unnecessary imposition of hierarchy. His thinking reflects the work of theorists like Joyce Rothschild, who sees workplace democracy as a countertrend to the prevailing ethos of hierarchical management. Embracing worker leadership allows these institutions to grant workers more autonomy, engagement, and voice and leads to greater satisfaction and commitment to the organization.[38]

Once Headlong's directors established that its workplace would be a democracy, they needed to find a way to equitably share the work. There was a division of labor in which Amy did the finances, Andrew did the fundraising, and David did the outreach and communication. According to the codirectors, this was an easy decision. Each person got to perform the function suited to their skills and personality.

Seven Votes Apiece

In order to express their individual preferences, Headlong developed an innovative decision-making methodology. From Headlong's beginning until the creation of *More* in 2009 (a project I discussed in the previous chapter), Amy, David, and Andrew made decisions by consensus. But rather than one person, one vote, Headlong initially allotted seven votes to each of the codirectors.[39] Amy related that their working method was really time-consuming, but ultimately it was really important work. Here is how she explained the method:

> Each of us has seven votes. If we're trying to decide something and we're at loggerheads about it, you can put your seven votes to the two sides of the question based on however strongly you feel about it. If I feel really strongly, I put all seven into "yes" and zero towards "no." If I'm kind of, eh, then I might put four and three. Tally the votes and find the clear winner.

The seven-vote method caught on with some of Headlong's collaborators as well. Longtime ally Christopher used it in his work in the theater department at a nearby college. He told me that he found it a smart way to account for the depth people felt toward both sides of an issue. But using the method requires good faith among participants: "Every time I've used that at Bryn Mawr, people have cheated. The only way that system works is if you really check in with yourself and you say, 'Deep in my heart of hearts I really feel five-two on this.'" The value in any consensus method lies in a process of individual and collective inquiry into what is good for the practice at the heart of the matter.

In the early years, Headlong was so committed to consensus decision-making, they even applied the process to their shared living arrangement. When they first moved to the city, the three codirectors shared a tiny two-bedroom apartment in Southwest Philadelphia. After a while, they felt it was too small to live together—so they rotated moving out. Amy remembered, "We were like, 'Well, what's the equitable decision-making process to figure out who's allowed to move out, basically. Or is it based on who can afford to move out?" Since the codirectors all had day jobs in those days, different people had more money coming in at various points. Amy laughed at the extent of the seriousness with which they deliberated in those days: "It's just absurd when you think about it, but that was what we did."

The Arbiter Emerges

Despite getting very good at making collective decisions, Headlong was nevertheless run by very strong-willed, opinionated people. Over time, the decision-making process needed to be reevaluated. The codirectors realized that not every artistic decision could be made communally. (The codirectors' administrative roles remained stable and intact.) As the complexity of their shows ramped up, along with their success, there was a need for one person to sit in the light booth with the lighting designer making the decision about what the lighting should look like. Someone else could therefore be figuring out what stage shots they wanted the photographer to take, Amy remembered. They came up with a new idea: the arbiter. In a given artistic process, the arbiter would have final decision-making authority. Even when projects originated as a communal effort, all the minute decisions that make up an artistic process would be handled by the agreed-upon arbiter. It allowed the codirectors to step outside of their given roles and learn how to do new things. This was David's vision of leadership without oppressive hierarchy put into action.

The arbiter was a different person for every Headlong piece. Job rotation of this kind recalls a key element of what has been termed the collectivist organization.[40] Because Headlong pieces took time to generate and build toward a public performance, sometimes having a single arbiter would create an issue. Amy recalled, "As the pieces got bigger and longer term, you could go two years without being in charge of a piece. That, sometimes, start to feel like, 'Why am I always in a back-seat role?'"

In a sense, Headlong's evolution represented the continued engagement with ego and egolessness that David mentioned at the outset. They were trained as creators to "go into discomfort," as David related: "If there is something that is uncomfortable or that you don't like, that's a site for you to investigate and kind of work against. Your red flags are places that you should . . . engage." Over time, the work of balancing the individual's and the collaborative's needs led to an ongoing struggle with the power dynamics in the company. In particular, the other co-directors struggled with a perception that Andrew Simonet dominated the organization. As the grant writer, it fell to Andrew to articulate Headlong's creative projects to funders. That work of envisioning, describing, and bringing in financial backing, though behind the scenes, is a very real locus of organizational power. It is certainly more widely respected work than keeping the organization's books. Speaking just after his departure from Headlong, Andrew simultaneously maintained the importance of his partnership with the other codirectors, while feeling uncomfortable with the amount of responsibility he felt he shouldered.

Family as Metaphor

These private tensions that both sustained and challenged Headlong's collaboration stood in contrast to a perception in the Philadelphia arts community that Headlong was a happy family. This metaphor of family felt alternately apt and constraining to the people I spoke with about Headlong. Two of the company dancers reflected on the feeling of family at the time of Headlong's difficulty during the making of *More* in 2009. Jasmine highlighted the challenges of a three-way collaborative relationship: "It's hard enough being in a two-way marriage, but when you're two you can go back and forth. But three people changing, it's a lot . . . when that burning fire and magic became more complicated." Over years of working together with a small cadre of devoted dance company members, the notion of Headlong-as-family had become an operative way of thinking about the organization. Wendy also used the marriage metaphor:

> We had become such a loving family and to see our three-headed parents fighting . . . It had always been kind of present and quiet [in the background], but it was like Mommy, Daddy, and Daddy are fighting in the other room!

Andrew Simonet reacted with distaste to the notion that Headlong was a symbol of effortless married or family relationship. For him, the relationship was more complicated and should not be viewed reductively:

> I worry about the ways that we are a symbol for people of . . . good old Headlong getting along. Not that we didn't. We did. But we did by doing the hard shit. It's like a real marriage versus a Hollywood marriage. Being actually married is fucked up! [laughs]

It was Andrew who was the first to leave the orbit of Headlong, marriage or no. Some observers might suggest that the structure they had built was not strong enough to sustain the original collaborators any longer. Company member Eve pushed back on such a simplistic reading of Andrew's departure:

> A positive reading of that same thing would be that the structure was so strong that it announced itself, and that Andrew had to leave, because the structure enabled him to make that decision in a way that was consonant with the values and the processes of the organization.

A Structure That Sustains

Looking back now at Headlong's decades of cooperative inquiry, struggle, and artistic creations, I am reminded of the heart-wrenching beauty of it all. They made decisions on their own terms and changed along with the ebb and flow of funding, the requirements of aging bodies and growing families, and of their artistic vision. Amy recalled with pride that the decisions Headlong made about their practice of cooperation were all internal decisions. She did not blame any entity or force outside of Headlong for anything that occurred. Amy reflected on Headlong's focus on internal goods in the face of a system that actively works to subvert Headlong's brand of ethical artistic practice:

> I do think it's really hard to be a collective anything in a hypercapitalist environment. It wasn't money or reputation or fame. It wasn't any of those things that made us individuate more, so I'm happy about that too.

Money and fame—the external goods of any artistic practice—were not the motivators of Headlong's artistic project. The motivators were the pursuit of virtues through artistic courage, hard truth, and a daring, loving cooperation. After our interview, Headlong dancer Jasmine sent me a letter, reflecting on her own time with Headlong and what it meant to her. Her words express the diversity and depth of the Headlong experience quite beautifully:

> When meeting with you it was most palpable to access the sadness and hope of the transition they were in. But I will always be in awe of the ways that Headlong functioned and blossomed so beautifully, so infectiously, for so many years. There were definitely moments when the chaotic co-run ship seemed about to careen into a wall. But someone always grabbed the wheel, either with sass or with humility, or with a democratic vote, and at that moment the group would rally to support the vision. And afterwards there were debriefs and jokes and there was love.

VIRTUE IN INSTITUTIONAL PRACTICE

Effective cooperation requires organizations that can ethically sustain practices. Organizations are containers for shared labor, affect, solidarity, and conflict. At their best, they strive to balance the pursuit of internal goods with the necessary achievement of external success and validation. In this chapter, I shared a set of practice stories to illuminate some of the struggles and triumphs I encountered in the course of my research. These stories are meant to illuminate, to inspire introspection and dialogue. There are many more stories of cooperation, in these organizations and others, yet to be told. Before I conclude this chapter, I will offer a few takeaways, a few exhortations for practice, that speak to the level of the organization.

Resist Alienation through Cooperation

The pervasive condition of alienation in our workplaces can be counteracted by basing organizations and institutions on the notion of a social self. This alternate ontology understands identity as formed collectively, and any organization that grows out of this understanding must reject individualism and competition as its ideals. The cooperative movement already subscribes to a set of values and principles that can aid organizations in the deliberative work to turn ideals of cooperation into reality.

Cooperation in practice stands as a bulwark against alienation from labor. The forms of estrangement many workers feel from their labor lead to a sense of powerlessness and desperation. Alienation is not an individual problem, though it affects workers individually. Rather, alienation is a feature of the broader political economy, of business as usual. Thus, individuals who seek to overcome alienation can only do so as part of the social world. And the vehicle for the reclamation of self and world can only take place through a reinvention of social practices. Jaeggi concludes her study of alienation with a provocative question: "How must institutions be constituted so that individuals living within them can understand themselves as the (co-)authors of those institutions and identify with them as agents?"[41] It is my contention that institutions that embody ethical practices of cooperation are so constituted and that participants can assert their needs through them. Yet, ethical cooperative practices need to be continually revisited and renegotiated over time and across space.

Balance Internal and External Goods

Food co-ops like Mariposa and Weavers Way need to succeed as both enterprise and association. To forsake the business side of the equation (the external goods) means cooperative death, a fate that plagued many of the other consumer co-ops that started in the 1960s and 1970s. To forsake the association side of the equation is to become a co-op in name only, a charge frequently leveled at cooperatives that seem excessively focused on success in the capitalist sense. Many food co-ops around the United States bury the concepts of membership, shared labor, and the cooperative principles deep down, far beneath where the average shopper knows to look. Mariposa and Weavers Way both came to the conclusion that lifting restrictions on shopping and membership allowed them to serve a broader community, to be more inclusive. At the same time, it broadened the customer base enough to sustain store expansions and generate more jobs. Yet, member labor stalwarts like Park Slope Food Coop insist that costs can be better contained, and community can be better maintained, by the kinds of restrictions that the Philly co-ops recently lifted. As Mariposa and Weavers Way settle into their new policies, they work to foreground the importance of membership, and member labor (where appropriate), knowing that their success as associations depends on a strong sense of affiliation, as well as the provision of affordable goods.

Avoid Burnout through Leadership Cultivation and Shared Responsibility

POCA is an altogether different co-op from a consumer-owned grocery. Instead of being hyperlocal, POCA is a national network of independent businesses that have banded together in association to sustain the practice of community acupuncture. By creating a multistakeholder cooperative that receives investments and offers benefits to acupunks, clinics, and patients, POCA is building a movement that offers a counterpoint to conventional, expensive private acupuncture. It advances a tradition of acupuncture connected to a radical history and creates solidarity among practitioners who seek to be radically inclusive and democratic. By running its own acupuncture school, POCA can reproduce its model and populate clinics with punks trained in its particular ethos and treatment modalities. But POCA's long-term success as a cooperative depends on the continued thought leadership of people like Lisa Rohleder, the provision of mutual support among clinic owners, and the attraction of a high volume of patients to clinics throughout the network. If POCA is to mature and sustain itself, it will need to continually renew its human resources through the cultivation of leaders who can ensure the co-op continues to serve all its many stakeholders.

The same is true at Headlong. As the organization changes, leadership is at the heart of Headlong's effort to persist in collaboration in the precarious world of experimental performance. David Brick made the important distinction between leadership and hierarchy, teaching that real leadership empowers organizational democracy and a politics of care. From its earliest days negotiating who paid the rent in a tiny, shared apartment, to the eventual unbraiding of its creative process, Headlong's codirectors continually revisited the covenants that bound them to one another. They tried out innovative voting schemes; they allowed each creative piece to be shepherded by a single arbiter; they brought in company members who were made to feel like family, though this form of marriage and family harbored no illusions of effortless agreement. All the while, the internal politics of cooperation shifted and changed. Headlong's structure has morphed and changed, yet the company has managed to sustain the work of asking urgent cultural questions throughout it all. It leaves a legacy that includes its codirectors and company members, who continue to live out Headlong's values in their other projects. Not only that, but Headlong has supported the work of a broad community of artists in Philadelphia and beyond, in ways I will elaborate further in the next chapter.

Beginning with the body, this chapter has demonstrated that cooperation needs to scale up to the level of work and organization in order to make a broader impact in the world. These two scales reinforce and complement one another. The bodies of cooperators benefit from having their practices inscribed in organizational arrangements that lead to overcoming relationless alienation. But the organization is not the last stand for the practice of cooperation. Organizations participate in community and economy. They are part of the social and economic landscapes that surround them, which they influence in turn. The next chapter turns to cooperative projects as they fare in the production of community economies.

PRACTICES OF COMMUNITY ECONOMY

The opposite of alienation is the affirmation of life. Alienation is a product of forces that are life-defying and life-denying. Though it is felt by the individuals who absorb its impact, alienation will only disappear when economic and social relations are remade. In such an effort, there is a need to bolster the agency of individuals while simultaneously confronting structural inequality. Scaling up to address conditions beyond the body and the institution requires a discussion of how cooperation fits into—and hopefully alters—economy as we know it and the construction of community under capitalism.

One of the earliest critics of the life-defying effects of capitalism was John Ruskin, a Victorian art historian and social critic. Writing in a popular literary magazine in the fall of 1860, Ruskin implored his readers to recognize that, "THERE IS NO WEALTH BUT LIFE. Life, including all its powers of love, of joy, and of admiration. That country is the richest which nourishes the greatest number of noble and happy human beings."[1] For Ruskin, England, in the throes of the Industrial Revolution, was decidedly not a country that offered sufficient nourishment to its inhabitants.

A contemporary of both John Stuart Mill and Karl Marx, Ruskin was one of the most popular voices of his day. His admirers included William Morris, Leo Tolstoy, John Dewey, and Mahatma Gandhi; Ruskin's *Unto This Last* was rated the most influential book by the inaugural class of Britain's Labour Party.[2] Ruskin's early writing featured florid, tremendously complex passages full of allusions to classical mythology and Christian theology intended for the most highly educated readers. Later on, Ruskin shifted his approach and began to write directly to a working-class audience. The struggle to change the world around him led Ruskin to pursue utopian endeavors like starting an educational charity, the Guild of St. George, and an art museum for the working class in Sheffield. Both still exist today.

Ruskin is a fascinating figure, partly because he began his career writing about art and architecture. Like the founders of Headlong Dance Theater, Ruskin recognized that art is both a vehicle for individual creative expression and an important cornerstone of society, a practice constantly at risk of marginalization. Deeply passionate about craft and handiwork, Ruskin was driven by a concern for the plight of the artisan. This concern led him to elaborate a critique of the political economy of his day, with its emphasis on narrow economistic justifications for human behavior. He was interested in the relationships among aesthetic, economic, political, religious, and social aspects of the good life.[3] Ruskin was one of the first to view wealth as a social relation, recognizing that wealth distribution has consequences for the distribution of power in society.[4] He averred that the pursuit of riches was in truth a pursuit of power over people and natural resources.

Believing in the dignity of all work, Ruskin's ideas prefigured the welfare state as it would come to be implemented later in Britain. He argued for an early version of a universal basic income, finding it abhorrent that workers would be stranded in the economy. He was also committed to a vision of ethical consumption. He presciently understood consumption as the endgame of economic life, emphasizing the link between the choices of the consumer and the conditions of the workers involved in the production process, as well as consumption's effect on natural resources. To Ruskin, ethical consumption was a practice of moral imagination, uniting consumers, producers, and the environment. The act of consumption implicates all and creates a web of mutual obligation. Only when all of these elements are understood in a holistic manner can the morality of their relation be inferred. It becomes the consumer's responsibility to factor all of these things into his or her reading of the value of a good, not just examining the price tag.

Writing at a time of widespread increases in consumption among all economic classes, Ruskin foresaw the role consumption would play in driving the capitalist economy. Though that power is limited by regulation, competition, and the relative power of the individual consumer, consumer power is connected to our citizenship in a market economy.[5] Ruskin asks: "What priorities should people set together, especially as consumers? What activities, ends, and goods are best for fostering people's character and well-being and are most productive of a good community, a just society, and a sustainable environment?"[6] His writings on ethical consumption prefigure the consumer activism of our day.

Over time, Ruskin's political writing fell out of favor, partly because of his tendency toward scolding moralism and his mistrust of anything but small-scale, rural economic life. But Ruskin helped set the tone for a number of later moral economists, who realized that the reform (or replacement) of capitalism needed more than a technocratic fix based on adjustments at the margins. Rather, reform of the distribution of resources needs to be coupled with a hard look at questions of liberty and solidarity.[7] This moral critique has found expression in many activist quarters since Ruskin's day. Among others, the collaborators of J. K. Gibson-Graham, known as the Community Economies Collective, have taken up the charge of envisioning economic diversity as a generative way of building a more just political economy.

This chapter lifts up the moral critique of capitalism that Ruskin and others helped to inaugurate. Since the Victorian era, this critique has rung out time and time again, from Black, feminist, queer, Marxist, Indigenous, and other voices. And this critique, in various levels of intensity, exists in the cooperative movement as well. One of the primary opportunities of cooperation is to envision a future where alienation is overcome through social action. This work begins at the level of the body and expands at the level of shared labor. But in order to maximize its reach and potential, it has to operate at higher scales as well.

In what follows, I explore the scale of cooperation as part of a community economy. By "community economy," I mean the generative project of reimagining the economy in the face of entrenched capitalist thinking. I explain the way diverse economy scholars understand community economy and talk about the ways cooperative projects scale up, federate, and sustain their work. Finally, I explore how each of the cases in my research contributes to a community economy. It is worthwhile to step back and unpack these concepts to clarify the ways in which it helps our understanding of the potential of community economies to drive social and economic progress.

COMMUNITY ECONOMY: A GENERATIVE PROJECT

One of the cardinal contributions of the diverse economy approach is the concept of capitalocentrism. Gibson-Graham explain the concept this way:

> When we say that most economic discourse is "capitalocentric," we mean that other forms of economy (not to mention noneconomic aspects of social life) are often understood primarily with reference

> to capitalism: as being fundamentally the same as (or modeled upon) capitalism, or as being deficient or substandard imitations; as being opposite to capitalism; as being the complement of capitalism; as existing in capitalism's space or orbit.[8]

Under the sway of capitalocentric logic, capitalism is seen as the norm, and all other forms of economic activity are seen as exotic, lesser, or deviant. Capitalism functions as a hegemonic, totalizing discourse possessing massive shaping power. The harm of capitalocentrism comes not just from the demotion of every other form of economic activity but also from the rendering of these assorted activities as fundamentally "the same as, the opposite of, a complement to, or contained within" capitalism.[9] All forms of market exchange are misinterpreted as being simply variations on a capitalist theme. All motivations for social action are construed as calculated, rationalist self-interest in the capitalist mode. Economic difference is flattened; economic horizons are limited.

As a means of overcoming capitalocentrism, J. K. Gibson-Graham propose the concept of diverse economies. Diverse economies challenge the domination of reductive capitalist thinking by cataloging the variety of arrangements that coexist in a given economy. These arrangements include paid and unpaid labor, from household work and volunteering, to reciprocal exchange, to wage labor.[10] Diverse economies include market and nonmarket forms of exchange, from gift giving to gleaning, from underground markets to sale of goods in exchange for money. There are also capitalist and noncapitalist forms of enterprise, from independent to communal enterprise, from state-owned enterprise to nonprofit firms. Not all of these forms of diverse economy are benign; Gibson-Graham recognize the presence of slave labor, theft, and indentured servitude as very much present on an economic spectrum typically rendered as merely capitalism.[11] By deconstructing the unitary vision of capitalism, Gibson-Graham launch a project that opens up horizons for new readings of social and economic life.

The corrective to capitalocentrism is the concept of community economy. For Gibson-Graham and their collaborators, the community economy is a means to recognize that certain forms of economic diversity are fundamentally healthy and generative, while others are oppressive and harmful. This recognition forms the basis of a political program to highlight and strengthen these generative aspects of economy, to build a set of performative practices that lead to a "collective project of construction."[12] The performative practices highlighted in this book contribute to the building of community economies, from the ethical consumption efforts of Mariposa and Weavers Way, to Headlong's wry social critique and deep ethic of care, to POCA's endorsement of health as a collective right.

In order to demonstrate the depth and richness of community economy, diverse economies scholar Ethan Miller examines three interrelated elements of the concept.[13] He begins by exploring its ontology, followed by its ethics, and, finally, its politics. His effort is designed to clarify and strengthen the practice of community economy, and his observations deserve to be revisited here as they relate to the project of this book.

Ontology, for the uninitiated, is a set of relations and properties regarding a given phenomenon that defines its way of being in the world. In the case of community economy, Gibson-Graham reject any rigid way of conceptualizing community economy that fixes it as a universal category. This kind of fixity is precisely the problem with capitalocentrism, the conceptual trap that diverse and community economy thinking is designed to overcome. Rather, Gibson-Graham offer a contingent and contextual analysis, preferring exploration and experimentation.

Miller explores the dual constituent parts of the concept: economy and community. Both words are worlds in themselves, covering vast historical, cultural, and philosophical terrain. Regarding economy, it is a performative tool and set of social relations rather than a thing in the world that can be captured and examined under a microscope. Any reading of economy, capitalist or otherwise, that ignores the provisional and ever-shifting nature of such a variegated set of practices fails to adequately capture the diversity and possibility that economy offers. Instead, Gibson-Graham seek to queer the economy, finding in queer theory precisely that rejection of binaries and monolithic versions of identity that are so restricting of the performance of a range of possible identities.[14] In their rejection of economy as a definitive entity, Gibson-Graham recall the philosophical orientation of pragmatism, without naming it as such. (Pragmatic readings of democracy form the basis of the next chapter of this book.)

Just as Gibson-Graham seek to open up and destabilize the concept of economy, they perform similar work on the notion of community. Community is not a "shared positive essence, a unity, or a project of fusion to be achieved."[15] Such conventional accounts of community—rendered as something fundamentally positive and desirable, where individual identities are subsumed under a collective—have been widely critiqued as rife with the potential for oppression and silencing of dissenting voices. Rather, community should be construed as a function of being-in-common, similar to Mead's concept of the social self, as I discussed in chapter 1. To be in community is not to uncritically share a common identity, but to engage in an ongoing project of becoming. I will return to the theme of community in the next chapter when I discuss cooperative practices of democracy.

Therefore, the ontology of community economy requires both a rejection of fixity and an embrace of possibility. It seeks copresence and collective deliberation toward a community economy that is always in a state of becoming. Conceiving of community economy in this way requires an ethics of praxis, which is the next element to which Miller's attention turns. The ethics of practicing community economy require a constant negotiation of difference, an interrogation of interdependence.

A critique of capitalism is central to the ethical project of community economy. Under capitalism, both difference and dependence are obscured, as each economic subject is reduced to an atomized, rationalistic actor striving to serve her best interests. This is a project of closure, not of opening and finding commonality. Community economy seeks to make visible—and contestable—the terms of negotiation of social and economic difference. In this way, community economies seek to redistribute power by opening up deliberation about who has the capacity to act and participate in activist struggles to reshape economy. Miller finds a "radically democratic impulse" in this ethical project, as it seeks to open up spaces of possibility and offer tools to those who are committed to building a more just economic future.[16]

Finally, Miller highlights the political dimension of community economy. By "politics," he means the enactment of projects and processes that demonstrate the range of forms for emancipatory economic action. The work of community economy researchers represents a form of scholar-activism, as they simultaneously participate in progressive economic organizing projects as they theorize about them. Yet they are careful to attend to the particular conditions that undergird different projects, lest they succumb to the temptation to synthesize a fixed set of universal principles.

For Gibson-Graham and others, postcapitalist politics ought to be a site of continuous struggle, undertaken by particular actors in particular places. That struggle is designed to expose "the contestability of previously enacted institutions."[17] This constant revision of institutions recalls MacIntyre's understanding of tradition as continuity of conflict. The danger in this struggle is that in many traditions, the less powerful have been excluded from agency. This very real danger, a key theme of this book, can only be met by constantly revisiting the purpose and the ethics of community economy practices. Thus, the three elements that Miller identifies as constituting community economy—ontology, ethics, and politics—must remain in constant play, lest practices ossify into routines that marginalize, oppress, or exclude particular actors from manifesting their capacities. As a vital, generative space of possibility that is neither inherently capitalist nor socialist, the practice of cooperation offers the means to build a flexible, resilient strain of ethical economy.

Cooperatives' Ethical Coordinates

Cooperative practices offer the possibility of enacting community economies. They do so when they abide by Gibson-Graham's "ethical coordinates," a set of guidelines for transformative economic interactions.[18] The ethical coordinates include making use of a social surplus, encouraging ethical consumption, and building a commons. Social surplus is the value that is created by productive labor that goes above and beyond what is needed for sustenance. Rather than returning surplus value to capitalist members of the owning class, cooperatives redistribute the social surplus back to their stakeholders. Ethical consumption, a cardinal concern of moral economists like John Ruskin, proceeds from the perspective that all economic relations are social and interdependent. When cooperative projects support consumption that sustains the planet and stands for the values of human and more-than-human lives, they foster practices of ethical consumption. Such practices make and sustain a commons. Traditionally associated with the shared use of natural resources like grazing land, a commons can be broadly construed as the practices that resist the enclosure and privatization of vital resources, from clean air to safe drinking water, even collective knowledge. Today there are hopeful signs that cooperatives are coming together to build community economies. They view cooperation as a systematic, federated effort, generated from the labor of individual cooperatives but aggregating and coordinating their potentially transformative power.

Mapping the Ethical Coordinates

The ultimate goal of cooperative organizing is the making of a commons in which resources are shared equitably for the collective good. Building a commons, like cooperation itself, is a practice. It must proceed through phases of reclamation, maintenance, and expansion. Sustaining a commons through the long intervals of unsexy work is just as important to the process as the initial bursts of energy and organizing that initiate new projects.[19] In the same way, the projects I profile in my research resist the dominant trends of the political economy to ensure the survival and growth of their practices. In the rest of this chapter, I map these ethical coordinates as they are manifest in the work of Headlong, POCA, and Weavers Way Co-op. I find that each adhere to the ethical coordinates through a pursuit of internal goods over external success, that they are interested in scaling up while remaining rooted in local community, and that they prize different but complementary forms of ethical consumption that undergird their relationships with their stakeholders.

RESISTING THE NONPROFIT INDUSTRIAL COMPLEX

Headlong has maintained an uneasy relationship with the arts economy surrounding it. The organization resisted playing by the rules dictated by consultants, funders, and other promoters of received wisdom. Some keen observers have called this constellation of forces the nonprofit industrial complex.[20] In the United States, most performing arts groups rely on grants from philanthropy and individual donors to fund their activities. These organizations are run at the behest of massively wealthy individuals who are largely unaccountable to a public and are able to steward what work gets funded through tax-advantaged spending. Many of the staff of these foundations are highly educated, critical, and curious people. And they rely on outside experts to evaluate grant proposals from artists before making a selection. However, there is an in-built elitism to the process that has been widely critiqued for, among other things, failing to adequately engage issues of diversity, equity, and inclusion of underrepresented minorities.[21]

This reliance on philanthropy is especially true for theater and dance, where ticket sales alone hardly defray the cost of devising work, running rehearsals, renting theaters, and mounting performances. In a sense, there is no surplus labor; everything the artists have is necessary labor poured into making the work. This market failure results in a series of compromises, with arts groups proposing projects to please funders and sometimes pandering to audiences to increase ticket sales (e.g., perennial holiday season *Nutcracker* performances of most traditional ballet companies are there to defray the losses of the rest of the year).

Success in the arts, like other fields, is often measured by external goods: fame and wealth. In the case of theater and dance, it is a prestige form of fame that beckons young artists. These artists pursue prizes and commissions and the opportunity to perform in highly regarded festivals and theaters. They do not expect to be on the cover of a glossy magazine. The wealth they seek comes in the form of healthy organizational budgets that have enough headroom to hire staff and support the artistic mission, as well as commissions to make new work and pay their artists and designers.

Headlong has always had a fraught relationship with the arts version of the nonprofit industrial complex. By necessity, it has engaged with funders and donors, but its orientation has always been an intuitive anticapitalism. And as the years have gone by, individuals involved in Headlong (particularly Amy Smith) have become more vocally critical of the nonprofit industrial complex. This anticapitalism manifested in three ways: being concerned primarily with pursuing internal goods, the promotion of self-care as a radical artistic practice, and valuing community over individual achievement.

Headlong's anticapitalist approach came to the individual members early in life. Amy reflected that she, Andrew, and David came from liberal, hippie backgrounds. Her parents protested the Vietnam War and were active in progressive politics. She explained that the three of them shared a desire not to participate in capitalist or mass-market consumer culture, a trait shared with many experimental artists: "Most artists are . . . interested in the idea of making something that's not a widget to be sold in the free market society." While most artists do not expect to strike it rich from performing, there is always the possibility of leaving the arts for more lucrative careers, or the rare event of becoming an art world star.

Neither of these appealed to the members of Headlong, as Amy explained with pride:

> One of us could very easily have said, "You know what? I just need to make some fucking money. I'm going to go get a job as an investment banker," or whatever. . . . Or one of us could have been seeking

> or been plucked out for some kind of big famous opportunity. A solo career or running an academic department or being a choreographer for someone. That didn't happen. Thank God.

Instead, Headlong members made decisions to change their career trajectories in relation to each other over time. David Brick agreed, even as we spoke in the challenging aftermath of Andrew Simonet's departure from the group. He noted, "That was exactly the right thing to do to sublimate all of that [ambition] and hold out that principle as a way to keep figuring out how to focus on the work and not the career."

Focusing on developing work and not putting career ambitions first certainly had consequences for Headlong. The company did not tour extensively or produce work that was always easily palatable and filled with the accessible humor of some of its earliest work. Following the muse meant that Headlong probably gave up on a number of opportunities to achieve national or international prominence. Nevertheless, Headlong looked down on dance companies that relied on retreading old work or were populated by artists who could not stand each other but stayed together for the sake of their fame and careers.

Instead, Headlong worked to foster an ethic of self-care. Andrew Simonet saw Headlong in contrast to the arts environment around it. He wondered, "Why are the people who run nonprofit performing arts companies so unhappy?" To him, they seemed exhausted and overwhelmed all the time. By contrast, Headlong decided that no opportunity or work of art was worth the well-being of the people involved. That did not mean that Headlong would not push itself to go after artistic excellence or grow as a company, but it would not do it at the expense of physical and emotional health. As Andrew explained, "When you are like, 'I am losing it' then just cancel it. We're not going to do it." Imagine the directors of Amazon or Apple telling their creative teams that the newest product launch should not take place at the expense of their health. It is unfathomable, precisely because these corporate leaders brag about how mercilessly hard they push their employees, offering them wealth and prestige at the expense of self-care.

Headlong also pursued an agenda congruent with community economies through its support of communal needs over those of the individual. Albert, who served as Headlong's first managing director, put it this way: "I don't think the phrase 'anticapitalist' ever came up, but . . . the relationships between people were less about power, they were less about the exchange of money and they were more about an affective sense of mutual love." This mutuality stands in contrast to the prevailing ethos of modern liberal individualism.

Headlong dancer Carrie expanded on her vision of the difference between Headlong and the way she saw the mainstream American ethic operating:

> This culture, American culture, is so individual. . . . The American dream is like, move away from your community and build a house with a picket fence where you're separate. And the whole aim here is not about nurturing community. You really have to build your own communities if that's what you believe in, right? This is how people in the world live, right? It takes a village; there's villages, right? America's like "Me-me-me-me-me and my wealth."

From the start, Headlong devoted itself to cultivating artistic community. One of its earliest programs was Dance Theater Camp. Beginning in the mid-1990s, Dance Theater Camp was Headlong's answer to the more established dance festivals they could not afford to attend. Participants would teach the skills and techniques they knew best or were most interested in exploring. In addition, participants would take on responsibilities for the group, like childcare or preparing meals. At the end of Dance Theater Camp, Headlong would use its own or a donated space to show off what the group had prepared for audiences. No money changed hands, and everyone benefitted.

Similarly, Headlong would organize monthly First Friday showings at their loft studio, putting out a sandwich board on the street offering free beer and performances, two shows a night. Mostly, Headlong would perform, but guest artists participated as well. A donation jar covered the cost of the beer, and the rest of the night would consist of conversation and building awareness of the work Headlong and its associates were trying to convey artistically. These First Friday showings persist in different configurations today.

This emphasis on building community and supporting the next generation of creators became more formalized in Headlong's later years. In 2008, Headlong started an accredited academic program in partnership with Bryn Mawr College called the Headlong Performance Institute (HPI). HPI was designed as an intensive semester program each fall, either for advanced undergraduates or recent college graduates interested in experimental performance. Former managing director

Albert explained that HPI was a natural trajectory for Headlong as the codirectors entered their forties, a time when the bodies and ambitions of dancers start to change. As the codirectors became more seasoned, Albert reasoned, they found they had a lot to teach to the next generation and desired to serve as mentors and community builders.

Still going after more than a decade, HPI draws faculty from Headlong and its collaborators and provides instruction and performance opportunities. For Albert, the strength of HPI revolved around "the decentering of individual achievement and the refocus on what a community can do together." This was the primary contribution made to students' lives. This observation was borne out not only in research interviews I conducted with HPI alumni but in exit interviews I undertook while serving as a Headlong board member. Alumni from HPI have gone on to populate the Philadelphia performance scene and beyond, drawing strength and inspiration from the training they received being in the orbit of Headlong.

In addition to mentoring the next generation through HPI, Headlong began an incubated artists program in 2013. Incubated artists receive a suite of services from Headlong, including financial management, communications and fundraising support, subsidized rehearsal space, and strategic planning services. Headlong also serves as these artists' fiscal sponsor, which means artists can receive grants without needing to form their own nonprofit organization. The slots in the incubated artists program are reserved for artists who are women, trans, and/or people of color, extending a commitment to diversity and inclusion that became a priority for Headlong in recent years. Some of Headlong's incubated artists have achieved considerable prominence, including Nigerian American poet and performance artist Jaamil Olawale Kosoko and transgender playwright and theater artist MJ Kaufman.

Finally, Headlong's codirectors have taken on activities outside the organization itself that foster community economies in the arts. Andrew Simonet runs a program called Artists U that operates in Philadelphia, Baltimore, and South Carolina. Artists U is an open-source, artist-run organization that offers programs on building a sustainable life as an artist through time and money management, personal strategic planning, and more. Since 2006, the program has supported hundreds of artists in reclaiming control over their career and personal trajectories. Andrew Simonet wrote a book (distributed freely on the Artists U website) called *Making Your Life as an Artist*. As of November 2019, the book has been downloaded over 200,000 times. Amy Smith is also devoted to supporting artists in their careers. She travels the country, serving as a financial literacy consultant for the funder Creative Capital and others. She also runs a tax preparation business for artists in Philadelphia that helps artists navigate the complex finances of being a small independent business. All of these activities elevate artist capacity and confidence, strengthening the careers and contributions of independent artists with a deep commitment to equity, care, and artist self-sovereignty.

CRACKS IN THE COMMONS

Headlong's avoidance of the conventional path has not been without its challenges or pitfalls; this is not a Headlong hagiography. In its efforts not to play the nonprofit performing arts game, Headlong sometimes had a rough road toward the necessary level of professionalization that would help it achieve its own objectives.

One example is Headlong's resistance to being governed by a board of directors. The organization formed a board for legal purposes—doing so is a requirement of nonprofit incorporation in the United States—but it resisted investing that board with real governance responsibilities. In good times, a board can help manage growth and strategy for an organization. In bad times, it can help puzzle out the problems at hand. Boards are often composed of cheerleaders with some expertise in corporate management, such as accounting or law. And board members are often financial donors to the organization. Yet there are risks involved with boards pushing back on the organization or trying to co-opt it in a direction that goes counter to the wishes of the staff. According to early board member Francis:

> [Headlong's codirectors] just made sure that they had the board stacked enough that no one was going to give them a hard time and that if anybody ever did, they could just change the composition of the board. And they weren't really looking for anything from their board early on, except corporate formality positions so that they could get grants.

In the case of Headlong, the organization avoided the pitfalls of an unhelpful board, while missing out on some of the advantages that a strong nonprofit board can provide. As a member of Headlong's board for several years in the late 2000s–early 2010s, I can attest to the frustration of not being asked to do all that I could to foster the organization's success.

Headlong resisted professionalizing its staff just as it resisted giving the board a traditional role. Again, this was a deliberate choice, made in accordance with the group's desire to counteract the bureaucratic nature of many arts nonprofits. Amy Smith explained that funders wanted Headlong to professionalize by hiring a managing director, development director, a finance person, and the like. That notion ran counter to the codirectors' feeling that they could function effectively as self-taught professional administrators as well as artists.

In Headlong's early days, it was almost as if professionalization happened by itself. David Brick recalled that "there came a moment when we had job descriptions." The organic work of making dances started to necessitate more structure. Rather than deliberating with a strategic planning consultant for months, the codirectors just started to do what came naturally to them. It became David's job to do publicity, Andrew's job to fundraise, and Amy's job to manage the organization's finances. For Amy, doing the finances could be rather thankless: "In some ways it's a curse more than a blessing," she recalled. "I remember having budget meetings where David would say, 'Your budget, blah-blah-blah.' I'd say, 'No, dude. This is our fucking budget. You just can't use that term that this is my budget.'" Even when roles are assigned by intuition, negotiating accountability can be a fraught exercise.

Having the artists serve as administrators meant there was no separation between the creative versus executive functions and the people involved. When arts nonprofits professionalize, there is usually an artistic director who is different from the executive director. This way, in theory, the artistic work of the company can grow without also being responsible for the bottom line. In practice, these things are necessarily intertwined, especially in small nonprofits with the budgets to match. But Headlong's dedication to simultaneously administering the company and serving as a three-headed creative force meant the bulk of it fell on the codirectors. It is hard to say, in retrospect, whether the model limited Headlong or freed it. Because the company did not have the overhead of a large professional staff, it could afford to stay true to the founders' vision and keep the lights on with less stress. But one thing is clear: later on, it would make the managing director's staff position a difficult one to hold.

As the company grew, it became necessary to expand the circle beyond the three founding codirectors. That meant adding dancers, but it also meant adding some professional staff. Beginning in 2000,

Headlong employed a series of managing directors to support the operations of the company. It was a challenging transition to expect an outside employee to care as much about the company as the founders, and equally hard for the founders to let go of what they had created. Andrew Simonet reflected on that challenge:

> When it's the three of us, we're the owners. When you ask someone else to do that it's really weird; you're like, "How do I make this worth your while?" I think all of our company managers are extraordinary people and have come up against that: "This is really fucking hard and it's not my baby, and where do I draw the boundary?" Money would help but money's not the only thing. We kind of wrestled with that. And it's kind of exhausting.

Drawing the boundary was often hard for all the people involved, as employees worked extremely hard for the relatively low pay that is standard in nonprofit arts. And the codirectors struggled to figure out how to use their labor effectively and appropriately. Andrew admitted that while Amy was more businesslike, expecting employees to work according to set hours and job descriptions, he and David were more low-key about the arrangement, preferring to hire people based on talent and charisma and letting them loose on the organization. Andrew explained the strategy as: "Oh, let's just hire mission-driven geniuses and just let them do what they do." But he acknowledged that the difficult terrain of navigating among the three founding codirectors and their all-encompassing identification with Headlong could be tricky.

At the same time, according to Andrew, working at Headlong was a rewarding and useful professional experience: "I don't feel like, 'Poor them, they had to work for us.'' The work was varied and challenging, and those who did the jobs would leave the organization equipped to do lots of different things in the arts. After working successfully with a series of "mission-driven geniuses," a transition occurred when the codirectors realized that the managing director needed to be more of a boss than a subordinate. Around the time of working on *More* with Tere O'Connor (described in chapter 2), Amy admitted the codirectors realized that making administrative decisions by consensus was becoming an unnecessary burden. Therefore, the organization afforded the managing director at that time more executive sway in the organization. Still, it is not a coincidence that this was the phase of Headlong's existence when much of its communal process was up for reevaluation.

Perhaps the elevation of the managing director role was a sign of the changes to come.

The final challenge I want to relate about the community feeling at Headlong revolves around the role of the dancers in the company. In the early years, David, Amy, and Andrew were the choreographers, dancers, and administrators. But dancers Heather Murphy, Nichole Canuso, and Christy Lee soon joined on as consistent collaborators. These women were talented choreographers in their own right, running a parallel company, Moxie Dance Collective, for five years while they danced in Headlong. And over the years, other dancers became closely associated with Headlong's work. David Brick explained that the company grew organically, as they looked for people with a lot to contribute rather than just beautiful bodies: "We were looking for people who were thinkers, who were dynamic in the collaborative process, who were makers, because we dispersed a lot of the creative process into everyone in the room."

In interviews, the codirectors stressed the deliberative and democratic relationship between them and the dancers. But interviews with the dancers yielded a more complicated story. They questioned whether they were members of Headlong or just dancers for hire. Longtime collaborator Carrie recalled the dancers' frustration about their standing within Headlong:

> Between every Headlong project, the dancers would get together and be like, "Are we in Headlong? Is Headlong a company? What are we doing?" There was no transparency about anything about our relationship with them. We're building these artistic, spiritual, emotional ties to them as individuals and to Headlong as a company, but we have no idea what our role is.

Some dancers would take it personally, wondering what it meant to not be cast in a specific dance. These collaborators felt there was a lack of transparency between the codirectors and them. For some dancers, this meant they could continue their own careers outside of Headlong without feeling constrained, but for others, the lack of clarity could be galling.

Nevertheless, despite all of the challenges, the community that surrounded Headlong spoke about the way it created community with deep reverence. It is clear that being part of Headlong, while sometimes infuriating for everyone, involved no small measure of mutual aid and care.

ETHICAL CONSUMPTION AT THE CO-OP COUNTER

Ethical consumption is one of the key elements of Gibson-Graham's ethical coordinates. Food co-ops like Mariposa and Weavers Way endorse a philosophy of ethical consumption that hearkens back to the original pioneers of the cooperative movement, as well as other movements for food justice and food sovereignty. The continuity of past and present practices of ethical consumption allows us to imagine a hopeful future for societies facing economic and environmental volatility. An emerging ethic of consumption in the age of human-made climate change allows for the formation of new economic communities, new commons, and new possibilities.[22]

Rather than relegating market-oriented behavior as hopelessly capitalist and exploitative, it is possible to reexamine a broad range of types of markets. Such a re-presentation is necessary because a large portion of social wealth is noncapitalist in origin, as Gibson-Graham note. They further caution: "There is a tendency to conflate all market-oriented (i.e. commodity) production with capitalism. We need to resist that tendency if we are to theorize economic difference in the market sphere, and to acknowledge the many types of economic organization that are compatible with commodity production."[23] The same can be said of consumption, where noncapitalist businesses like cooperatives and sole proprietorships make up a significant portion of market activity.

Mariposa, Weavers Way, and other co-ops promote ethical consumption in their communities in a number of ways. They deliberately source products that advance sustainable farming practices or support minority- and women-owned businesses. They favor local brands that reduce the carbon footprint of their stock as well as recirculate money in the local economy. Over 30 percent of Weavers Way's stock is locally sourced, according to its marketing director.[24] An active membership and board are able to deliberate on the nature of the products the co-op ought to promote, rather than being at the mercy of a corporate owner. This is just one aspect of the democratic practice of a community-owned and -operated enterprise.

Both Weavers Way and Mariposa, acknowledging the premium prices of much of their goods, have programs to address affordability. At Mariposa, there is a low-income equity fund that enables low-income members to have their equity payments reduced while they can retain member status and build equity more slowly. Weavers Way has a Food for All program available to members who receive federal benefits like SNAP benefits or Medicaid. Food for All gives an automatic 10 percent discount on purchases and reduces the member's equity payment. And all members benefit from the Co-op Basics program, where lower-priced staple items are available throughout the store. Weavers Way and other co-ops are able to raise prices on certain items (beauty products, for example) and cut the prices on staples so that shoppers can have more access to healthy pantry items, fresh fruits and vegetables, and the like.

In addition to the efforts at ethical consumption relative to the goods for sale, these matters come into play in the design of the work environment at the co-op. Weavers Way and Mariposa pay workers above grocery scale and offer better benefits. Workers have a greater say in the management of the store than in corporate grocers, which leads to less turnover. Staff may also grow invested in the cooperative philosophy and the nature of the products they are selling, leading to a greater feeling of affinity to the cooperative project than would be found at a corporate grocer.

But there is one additional way in which Weavers Way, in particular, contributes to the development of community economy. It serves as an anchor and an organizer on the retail corridor of its Mount Airy location. In the rest of this section, I will discuss this anchor role and contrast it with the different relationships Weavers Way had at its defunct West Oak Lane location. It is my assertion that co-ops have the potential to serve as leaders in urban community economic development,[25] and the different ways this has come to pass for Weavers Way help to elaborate the spaces of possibility for that to be the case.

Weavers Way's Anchoring Effect

Weavers Way has been a stable presence in its original Mount Airy location since the mid-1970s. In important ways, the shopping district now called Mount Airy Village grew up around, and because of, the food co-op. Since 2010, when Weavers Way opened itself up to the general public, it is even more connected to the success of the district. Under Gary's leadership, Weavers Way has become a de facto community center and the anchor institution of the Carpenter Lane commercial corridor, in which it consciously took a leadership role. Along with the High Point Cafe, Big Blue Marble Bookstore, the Nesting House (a children's consignment shop and boutique), and several others, Mount Airy Village is a vibrant and successful commercial and community hub.

Although there had been some discussion in the 1980s of relocating to contain its growing membership, the members themselves largely rejected the proposal in favor of maintaining Weavers Way's Carpenter Lane location. The large, loyal, and steady clientele generated ample street traffic, and to accommodate that clientele, Weavers Way maintained longer open hours than most retailers. Weavers Way's public commitment to the Carpenter Lane location and the traffic it generated also provided stability that attracted other merchants. Even in 1993, Moving Arts of Mount Airy founder and owner Pamela Rogow noted of her decision to locate on Carpenter Lane: "I came here and thought, well, goodness, we're across the street from a market that has $4 million worth of business and 3,000 households. . . . I did this with intention. I wasn't naive about what I was building."[26]

The retailers attracted to Carpenter Lane by Weavers Way also clearly identified themselves with the basic ethic embodied in the cooperative: of being independent, local businesses concerned with creating a strong and specific sense of community with which many surrounding neighborhood residents also identified. As the owner of Big Blue Marble Bookstore put it: "Mount Airy is a neighborhood that supports local businesses and is really committed to homegrown institutions. . . . It's a very encouraging place to be starting an independent bookstore."[27] Notably, the owners of many neighborhood businesses are also members of the cooperative.

Interviews with Carpenter Lane business owners reflected that advancing the work of the corridor was led by Weavers Way, though the work is shared, primarily with High Point Cafe. Business owners related that the stability and dedicated marketing staff at Weavers Way made it possible for other retailers to scale up or down their participation in corridor activities, depending on their capacity, without feeling like the effort would stall. Cooperative membership is so closely identified with Carpenter Lane that one corridor business owner recalled having shoppers offer their Weavers Way member numbers at the cash register, forgetting that his business was independent. Yet despite the co-op's prominence, the corridor retailers related that the effort would be impossible without the space, money, staff time, and stability of Weavers Way.

A customer survey undertaken by Weavers Way in 2013 speaks further to a sense of shared norms among its stakeholders and provides a clear idea of what those norms are. Respondents reported that "the most important reasons for joining/maintaining membership in the co-op" were "Support for local growers/producers (93% consider it very important or important)," "Investing in the community (87%)," and "Supporting community programs (78%)."[28]

Weavers Way takes on an anchor institution role in Carpenter Lane in at least four different ways. First, it promotes its location to the benefit of all local businesses. Possibly its chief promotional tool is its extensive newsletter, *The Shuttle,* which, since 1973, has been mailed to each of its member households and distributed at its store and in neighborhood news boxes and, since 2006, has been available online. More than a store newsletter, *The Shuttle* is in fact a community newspaper, which serves to publicize not just Weavers Way but all of Mount Airy Village and the surrounding neighborhood. Second, Weavers Way has also sponsored a Mount Airy Village loyalty card that provides discounts at the cooperative earned by patronizing other corridor businesses. Third, the cooperative is an extensive property owner on the corridor, by which it controls four storefronts and can thus exercise significant control over the retail mix, to the benefit of all retailers.

Finally, Weavers Way sponsors annual events on the corridor. The two chief events are the Mount Airy Village Fair and the summer farmer's market, both begun under the previous general manager. Although Weavers Way is the primary sponsor of the fair, it is a joint effort of several other corridor institutions, most notably the High Point Cafe and the parent–teacher association of the neighboring public school. Recently, Weavers Way's marketing manager noted that the co-op maintains a focus on support for nearby local shops, pointing out: "This is ingrained in our values. We were born out of the community, so we want to give back as much as possible."[29]

More generally, as the customer surveys and the history of the corridor suggest, Weavers Way has both shaped and been shaped by the unique and distinctive social norms of the neighborhood and its commercial corridor. The role that these shared norms serve in creating a consensual space for Weavers Way to play an anchor institution role becomes more evident by looking at Weavers Way's role in West Oak Lane, where the cooperative never attempted to play an anchor institution role.

An Organizational Misstep

A cautionary tale stands at the heart of Weavers Way's story of co-op-led community development. For a few brief years from 2007 to 2011, Weavers Way operated a satellite cooperative in the majority Black neighborhood of West Oak Lane. While the failure of this project seems like a blip in the nearly fifty-year history of Weavers Way, it bears some important lessons for those who seek to expand cooperatives beyond their original geography and demographics. In its short tenure, West Oak Lane showed another set of organizational possibilities for Weavers Way—in terms of race, income, geography, and politics. The failure of the co-op in West Oak Lane was consequential for Weavers Way's potential as a builder of community economies.

Weavers Way was invited to open a branch store at Ogontz Avenue and 72nd Street by the Ogontz Avenue Revitalization Corporation (OARC), a local community development corporation. Weavers Way was asked to replace a corner store that was failing. Weavers Way's general manager encouraged the co-op to take a chance on taking over the store and secured funding for renovations from the Reinvestment Fund, a local community-development financial institution. OARC offered Weavers Way six months of free rent and a small monthly subsidy. Over the course of its tenure in West Oak Lane, Weavers Way tried a variety of approaches—including changing staff, product mix, and the look of the store—in an attempt to make it profitable. But the branch store never generated the kinds of sales necessary to keep it afloat, and Weavers Way decided to close it in 2011 and turn control of the property back to OARC.

Kelly, a Weavers Way board member, remembers that there was more at stake in expanding to West Oak Lane than just moving into another physical space. West Oak Lane was a different socioeconomic community than Mount Airy, where Weavers Way had been for thirty-five years by that time. She simultaneously felt excitement about the opportunity to diversify the Weavers Way membership and concern about the process behind preparing the community for the co-op. On one hand, Weavers Way prided itself on having an open, democratic membership and wanted to expand the diversity of that group. On the other hand, Kelly explained, nobody in West Oak Lane had asked for a co-op to open in that neighborhood. Given that many co-ops are organized from the ground up, this presented a challenge to Weavers Way's legitimacy. She noted, "We weren't organically settled from the beginning.

It was more of an outside decision. And I think that's why ultimately, we're closing it."

Another board member, Sandra, concurred, explaining that while West Oak Lane fit Weavers Way's mission of wanting to "put cooperatives in underserved areas," it was done without the proper preparation or research into what people in the neighborhood actually wanted. This lack of community organizing makes plain the problem with simply dropping a co-op into a neighborhood that did not ask for one, especially one that was run by outsiders.

Weavers Way leaders cited other reasons for the failure of the store, beyond its lack of connection to the local community. Many participants made the surprising suggestion that the co-op should have carried more unhealthy or low-end products to cater to the lower-income clientele in the neighborhood. Some suggested that if the co-op had sold junk food, cigarettes, and lottery tickets, it might have had higher sales. Such a suggestion was completely at odds with the product philosophy of the rest of Weavers Way. While widespread, this sentiment was not unanimous among the people with whom I spoke. Karen, a Weavers Way supporter from the Reinvestment Fund, explained that other grocers they have funded solve the food relevance problem not by supplying junk food but by providing culturally appropriate food. Sometimes, she explained, stores that normally focus on the local also feature non-locally sourced products like tropical fruits and vegetables to provide relevant food for communities that base their diet around these foods.

Cynthia, a longtime board member who is Black, stated that she did not think that the lack of support for West Oak Lane was due to the culture in the neighborhood. For her, "the fact that Ogontz is predominantly an African American community is not the plus or the minus of it all." Cynthia went on to explain that her sense of the shortcoming of West Oak Lane was that there was a full-service supermarket quite nearby that already served the community and that there had been no constituency built up to support the co-op as an alternative.

Despite not having an established membership base in West Oak Lane, Weavers Way's management had other reasons for pursuing the opportunity. First, they felt they could learn valuable things that would help in a planned expansion to the more affluent Chestnut Hill neighborhood. The West Oak Lane store served as a proving ground for operating a second store, since Weavers Way at that time had only been in one store in Mount Airy. Second, by partnering with OARC, some interviewees suggested, Weavers Way could curry favor with OARC's founder, prominent Pennsylvania state representative Dwight Evans (now a member of the United States House of Representatives). After working with OARC on the West Oak Lane project, Weavers Way was able to secure nearly $1 million in state grants for its Chestnut Hill expansion with the support of Dwight Evans's office. Notably, while the West Oak Lane store has come and gone, the Chestnut Hill store remains in operation.

How should West Oak Lane be understood within the organizational project of Weavers Way? It raises more questions than it answers, especially since it is an abandoned project and it is not clear what institutional lessons Weavers Way took from it. To begin, it is clear that West Oak Lane was not Weavers Way's attempt to do community development. It was an opportunistic move presented to the co-op by an outside group. But many at Weavers Way thought of West Oak Lane as a trial run for the expansion to Chestnut Hill. To that extent, it is not clear that the specifics of the neighborhood really mattered when moving to the new store. The co-op did not lay groundwork or plan strategically with the West Oak Lane community. As the interviewees mentioned, there was not a lot of community outreach or a proper market study to determine demand.

This is partly a story about the dangers of exporting a successful cooperative into a new community setting. Pushing beyond a co-op's existing social and cultural milieu has particular challenges. The discussions about not knowing what types of food people in West Oak Lane wanted to eat is a symptomatic one. Food cultures are specific and fraught; getting the product mix and price point right is essential to the success of any retail grocer. This challenge is another instance of the paradox of exclusivity, as Weavers Way is oriented around selling certain kinds of food that demand certain prices. But the low sales proved that something was not working.

The West Oak Lane story is also an example of a lack of authentic and sustained stakeholder engagement, which is a precursor for building community economy. In a different class and racial setting from Mount Airy, it is unclear whether the Weavers Way project could have succeeded anyway. But without an attempt to foster dialogue with local residents about what kind of store made sense, and to codevelop it in a planful manner, it is no surprise that the store did not succeed. Weavers Way had only to examine the international cooperative principles to have a road map, if it so chose. These principles enshrine not only concern for the broader community but also the importance of consumer education. Cooperatives are not widely recognized as a business form in the United States, and there are no other co-ops in West Oak Lane. If Weavers Way had taken time to work collectively alongside neighbors to make a case for the benefits of a cooperative, that might have made a difference. Finally, OARC, the local community development corporation, bears responsibility as well. If OARC had been interested in sustainable commercial corridor development, with a cooperative as anchor (the role Weavers Way plays in Mount Airy), it would have put significantly more organizational energy into building a rapport between the co-op and its own neighborhood constituency.

COMMUNITY ACUPUNCTURE AND ITS OTHER

POCA creates community economies by building and sustaining a national movement of clinics, all organized around the same emancipatory, anticapitalist, cooperative philosophy of practice. It is a kind of acupuncture commons. POCA clinics are all committed to a mission that requires the cooperative to work toward increased accessibility of affordable group acupuncture treatments. Its goal is to build a long-term, stable economic relationship based on fair treatment for everybody. It also commits POCA to building alliances with organizations that build community and foster sustainable economies.

Part of what makes POCA notable is how it differs from the provision of private acupuncture in the United States. In private acupuncture, patients are seen one at a time, at considerably higher cost. The private acupuncture movement is designed to serve middle class patients and above. For poor people, there are sporadic and underfunded public health acupuncture programs, treating conditions like addiction. And there are Chinese acupuncturists that treat patients in urban ethnic enclaves. But by and large, the acupuncture industry in the United States is dominated by private acupuncturists, who have held sway from the late 1970s until being joined by the community acupuncture model in the mid-2000s.

Interviews with both POCA affiliates and other private acupuncturists revealed polarization and a difference in philosophy between the groups. Both groups saw the other as an antagonist with a fundamentally flawed vision of how acupuncture should be delivered in the United States. In this section, I present the different perspectives on how acupuncture should work, contrasting POCA for the most part with private acupuncture. In doing so, I highlight the important contribution made by POCA to the practice of cooperation. At the same time, I do not intend to devalue the relevance or importance of private acupuncture, which varies from practitioner to practitioner. I think it has a place in the complementary and alternative medicine ecosystem (I also find it, as well as treatments in POCA clinics, to be personally helpful). The goal here is to flesh out what makes POCA successful as a movement that has a particular ethos and worldview that it defines, in part, in opposition to the way acupuncture is generally offered.

POCA's worldview is based on several strongly held beliefs about the way clinics should be run, the qualities needed by acupuncturists to be successful, how acupuncturists should view income and stature, the way acupuncture education should support the community acupuncture movement, and the politics of systemic change. I will review each of these and contrast POCA acupuncturists' claims with assertions made by several acupuncturists in private practice whom I interviewed in Philadelphia.

Clinic Administration: Two Different Views

The first major difference between POCA and private acupuncture is that private acupuncture practices are usually founded by a single practitioner who is the face of the business and attracts a patient base. If demand is high enough, they might add additional acupuncturists or complementary services like massage. But the identity and brand of the clinic revolves around its founder and main practitioner. POCA organizes clinics differently. Lisa Rohleder's philosophy of the Big Damn Clinic, which I discussed in the previous chapter, states that the clinic is not any one acupunk's business. It should stand outside and apart from any one person. To POCA, clinics, not acupunks, should build a reputation. Acupunks are important but fundamentally interchangeable parts of a clinic that is set up to serve a specific geography and population. The goal is the avoidance of ego by each practitioner, so that patients feel they can see anyone at the practice and get an equally effective treatment, rather than waiting for a specific shift to see their specific acupuncturist. According to POCA, the goal is to support jobs for many acupuncturists, not to build up a cult of personality. Lisa explained, "You're not trying to create a business for yourself; you're trying to create a job for yourself."

According to everyone I spoke to, success is hard to come by in acupuncture. There are a few practitioners who achieve tremendous success, many more who struggle to make a living, and still others who begrudgingly leave the profession after failing to find a foothold. For private acupuncturists, success comes from hard work, marketing skills, and business acumen. One interviewee told me that good businesspeople do well in acupuncture; if someone does not succeed, the fault lies with them. Some argued that acupuncture schools should do more to teach business skills and clinic administration. But a leading Philadelphia private practitioner thought success had to do in part with how acupuncturists present themselves:

> Maybe they present as too counterculture. It doesn't matter if you're transgender or covered in tattoos, you need to just dress up like a grown-up. If you are in a medical, healing profession, you need to present yourself in a certain way . . . that really creates confidence. Even if you're faking it. When you look and dress and act like a punk rocker, that's what you are going to attract. And that's going to attract a demographic that doesn't have as much money.

The private acupuncturists with whom I spoke, for the most part, had an explicitly capitalist orientation to their vision of success: hard work, business acumen, and proper presentation leads to profitable businesses.

According to POCA members, success comes in a different guise. It comes from having lower, more realistic financial expectations and participating as part a successful clinic. They believe the movement is structured in a way that provides a higher chance of success for more acupuncturists. Rather than a few stars in each city, POCA's goal is to create lots of acupuncture clinics, with lots of opportunity for acupunks who are good at giving treatments but would not necessarily make it as entrepreneurs. One owner of a few successful clinics admits that not all of his employees would have made it outside of POCA: "[If we were] depending on capitalism and pure entrepreneurial spirit, most of us don't have that. Most of the acupuncturists we have hired would have failed—they would have tanked right away—and they would probably be doing something else." Rather than losing those people to the profession, this owner relies on them to staff his clinics and meet the needs of hundreds of patients per week.

One clinic owner in the Midwest saw it as a numbers game, that the odds of success are better working within the POCA framework.

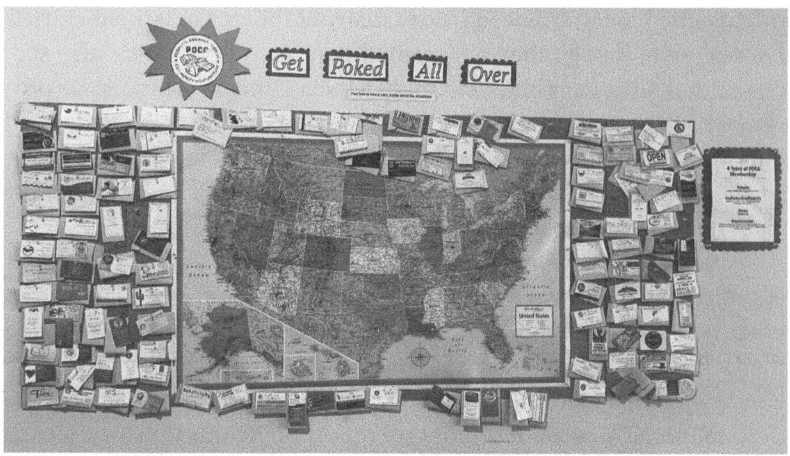

FIGURE 12. Map of POCA clinics across the United States. Photograph by Andrew Zitcer.

She played out a thought experiment in our interview, explaining that if a hundred people go into private practice, only five people will start making $100,000 annually after years of building up a practice. But the rest will struggle to get by, making maybe $30,000 or $40,000 and just barely surviving. She contrasted that example with POCA, explaining that the odds of a modicum of stability are better. To her, twenty out of one hundred people can make $40,000 or $45,000 in POCA practices and build stable lives.

The Pursuit of Money in Acupuncture

Financial success was a fraught topic in all the interviews. Each side thought the other was lying about the money being made. POCA punks thought private acupuncturists overstated their success because they also taught acupuncture or sold expensive supplements. Private acupuncturists thought POCA was lying because they assumed that a high volume of patients, even at a low cost per patient, would translate into high gross revenues. I did not ask to see the finances of any of the clinics I visited, and the private acupuncturists I interviewed were generally the most successful and well known in Philadelphia. But everyone disagreed about what made clinics financially successful.

Lisa Rohleder was deeply skeptical that many private acupuncturists could earn high incomes from acupuncture alone. She claimed that acupuncturists made money from teaching acupuncture on the side and selling expensive supplements to add to the revenue from acupuncture treatments. This was indeed true of many of the private acupuncturists I spoke with, though they maintained that their clinics were also successful in their own right. One Philadelphia clinic owner proudly proclaimed: "I know that the people that work at my office do really well financially. We have two receptionists [in addition to acupuncturists] so we've created five to six jobs and we hire the occasional window guy from the street. So that counts, too!"

Although POCA clinics offer a steady income, that does not mean it is sufficient to maintain a financially stable household. Very few POCA practitioners were willing to admit this. One veteran acupunk decried the lack of money in the profession, while defending his belief in the POCA system: "Where is the money [in acupuncture]? Actually, there is no money. There are just jobs. We're just doing this to have a job, so a few other acupuncturists can have job. That's the ethic that drives 85 percent of the clinic. How can we possibly stretch these fees out so we can have jobs and do this work that we love to do?" At the same time, he was willing to admit how it affected him personally: "A week doesn't go by where I am not like 'I need to do something else! I need a fucking different job. I can't do this.' Because I don't have a partner or family who got any money. It's not really sustainable unless we keep growing. That stuff kind of hits me as silly, and I am surprised how much it rattles me too." His candor was poignant. Even as POCA is building a movement of acupuncture for everyone, it is still very difficult to raise a family on the wages it affords.

What Makes a Good Clinician?

Private acupuncturists and POCA adherents even disagreed about what makes a good clinician. From a POCA perspective, the goal is to get patients in the clinic for as many treatments as necessary to achieve healing. The low-cost structure means that patients can come frequently without incurring the high costs of private acupuncture that they believe deter patients from seeking the number of treatments they require. But high volume and low cost requires the acupunk to work quickly, doing a limited number of points, with a limited time window for diagnostics. According to POCA, seeing a tremendous volume of patients makes better clinicians. Acupunks see all kinds of patients with all kinds of conditions, they argue, rather than seeing one or two patients per hour, like some private acupuncturists. Acupunks get more acupuncture experience in less time than private acupuncturists.

Unsurprisingly, private acupuncturists disagreed. They pride themselves on taking time with patients, even when they see several in an hour, and on doing detailed diagnostics that include looking at patients' tongues, feeling their pulses, and conducting short interviews. To them, it seems ridiculous that a POCA acupunk can look at a patient, ask a couple of hushed questions in a potentially crowded room, and insert needles into a number of points limited by patients sitting fully clothed in a chair. For private acupuncturists, even the publicness of the treatments was an issue. Patients might be less likely to talk about health challenges affecting them if they could be overheard by others in the same room. Some POCA clinics have a private room where patients can talk to acupunks, but that is usually by request, and some patients might feel too sheepish to ask.

According to one private acupuncturist, the community acupuncture movement is overly simplifying traditional Chinese medicine. This acupuncturist considers herself a lifelong student of these modalities and takes offense at POCA's simplification of the model. She reacted with indignation: "Chinese medicine is deep. If I were doing the same fucking ten points for thirty years, I wouldn't be in this field. I still have so much to learn. And I study all the time. Doing this for thirty-one years, I feel like a beginner. I feel like the community movement, they're asking too little of themselves." Though POCA members disagree that they are overly simplifying acupuncture, they argue that the practice requires a different sensibility. Some interviewees openly cast doubt on the efficacy of a lot of diagnostic tools and acupuncture points, viewing treatment frequency at low cost as the more important element. One central figure in POCA leadership explained that acupunks should develop a plumber-like mentality about acupuncture and that acupuncture is more like a trade than a profession.

Low-Cost Acupuncture Education

Given that POCA is trying to democratize acupuncture, it needed to eliminate a major barrier to financial stability for acupuncturists: high-cost acupuncture education. The cost of acupuncture education came up in a number of interviews, as educational debt had a negative effect on the careers and financial lives of acupuncturists. Like other forms of education, acupuncture school used to cost less, so older private acupuncturists had a much lower debt burden than those graduating today. Both POCA members and established private acupuncturists felt they had more freedom in their career choices than younger people weighing the costs of today's acupuncture schools.

Today, acupuncture school can cost up to $60,000. By contrast, POCA Tech costs less than $20,000. POCA Tech is able to keep its education affordable by relying on the volunteer labor of POCA members to develop curriculum, obtain and maintain national accreditation, and oversee policies and procedures for the school. The explicit goals of POCA Tech are the provision of affordable acupuncture education and a steady flow of acupunks for POCA clinics, trained in the co-op's unique philosophy.

But POCA Tech is not for everyone, as its marketing materials make clear. POCA Tech is steeped in the same politics and treatment philosophy as POCA proper. POCA Tech's curriculum has a thoroughgoing commitment to talking openly about topics like racism, class oppression, and Orientalism in acupuncture. POCA Tech is only open to POCA members, and students have to commit to working at a POCA clinic for three years after graduating. The expectation is that POCA Tech students will make a serious contribution to the POCA community. As the website communicates to prospective students: "If you're looking for a situation where you can pay your tuition and be a passive consumer of your education, this absolutely isn't it. The school and the co-op were built by communities of (imperfect) people who put in everything they had, and they'll expect you to reciprocate. Co-ops are hard and guaranteed to push you out of your comfort zone."[30]

Liberation through Acupuncture

POCA and private acupuncture both share the goal of improving health through alternative medicine. Both groups participate in an industry where it is difficult to succeed financially. And both believe they have special insight on what it takes to achieve success. For the private acupuncturists I met (and they do not speak for all the acupuncturists in America), hard work, good business acumen, and sound marketing were the drivers of success and stability. These practitioners acknowledged that not everyone succeeds in acupuncture but seemed to feel that those who did not had themselves to blame. For POCA members, the acupuncture industry and the capitalist system are to blame for driving talented acupuncturists out of practice. By contrast, the POCA model centers the clinic rather than the acupunk. They believe that clinics will find a high volume of patients by meeting people's need for low-cost, culturally aware treatment spaces.

POCA has created its own acupuncture ecosystem, both to counter the practices it finds faulty and to create another mode of treatment designed to include more, and more diverse, patients. This ecosystem features different treatment methodologies and its own accredited acupuncture school and encourages a very different expectation about the kind of money that acupunks can and should make from community acupuncture. This parallel acupuncture ecosystem has both goaded the mainstream acupuncture profession and inspired copycat behavior. In the next chapter, I will detail POCA's efforts to define and control the practice of community acupuncture as a practice of democracy, even as private acupuncturists take pieces of the POCA model and adapt it for a more capitalist framework.

The leaders of POCA are not in search of reconciliation. The ones I met oppose the subsuming of acupuncture into what they see as corrupt Western medicine. They oppose efforts to get acupuncture covered by health insurance (because of the confusion and brokenness of the American health-care industry) and the granting of acupuncture doctoral degrees (and the additional cost that implies), both of which are supported by mainstream acupuncture. For POCA, these practices conform to the worst aspects of capitalism. And so POCA is content to separate itself and pursue success on its own terms.

I will give the last word on the matter to an acupuncturist from Providence, who admitted she had very high levels of debt from acupuncture school and was taking a risk working in POCA clinics. Yet for her, community acupuncture is a vocation. She needs to make a moderate income to meet her needs but is not seeking anything more than that. Why? Because she feels that mainstream acupuncture leaves the people she wants to serve out of the picture, and she cannot abide that. She explains:

> I want no part of any system that would leave them out again. And I think that this is sometimes at the root of the tension between community acupuncture and other acupuncturists. It feels like the system has repeatedly left these people and no one wants to admit it or do much about it. And on top of that, folks get irritated at us for treating these people affordably.

She goes on to contrast community acupuncture with private acupuncture, stating that mainstream acupuncture does not understand that POCA acupunks would actually choose the salaries they have, even cap them in order to create more jobs for other acupunks and grow the movement. For her, "it's a different kind of selfish motivation . . . [that] gets rewarded in the stability of social capital and stronger networks rather than strictly money."

TOWARD A COOPERATIVE COMMUNITY ECONOMY

Cooperatives possess a comparative advantage when it comes to community development.[31] Cooperatives, when true to their principles, are already grounded in a vision of social and economic justice. Though that vision may take different forms in different contexts, cooperatives often find themselves participating in larger social justice movements while remaining rooted securely to local communities. They are also able to prioritize the long-term health of their community over short-term financial gains. Therefore, cooperatives are a key component in a more resilient community economic system. The cooperative projects featured in this book share these qualities and demonstrate different ways of building community economies despite their organizational and material limitations. I offer three takeaways for practice derived from this chapter's focus on community economy.

Cultivate a Social Surplus

For many of the people I met, the scope of their practice was determined by internal goods rather than the achievement of external success. This is most obvious in the work of POCA's acupunks and Headlong's dancer-choreographers. These are already professions without much in the way of surplus earning; an internalized measure of success supports practitioners through rocky economic times. But in contrast with capitalist private acupuncturists or dance companies that chase external rewards, these practitioners maintained a focus on ethical questioning of the status quo and building economic systems in response that supported their practice from the ground up. These interventions, including POCA Tech and Headlong Performance Institute, contributed to a social surplus where the values of the organization are shared much more broadly.

The concept of a social surplus informs the work of Mariposa and

Weavers Way, as they contribute to citywide, cross-sector, and regional organizing to strengthen the cooperative economy. Their participation in the work of the Philadelphia Area Cooperative Alliance and the Mid-Atlantic Food Cooperative Alliance and their partnerships with national cooperative organizations demonstrate that they see themselves as part of a movement that is locally grounded but affects scales beyond the local.

Create Opportunities for Ethical Consumption

These organizations all facilitate a kind of ethical consumption, another of Gibson-Graham's ethical coordinates, that fuels the development of a community economy. When member-owners purchase sustainably produced goods that strengthen minority-owned businesses, that is ethical consumption in action. When I pay a community acupuncturist $40 for a treatment, so someone with less means can pay $20 or less for the same treatment, that helps to stabilize an acupunk's livelihood. When Headlong insists on paying its dancers fairly and subsidizing HPI tuition for lower-income students, that means Headlong's ticket buyers are engaging in a form of ethical consumption.

Operate on Multiple Scales Whenever Possible

Each of these projects participates in community economy at a variety of scales. Their projects have local impact but reach more broadly. For more than two decades, Headlong has been part of a national conversation about alternative performance practice. And its company members and HPI alumni have reputations that go far beyond Philadelphia. They bring with them the values and commitments they learned in their time at Headlong, as they asserted in interview after interview. Weavers Way and Mariposa contribute to a regional conversation through their participation in networks that grow and sustain a cooperative economy. And they are part of an international cooperative movement that grows and changes in response to global political, cultural, and economic forces. Finally, POCA has changed the national conversation about acupuncture, with nearly two hundred clinics all over the country proving the point that this mode of health care should be accessible to everyone.

As these projects struggle in the generative work of ethically enacting community economies, they allow a glimpse of a new way of ordering society. Cooperative practices like these prefigure a world in which organizational democracy, radical inclusion, and the resistance of oppression are possible. In the next chapter, I will trace cooperation as a practice of democracy. By exploring democracy through my research sites and beyond, I make the case that cooperative practice is urgently needed at all scales, beginning with the body, through work and organization, in community economy, and at a societal level.

PRACTICES OF DEMOCRACY

It has become fashionable for pundits to speak of democracy in turmoil. This concern has come to the fore in the United States particularly since the election of Donald Trump in 2016, but there are similar disturbing developments all around the world. While I agree about the seriousness of the challenges facing democracy partway into the twenty-first century, these challenges are hardly new. Historians, political scientists, and astute observers of all backgrounds note that democracy is fragile, fraught, and only ever partially realized. Journalist and left-wing activist Astra Taylor's 2019 book title states it well: *Democracy May Not Exist, but We'll Miss It When It's Gone.*

Among the elements of that wide-ranging book, Taylor includes reminiscences of Occupy Wall Street's attempts at consensus governance in its large-scale general assemblies. Taylor's awareness of the limits of that model brings to mind similar challenges regarding consensus governance that occurred at Mariposa Food Co-op as it was in the throes of deciding to expand and open the store to the general public. At that time, Mariposa relied upon consensus to manage its operations, just like Occupy, but at a much more intimate scale. A quick visit to that place and time at Mariposa provides further exploration of the benefits and challenges of consensus as a tool.

From its inception to its expansion, Mariposa used a form of consensus decision-making of the general membership. In its membership meetings, anyone present could vote to block a proposal, and deliberation would go on until everybody was satisfied with the proposal at hand. Mariposa used a system that really required unanimity rather than consensus. This unanimous-style consensus formerly in use at Mariposa is difficult to achieve, with any one member able to block the larger motion from going forward until that person is satisfied. The membership could debate a decision for hours without a tangible policy yield. This process might choke out the opportunity for change.

However, decisions made in this way were strongly supported by the active co-op membership.

Former employee Sam found the consensus system frustrating, believing that people misused it to benefit their own individual preferences: "[The consensus] system is incredibly conservative. Everything stays as is as long as there is one person who objects. People weren't open to consensus being against their own desire or motive—or they weren't trained enough to make their desires subservient." Meetings where controversial policies were proposed lasted for as long as four hours, well beyond the scheduled duration. At one meeting I attended, the meeting lost quorum because of the length of time it took to work through the issues involved early in the agenda. At that point, none of the decisions arrived at could be binding, since the meeting was not an adequate representation of the co-op.

When such a small percentage of the overall membership is represented, decisions that get made may have the consensus of all assembled, but that body does not represent the will of the whole co-op. Randy, a longtime Mariposa employee, reflects on the conundrum: "There were a handful of people that were active in the membership meetings. . . . [It depended on] whatever members randomly turn[ed] out at the membership meeting."

The issue of consensus at in-person meetings brings up a larger issue of how much of the membership was represented in these discussions. When Mariposa began, it was small enough that all of its founding members could sit in a common room at a neighborhood group house. It was not until the 2000s that meetings started to occur in public venues. Perhaps in these very early days, the membership was represented adequately for decisions to reflect the will of the whole organization. But as the co-op grew, the number of people who showed up for membership meetings declined, both in relative and absolute numbers. In response, the co-op moved to an elected board of directors rather than relying on consensus for decision making.

Whether it is direct democracy in the form of consensus governance or representative democracy with elected officials, democracy, with its elusive challenges, is the ultimate scale at which to evaluate the practice of cooperation. Once cooperation is established in bodies, in organizations, and in local economies, it becomes possible to imagine how cooperation might animate these discussions of democratic governance. Democracy as a cooperative practice needs to stem from the level of the individual body and inhere in all of the other forms of social interaction that undergird a democratic polity. It is more likely that cooperative practice of democracy will come to occur in democratically run associations, workplaces, families, and movements rather than in electoral politics. Periodic acts of voting or discrete decision-making are not the same thing as ongoing, thoroughgoing acts of deliberation throughout social and economic life. Electoral politics matter, but they are not the focus of this analysis.

Instead, this chapter explores moments of democracy (and its lack) in the cases featured in the rest of the book. Before doing that, I delve into some of the constituent issues that must be understood in order to conceive of democracy as a practice of cooperation. These include the notion of community; the relationship between democracy, liberalism, and communitarianism; and theories of democracy that are more expansive than those that merely focus on political democracy. Then I will turn to the cases to highlight the ways they build toward a form of creative democracy. In the end, it is the return to the body that completes the multiscalar analysis at the heart of this book's project. I conclude with some recommendations on how to instill democracy into the practice of cooperation. But first, I want to spend some time thinking through how democracy is related to the complicated question of being together in community.

THE (MIS)USES OF COMMUNITY

In my own work as an urbanist and practitioner, there are often appeals to the wisdom of some mythic version of community. Such a community, often constituted by poor people and people of color, are presumed to have deeper insight into the matters at hand, and if planners, developers, and others were to leave control to community, things would work themselves out better and more equitably than they do today. While I believe strongly in the need for power realignment and the relevance of local knowledge to planning, I reject the idea that the community is some singular, formed entity that lies in wait to correct the actions of powerful, wrongheaded decision-makers. There is a danger of idealizing community as a place from which to pursue democracy rather than working within community as an active site of struggle and contestation.

Another setting in which I find community deployed is by urban higher education institutions (like the one where I teach) regarding their public-facing mission. In this setting, the romantic discourse of community has a variety of uses. In one sense, communities (again, usually poor people and people of color) are there to be saved from poverty, poor education, poor health outcomes, and other indicators of distress. The higher education institutions seek to address these problems through research, service learning, and institutional policies that are supposed to illuminate and alleviate difficulty in the neighborhoods around the institution. While this work can produce good outcomes, particularly in the form of workforce development and local purchasing, often it helps faculty, students, and administrators more than it helps the community. After all, students get degrees and jobs and move out of the university neighborhood. Faculty get research funding, tenure, promotion, and other benefits that accrue to them in part because of their work in the community. And administrators gain reputation and cachet from the compassionate stance they take toward the institution's neighbors. At the same time, indicators in poor neighborhoods around universities are notoriously hard to change and life for people in these neighborhoods often remains difficult while the university's reputation rises. (I recognize that I am fully implicated in these processes, as a teacher and researcher who works in the West Philadelphia neighborhoods surrounding several major research universities.)

At the same time, the community can be seen as a thorn in the educational institution's side. When neighbors try to exercise power in ways that go against the university's priorities and plans, the relationship becomes fraught. I have seen this take place when neighbors try to assert their power and make demands, including struggles around community benefit agreements or PILOTs (payments in lieu of taxes). In these moments, it becomes clear that community has its place—to participate in partnerships and serve as fodder for research and other interventions. As one neighborhood resident recently told me, the universities want to partner, but they set all the terms of the partnership and do not want to be pushed to do otherwise. In writing this, I recognize that university-community partnerships vary from place to place, and some probably approach a higher standard of equity. The point is that the reliance on community as a signifier of all that is wholesome, authentic, folksy, and passive is problematic for a number of reasons.

In order to operationalize cooperation as a practice that begins locally and scales up, it is necessary to recognize the shortcomings and possibilities of local, face-to-face community as it is construed in urban life. In addition to the way community is employed by conservative critics of modernity, by some activists, and by urban universities, there are a number of problems with reliance on an ideal of community. These include conceptual fuzziness and nostalgia, the potential for exclusion and chauvinism, a failure to recognize how capitalism is implicated in community, and the problem of scale. After discussing these shortcomings, I will talk about a way of reconceptualizing community as a site of social action and agitation. Community, construed differently, can and should be rescued and operationalized toward democracy and justice. This insight leads into a discussion of creative democracy as an ideal method for living out cooperation's most expansive potential.

A Fuzzy, Problematic Concept

The first problem with the concept of community is its fuzziness. According to regional economist Ann Markusen, "a fuzzy concept is one which posits an entity, phenomenon or process which possesses two or more alternative meanings and thus cannot be reliably identified or applied."[1] Community can mean a variety of different things: a geographically bound area, a group of people who share habits or identities, or many other ways of drawing the distinction. Yet community is often evoked as an affective, or felt, value rather than being explicitly explained.[2] This conceptual fuzziness leads to what philosopher Iris Marion Young calls an ideal of community, in which real differences among people and groups are denied. Instead, the ideal of community seeks to lump people together into a unified and undifferentiated metaphysical whole. Young maintains instead that individuals possess multiple and overlapping group identifications and that even members of the same group do not necessarily hold the same views or priorities. Instead, she argues, group members are differentiated from others by their practices, relations, special needs or capacities, and structures of power or privilege rather than some ideal of sameness.[3]

Often, those who decry the dysfunction of American democracy and society contrast that dysfunction with an appeal to local, face-to-face community, like Occupy's assemblies at their most functional. This is a long-standing tradition that goes back to Alexis de Tocqueville's observations of American associational life in the 1830s. Tocqueville did find value in the political processes of the New England town meetings he observed, comparing them to the heyday of participatory democracy in ancient Athens. This comparison has led a lot of observers to follow

Tocqueville in nostalgia for a past of face-to-face local deliberation. But, according to feminist and queer theorist Miranda Joseph, this nostalgic conception of local deliberation is a misreading of Tocqueville.

Tocqueville lauded townships because they served as sites of active political contestation and opportunities for the forming of associations, not because of their small-scale, face-to-face character. Joseph explains that this misreading of Tocqueville ushers in a romantic discourse of community.[4] In this reading, contemporary political fragmentation and mistrust is a feature of modernity, and community (of the sort Tocqueville recognized) represents a premodern ideal worthy of rebirth. This romantic discourse idealizes earlier forms of community, when in fact those communities were also beset with disagreements, hierarchies, and exclusions alongside the benefits they offered. To view community with nostalgia is to misrecognize the past.

This romantic, nostalgic view was also embraced by an influential body of thinkers called communitarians who emerged in the 1980s as critics of liberalism. Communitarians took a page from thinkers like George Herbert Mead (discussed in chapter 2) who assert that identity derives from a social rather than an individual self. Communitarians ascribed recent social problems to a decline in trust, civic virtue, and civil society.[5] Therefore, communitarians often embraced a politics that reflexively valued communal institutions like the family, the church, and the nation.[6] Critics of communitarianism aver that those institutions frequently oppress their members. For all the good they can do, members are unavoidably embedded in them rather than being there as a function of choice.[7] The claims these institutions make on their members are often affected through hierarchy and domination.

One consequence of this nostalgia or preference for community as a function of traditional relationships is that the desire for community can lead to racism and ethnic chauvinism.[8] Alongside progressive organizing efforts, there is a right-wing "anticanon" of community organizing that achieved massive influence, embedding conservative Christian politics in local school boards, city councils, and state legislatures.[9] Unlike the paradox of exclusivity in cooperation, where exclusivity of some kind is desirable to maintain group affiliation, the kind of exclusivity embraced by some communities is pernicious. Efforts to curtail voting rights, deny reproductive rights to women, and thwart gun control are every bit as much projects of the community as any progressive political goal. Those who embrace nostalgia for community need to be prepared for the varied uses to which community can be deployed.

Critics note that the overwhelming share of both liberal and communitarian political philosophy is written by white men, who may themselves be nostalgic for eras in which they were even more politically and socially dominant. The majority of philosophers have been men; they have held social positions in which they have not been forced to experience many of the detrimental effects of the institutions they endorse. Communitarians and liberals both imagine an atomistic, unattached self (one group against the concept and one in support of it). Feminists point out that this unattached self simply does not reflect the reality of many women, who frequently hold a foundational role as caregivers. Feminists also maintain that understandings of self and community must account for differences in sex, age, ability, race, sexuality, gender, and class rather than focusing narrowly on family, neighborhood, and nation, as the communitarians would have it.

Liberalism and communitarianism are both implicated in a racial project that has traditionally excluded and oppressed people of color around the world. Political philosopher Charles W. Mills notes that both schools of thought, even in their disagreements, share fundamental, taken-for-granted assumptions. Cardinal among these assumptions is a condition of political equality for all people. But people of color, Mills relates, have never held political equality in the societies cataloged by communitarians and liberals, particularly in America with its legacy of slavery and Native American genocide. When it comes to the life of the community, "the existence of people of color necessarily transgresses and disrupts the key assumptions of both of these political framings. Expropriated Native Americans and enslaved Africans are clearly not part of the European and, later, Euro-implanted/Euro-imposed 'community' in question."[10] Clearly, discussions about community as a core component of democracy are infused with questions of power, and the project of advancing political community requires a realignment of people and resources to adequately represent the full humanity and complexity of all participants.

The next critique of a romantic vision of community regards the relationship of community to capital. Joseph notes that community as a concept is supposed to stand outside of economic relationships and comprise a purely altruistic set of relationships, balancing and harmonizing capitalism. Joseph finds instead that capital affects communities and connects them with one another. Historical analysis shows that early nineteenth-century yearnings for community were based on anticapitalist efforts to resist commodification and mechanization of the economy.[11] According to scholars of political economy James DeFilippis, Robert Fisher, and Eric Shragge, "Historically, factories, mines, and other components of the wage-labor productive economy were rooted in communities, and the divide between places of employment and places of residence was much narrower and less dichotomous." They go on to note that today's care work and reproductive labor have been hired out to low-wage workers and are part of the wage-labor economy as well.[12] However, conservative champions of community view it as an apolitical source of the solutions to problems of crime, drugs, and the like—rather than viewing these as structural problems that deeply implicate the state and the structure of the economy, as well as the local community. The neoliberalism of the 1980s and beyond has sought to depoliticize community and make individual and small-group responsibility for their own well-being a replacement for demands to change systems to better support local community needs.

The last consequence of a nostalgic view of community is that it does not scale up, that it cannot address systemic problems because of its local character. Not only does MacIntyre endorse this view, he also prefers that solutions be found through practices at the face-to-face level. This is one of the places I part with him. Indeed, history is populated by examples of local community organizing that affected much larger scales of influence. The settlement house movement of the early twentieth century worked with recent immigrants to provide education, social services, and cultural opportunities. Some of its most prominent leaders changed the national conversation around early childhood education, civic infrastructure like playgrounds, and labor reforms. The "backyard revolution" of the 1960s and 1970s saw community mobilized in service of national policy changes around civil rights, workers' rights, and more.[13] The cooperative movement itself represents a decentralized but federated structure of economic and political organizing that has resulted in a significant number of the planet's inhabitants participating in an alternative or anticapitalist economic initiative of one kind or another.

Community holds even greater political importance and urgency in a time of democratic dysfunction. Community is the place where citizens interact with the services provided by the state, where they form political consciousness, where they participate in political life, and where they interact with social movements.[14] Therefore, communities need to be mobilized and activated to address the local and systemic problems that affect them, while making democratic demands. Ending oppression means letting go of both nostalgia for the past and relying on the romantic notion of community. Instead, local and chosen communities of affinity must organize to "occupy liberalism" and insist on the full inclusion and participation of an intersectional coalition of changemakers. Iris Marion Young calls this organizing strategy a "politics of difference" in which groups, not just individuals, fight for justice in community.[15]

Search for the Great Community

Like Iris Marion Young, pragmatist philosopher John Dewey also believed in fighting for justice through community. For Dewey, the search for what he called the Great Community was the cardinal goal of solving the problems of the public, of democracy.[16] The Great Community can be achieved through deliberation and communication, and it is a site of constant progressive struggle. Dewey's philosophy of creative democracy, espoused throughout his long life and career, resonates deeply with the objectives of this book. Dewey sees democracy as a form of moral and spiritual association that composes the backbone of social life. Rather than anarchic mob rule or the mere quantitative aggregation of individual voter preferences, creative democracy is a framework for being-in-common that simultaneously respects the capacity of citizens to self-govern while challenging them to function at the highest possible level of self-actualization.[17] Dewey's creative democracy is a call to action in the face of startling levels of public fracture around the globe.

Creative democracy fundamentally respects the personhood, intelligence, and agency of each participant in the collective project of figuring out how to lead a good life. By granting the capacity to meaningfully self-govern, Dewey sees democracy as an individual and collective political responsibility. He rejects the ontology of atomized individualism in favor of a social body composed of unique and complementary perspectives, collectively able to discern the most effective course of political action. Thus, democracy is a way of life rather than something institutional and remote. According to planning scholar Robert Lake, Deweyan democracy is collective, relational, and constitutive. It is collective in the sense that individual autonomy is achieved through sustained engagement across a variety of social contexts. Democracy is not something that is limited to sporadic, periodic engagement like voting. It is relational because it goes beyond mere deliberation to form the backbone of social cognition based on collective exploration and experimentation. Finally, it is constitutive because the combined intelligence unearthed in these cooperative spaces yields better solutions to the problems of the day.

Framed in this way, as a continuous and open-ended practice, creative democracy fosters the development of democratic subjects who are capable and inclined to do the hard work of sustaining an ethical way of living. Dewey's social hope and faith in democracy is grounded in the many examples he saw around him in everyday life. I too am heartened and sustained in my belief in democracy by the examples of the cases profiled in this book. Creative democracy is more than a pipe dream. It is manifest by those courageous enough to enter into relationship with it as both a value and a practice.

Democracy is thus a practice in the same sense as cooperation. Perhaps it is the ultimate expression of cooperation as a practice. As with any practice, there is the dilemma of how to best make it manifest. Though democracy serves an educative function, it requires education and preparation in order to set the conditions for its success, a chicken-and-egg challenge famously laid out by Rousseau in *The Social Contract*.[18] For Dewey, this work must begin in childhood and continue throughout a life of learning. In any democratic setting, it is the values of generosity, openness, and respect that must be in place, alongside a commitment to collective experimentation and a focus on improving results. Practiced in this way, creative democracy is an avenue toward a more equal and more desirable social life.

Back in 1927, Dewey wrote, "The idea of democracy is a wider and fuller idea than can be exemplified in the state even at its best. To be realized it must affect all modes of human association, the family, the school, industry, religion."[19] To date, these areas of social life have not been democratized. Through cooperation, a more participatory form of democracy can triumph over hierarchy and individualism. The cases in this book all pursue their objectives in service of participatory, creative democracy, a state of political affairs that has yet to broadly take hold across the political sphere. In anticipating such a future, they practice a form of prefigurative politics. By "prefigurative politics," I mean social practices that embody the kind of society they seek to bring about, rather than waiting for ends that are radically dissimilar from the means used to achieve social change. Prefiguration can be seen as a hopeful gesture that points toward the ways in which a just future grows from today's practices.[20] Each of the practices of cooperation profiled in this book seek to create a new society in the midst of existing, less just arrangements in order to help usher in a different future.[21] In the sections that follow, I describe how each of the cases prefigures the conditions of democracy they wish to see, while facing all of the challenges that occur when trying to pave a way for a more democratic state of affairs.

I SLEEP WITH STRANGERS

In the previous chapter, I detailed how POCA's community acupuncture movement distinguishes itself from the conventional, private provision of acupuncture in the United States. In this chapter, I will continue to draw that distinction, as it has democratic as well as economic consequences. POCA practices democracy in a number of ways. First, POCA turns an individual, atomistic practice of alternative health care into a collective and communal one. This transformation occurs by POCA staking a claim as a comprehensive movement for social change that prefigures a realignment of the way health is fostered. Second, POCA pursues democracy in its clinics by respecting the full personhood of patients, particularly along class and racial lines. Third, POCA has begun to implement a trauma-informed praxis that is grounded in narratives of personal and community liberation. I will address each of these in turn, demonstrating how collectively they work to achieve POCA's goals of what it calls liberation acupuncture.

When it comes to cultivating social solidarity through acupuncture, POCA's primary method is treatment in groups. Even though patients do not speak to one another, there is a sense among clinic owners and acupunks that some sort of community has been formed. The image of a dozen people, each dozing in recliners while soft music plays, each with their own personal story of struggling to find health, may indeed conjure impressions of a somnolent democratic space. I asked Jack, an acupuncturist in Portland, about the advantages of group treatment. He replied that the advantages accrued both to the patients and the practitioner. Even though there is no talking among patients, he finds a certain camaraderie that is formed, that the patients are all in it together.

Jack contrasts this camaraderie with the social isolation that many of his patients face in the rest of everyday life. Several acupuncturists told me that they were aware that treatments in a POCA clinic are the only times in a given week where some of their patients are touched by another person at all. Given that condition, Jack finds it important that the clinic provide a safe place. He explains, "It's a public place, but it's a safe place where they can let their guard down and relax. There's this unspoken sense of hope and relief for humanity. It's something that's unfortunately missing in most of the day-to-day interactions that we have." Carol, an acupunk from Providence, concurred when I spoke with her. She explained that everyone is facing something different, but they are all doing it together: "The person next to you might be there for headaches or sleep or they might be there for prostate or lung cancer. To me there's just an amazing grace there."

POCA's acupunks take this responsibility both seriously and lightly (witness the bumper stickers for sale at some clinics that cheekily state "I sleep with strangers"). But it was clear in my many conversations that the democracy of the clinic is mirrored in the democracy of the cooperative itself. In other chapters, I have written about the ways in which the cooperative supports the enterprise of community acupuncture across the nation's clinics. But this point was made poignantly in an interview with Tamara, one of the co-op's most active members. She explained that being in the cooperative taught her that humans are not parasitic and destructive; rather, they can come together and build beautiful, mutually supportive structures. This is the kind of creative, participatory democracy Dewey advocated back in the 1930s. Tamara made it clear why she values being in a co-op, while busily operating a rural clinic by herself: "It helps with the isolation of capitalism, because living in this capitalist society where we're just mostly competing with each other, there are these communities where we're not and that's just awesome."

POCA in many ways is a political organization, with a set of goals that members perceive as oppositional to capitalism, to mainstream health care, and to conventional private acupuncture. POCA members draw strength from affiliation with these political goals and from a sense that they are creating something revolutionary in the face of difficulty. (One of POCA's taglines for the movement is "The Calmest Revolution Ever Staged.") Given their firm commitment to POCA as an organized approach to transforming acupuncture, it is not surprising that POCA's key players defend its approach against its critics. Though many of them espouse support for other ways of doing acupuncture, they make it clear that POCA's vision of community acupuncture is not amorphous.

FIGURE 13. Bumper sticker for sale at West Philadelphia Community Acupuncture. Photograph by Andrew Zitcer.

They are not open to individual clinics "making it up," in the words of Emily, one of the organizers of POCA in Portland. Megan, a clinic owner in Providence, did not mince words: "We're fine factioning off and just being a different thing and calling ourselves a different thing. We're calling ourselves community organizers with needles." As POCA Tech's leaders phrased it in a letter to the national accreditation board: "Community acupuncture is not half of something. It is something whole in and of itself. It just happens to be something different."

POCA's partisan identification has led to disagreements with private acupuncturists, who frequently see the goal of widespread acupuncture as something all parties ought to share. Private acupuncturists, and even community clinic owners who choose not to affiliate with POCA, expressed consternation over POCA's insistence on holding fast to its political goals. One private Philadelphia clinic owner exclaimed, "They are replacing Chinese medicine with politics!" Another stated that POCA had such reverence for its model that it was ignorant of the contributions that others could make: "You shouldn't say my god is better than your god—there is no one best."

Some felt that POCA ought to participate in the conventional health-care system to try to make acupuncture more widespread. Why not work within the system and collaborate with doctors and hospitals and advocate for acupuncture to be covered by insurance? (It is now covered in a limited way in Pennsylvania as of 2019.) But POCA, to the chagrin of some private acupuncturists, is not willing to engage in that kind of collaboration with the forces of the capitalist health-care industry. Instead, it is focused on its own anticapitalist agenda. The

Philadelphia clinic owner quoted above exclaimed, "We are not in a Communist country. We're in America! You can be as political as you want but at the end of the day you have to pay people, and then guess what? You're in business."

POCA clinic owners and acupunks do not deny that they are in business. They know firsthand the struggles of operating a successful clinic while trying to preserve affordability and access. Daniel, a clinic owner from New England reflected on these disputes, calling out a "fundamental philosophical schism" between POCA and the rest of mainstream acupuncture. For him, mainstream acupuncture's focus is on self-preservation and the well-being of the clinics and practitioners rather than the needs of marginalized patients. Although I had conversations where practitioners expressed respect or even admiration for the other side, such expressions of mutual support were rare; I recall only two practitioners, out of thirty-two interviews, taking that position. It is clear that POCA holds fast to a set of values and practices that prefigure the world it wants to see for its patients and practitioners, and it is not willing to dilute that vision to compromise with mainstream acupuncture.

POCA pursues a prefigurative politics of democracy through a recognition of the personhood of its patients along class and racial lines. One concern that arose in the interviews is private acupuncturists who expect patients to return again and again for costly treatments that strain their finances. In a political economic environment where health care is a luxury and not a right, patients may turn to complementary and alternative modes of treatment whose costs come in addition to monthly premiums, copayments, limited coverage, and more—if they are even insured in the first place. For those who are uninsured, alternative care like acupuncture may be a relatively affordable hope to get a handle on a chronic medical condition like back pain or infertility. But at $80–100 per session, conventional private acupuncture's cost makes frequent return visits a challenge to many patients.

One POCA acupuncturist in Philadelphia lamented the practice of mainstream acupuncturists encouraging patients to get treatments they cannot afford. She explained that some acupuncturists make patients feel badly about wanting less expensive treatments, urging the patients to "value their health" and make a deeper investment in acupuncture treatments. In response, she wondered, "If you don't have that money, how can it be about valuing your health? If you literally don't have those dollars? It's not about valuing your health, it's just about not having the money." By contrast, POCA clinics limit the cost of their treatments (and the income of their acupunks) in order to make it possible for patients with limited incomes to seek out more frequent treatments, without the guilt.

Another mainstream acupuncture practice decried by the POCA acupunks I interviewed is offering community-style treatments on some days or in some locations. POCA clinics across the country all work off the same sliding scale, and while they will offer seasonal discounts or POCA member discounts of a few dollars, they do not have alternative clinics that charge a higher rate or charge different rates on different days. Acupunks felt that these differential rates were confusing for patients, as well as making patients who sought out lower-cost treatments feel less worthy than those who "valued their health" enough to pay for more expensive treatments. A consultant who helps out with POCA and POCA Tech explained why he felt the practice was problematic: "If you are treating some people for $100 and other people with $20, the people are paying $100 better get some kind of extra service. At the same time, how do you make the people who are paying $20 feel like they're not getting half a treatment? They're not getting shorted." In this context, it feels like valuing patients differently at different price points.

On some level, this distinction reflects a difference in the treatment philosophy of private versus community acupuncture. In the $100 treatment scenario, the private acupuncturist is likely seeing one to three patients per hour and offering a consultation to each person. They are likely being seen in a private room and being given the opportunity to get more needles in places that community acupuncture clinics cannot offer because of the group nature of the treatments. As I have said before, there is an important role for private acupuncturists to play in the acupuncture ecosystem. In this case, the issue is when private acupuncture tries to have it both ways, offering expensive treatments that appear to hold more value on some days or in some clinics, while offering less expensive treatments in other venues that might make patients with less means feel less valued.

Another element of acupuncture personhood concerns the issue of race and cultural appropriation. In this case, the issue that arose in interviews specifically concerns the use of Asian iconography, Chinese characters, and other Asian decor. In some cases, this seems to be part of a larger effort to turn the clinic experience into more of a spa treatment. But POCA clinics make an effort to look neutral. And an interview I had with a Chinese American POCA clinic owner revealed her discomfort with the appropriation of Chinese symbolism in clinics owned by white acupuncturists. From her perspective, Asian acupuncturists are already fighting racial discrimination and threats to their legitimacy because of cultural and language barriers. Therefore, they try to legitimize their clinics by pursuing a more Western medical decor, including wearing white coats, which is not the custom among either private acupuncturists or POCA acupunks. She laughed as she explained, "I don't need all those weird Buddha statues and fountains and fish. I guess it's just a bunch of white people trying to seem Asian and Asian people are trying to seem medical."

Lisa Rohleder concurred with this assessment, having been in the acupuncture profession for a few decades: "That orientalism thing is hugely problematic. For a lot of these people, acupuncture, it is their religion and it's the center of their lives. I don't need another religion. My god, I've got one and it's pretty fucked up. I don't need another fucked up one where people tell me what to do and how to think, but at least that's a religion [meaning her Catholicism]. This is a pseudo-religion for rich, white people." In addition to being problematic from a perspective of cultural appropriation, several interviewees mentioned that Chinese imagery may be alienating to some, particularly working-class patients. For these patients, acupuncture may already feel risky and foreign, a departure from the medical environment they know. To layer in unfamiliar language and customs, especially out of their proper cultural context, may make some patients confused or uncomfortable. This instinct to shield patients from traces of Asian imagery cuts both ways, reducing the potential for Orientalism by white acupuncturists while potentially contributing to an erasure of a very relevant Asian historical and cultural influence.

Finally, POCA creates a space of democratic inclusion through what it calls liberation acupuncture. If community acupuncture is the model of low-cost, high-volume group treatments, liberation acupuncture can be thought of as the ethics of community acupuncture. Developed in concert with the curriculum of POCA Tech, liberation acupuncture takes liberation psychology as its lodestar. Liberation psychology has its origins in the 1970s in Latin America, where a Jesuit priest and psychologist named Ignacio Martín-Baró challenged the neutrality and universality of psychology. Instead, he focused on the particular needs

FIGURE 14. Portrait of Ignacio Martín-Baró, one of seven "Liberation Acupuncture Ancestors" portrayed by artists and acupunks James Shelton and Kate Kampmann. Image by James Shelton and Kate Kampmann. Courtesy of POCA Tech.

of oppressed people in places like El Salvador, finding that the conditions of their structural oppression were more germane to their mental health than a focus on individual pathology. Thus, liberation psychology is a form of critical social psychology.

Liberation acupuncture proceeds from the same sorts of assumptions with acupuncture as the treatment methodology. In doing so, liberation acupuncture creates an alternate justification for POCA's acupuncture praxis, grounding it on a different foundation than the way traditional Chinese medicine is taught in other acupuncture schools. POCA Tech takes a pragmatist approach to treating the patients who come to its clinics. Lisa Rohleder explains, "Acupuncture works if it works in real life, for ordinary people, and whatever allows ordinary people to use acupuncture in a way that works for them is more valid than an academic theory that you can't/shouldn't do acupuncture like that. Apparently, the way to say that so academics can hear it is 'Liberation Acupuncture.'" This justification has echoes of Dewey's vision of pragmatic, creative democracy. It works if it is better in its effects than the alternative. In this case, if it is better for marginalized and oppressed patients, then liberation acupuncture is the best acupuncture on offer.

Foundational to liberation acupuncture, as conceived by POCA, is the idea that disease does not exist outside of social conditions and cannot be treated without attending to those social conditions. Thus, liberation acupuncture proceeds by recognizing and working with the needs of the oppressed, exploited, and excluded. As awareness of the pervasiveness of trauma is becoming more widespread, there are efforts to try to make trauma-informed care more widely available. POCA has made an organizational commitment to making clinics trauma-informed spaces and to incorporating trauma-informed care as a fundamental component of the POCA Tech curriculum. POCA clinics strive to be trauma informed by serving as spaces for physical and emotional safety through the mostly clothed, public group nature of the clinic setting. There is no opportunity for an acupuncturist to be alone in a room with a patient, stand over them while they are without clothing, and administer a treatment. There is often no structure for a thorough consultation, which means that patients do not have to go into detail about their trauma (though some clinics do offer a private consultation space as an option). In addition, practitioners are trained to ask for consent before touching patients, avoid language that shames patients for their health issues, and offer the clinic as a predictable, reliable, and low-cost way for patients to receive care that can help them move forward with their treatment plans.[22]

Ultimately, this focus on trauma-informed care brings the story of cooperation back to the body itself. In an article in *Gay Mag*, a new magazine from author Roxane Gay, a mother describes her experience of surviving after losing a child in childbirth. It is so beautiful and poignant that I will quote it at length. In the piece, she tells of her experience visiting a community acupuncture clinic, which she had visited before experiencing trauma. This time, her experience was different, and she found herself weeping after the acupunk put the needles in. The weeping did not stop:

> There were other people in the room, and I knew they could see me, but still I wept. I didn't attempt to wipe away the tears. I didn't make any noise, but it's not that I held myself back, it's just that my body was somehow soundless. I felt myself in my body and in the room. I was close to sleep but fully aware of everything. I listened to the soft shuffle of shoes, small coughs, and the crash of the footrests. I felt the needles in my arms. I wouldn't have been able to reach up to wipe my tears away, even if I wanted to. Which I didn't.
>
> After a lifetime of worrying about making people feel uncomfortable, I let go. In a room made for bodies, there was no choice but to know my own, to recognize the ways it had been broken open and was being put back together again. I was merely mortal, merely making peace with empty space. Instead of making it harder, the existence of other humans in the room made it easier. They were strangers, but I recognized them—their knit hats, their scruffy beards and bike pants, their rain-frizz and their sighs. . . . No one ever asked me why I was crying or said a word about it, and I felt better every time I left.[23]

POCA's goal is to achieve, through bodily care and social transformation, a movement that will reshape the way acupuncture is delivered around the United States. Today, it practices its own form of prefigurative politics, in the face of an acupuncture establishment that is only grudgingly accepting its presence. Mark, another of the Portland acupuncturists, described a vision for a global community acupuncture movement to me. For him, it consists of a cooperative where POCA clinics are so numerous that they are able to use their purchasing power to get better deals on purchasing and disposing of acupuncture needles, sustaining a low-cost POCA Tech that graduates acupunks ready to staff and run successful clinics, and the presence of such clinics in every major population center. He speaks to the prefiguration of a reality suffused with community acupuncture: "Instead of treating 1 percent of people in America, you know, maybe we would treat 80 percent. That would be a great normal."

I OWN THIS PLACE!

Organizational democracy is a key component of participatory democracy. In the case of cooperatives, it is enshrined in the international cooperative principles themselves, which call for democratic member control, open and voluntary membership, education and training of members, and concern for the broader community. At different times in the evolution of a cooperative project, these principles may be enacted in different ways. There is usually more participation in the startup phase of a cooperative, at times of major change, and in times of struggle. The challenge to keep members engaged in sustaining the organizational democracy is a challenge for any cooperative project over its life span.

Nevertheless, for some members, participation in governance feels natural and thrilling. One active Mariposa member expressed excitement to be an owner of the co-op: "When you walk in, you are like, 'I own this place!' There is something to be said for 'What do we have?' Not 'what do you have?' Just difference in language, but it's significant. And it's indicative of people feeling an ownership stake in the co-op." Community ownership provides a unique relationship with the places on one's daily round. It certainly stands in contrast to the nexus of Amazon's ownership of Whole Foods or the ongoing consolidation of the rest of the grocery economy under large-scale corporate control.[24]

At the same time, this excitement needs to be met with a widespread sense of responsibility for the stewardship of the cooperative enterprise. Democracy within cooperatives depends on it. Co-ops need to be run as a balance of association and enterprise. When they are too much of an association and too little of an enterprise, there is a risk to the integrity of the whole endeavor. In this section, I will relate two instances in the history of these Philadelphia food co-ops where an excess of trust led to serious consequences for the health of the co-op. In both cases, a kind of radically democratic impulse to have the stores run less formally and more along the lines of the countercultural cooperative enterprises of the 1960s was detrimental.[25] In the case of Weavers Way, this led to a major financial crisis. In the case of Mariposa, it led to a set of shopping and accounting practices that were sorely lacking as the store prepared to expand. Rather than being curtailed by better organizational controls, democratic cooperative practice increased, allowing the stores to be able to expand and provide more healthy food, more expansive community ownership, and more jobs in the neighborhood.

CRISIS AT THE CO-OP

The headlines in the *Philadelphia Inquirer* in December 2002 depicted a dire situation: "Money Woes May Kill a Popular Co-op," "Money Crisis at Co-op Shakes Members' Trust," and "Money Picture Gets Worse for Troubled Co-op." That winter, Weavers Way faced the possibility of its own demise due to a financial crisis. When the final accounting was done, $618,000 of members' equity in the co-op had disappeared. The co-op's long-time general manager resigned. And the co-op's bookkeeper faced criminal charges. What happened? In late November 2002, Weavers Way planned to purchase two buildings across the street from its original location in Mount Airy. This was to be an incremental expansion, one designed to convert two small buildings into a site for a café and a location for prepared foods. The then-general manager went to the loan closing, expecting the long-time financial manager to attend as well. She was not seen or heard from for several days as the crisis began to unfold. Upon examination, the general manager found out there were not enough funds in Weavers Way's accounts to cover the check, meaning the purchase of the properties could not go through. Over the next several weeks, Weavers Way's board investigated the co-op's finances and discovered that funds had been transferred from one bank account to another to cover shortfalls at the co-op. As time went on, understanding of the scope of the problem deepened. A subsequent accountability report put together by Weavers Way brought to light problems that went back at least as far as 1996, possibly even as early as 1994. It may have taken Weavers Way's board as long as eight and a half years to become aware of the financial mismanagement in its midst.

The co-op uncovered a number of actions that comprised the mismanagement of funds. First, Weavers Way consistently paid its vendors late and owed them hundreds of thousands of dollars more than what it reported on its internal financial statements. Because no one besides the financial manager ever looked at the co-op's bank statements, no one noticed the massive discrepancies. In addition to the late payments, there was also a tremendous volume of bank overdrafts on all of the Weavers Way bank statements. These ended up costing the co-op $140,000 over approximately 4,500 overdrafts. The financial manager hid most of this activity from the finance committee and board. Nor did anyone notice the volume of mail coming from the bank or look at any bank statements. The ultimate consequence is that the inaccurate financial picture made it appear that the co-op was more profitable than it actually was.

The financial manager was hardly the only person at fault for the financial crisis. The accountability report makes clear that blame was shared throughout the organization, including the board. Surprisingly, the Weavers Way board never conducted audits of its finances. One of Weavers Way's board members puzzled over the disjuncture between the board members' own business savvy and their failure to apply it to the co-op setting:

> The thing that I always found amazing is the people who had been the presidents, treasurers, senior officers of a co-op board—they were serious people. They weren't Moonbeam Jones and Sunshine Smith, you know, and running this wonderful hippie little organization, they were business people and they were lawyers and—and so, what they would do is somehow here they put on blinders, I said, "Oh, but that's the co-op."

What this board member brings to light is that these businesspeople somehow saw the co-op differently than they viewed their own businesses. The co-op, perhaps by virtue of its social, community-based mission, was exempt from the kind of hard-nosed scrutiny that other businesses required.

Weavers Way responded to the threat of financial ruin by making several serious asks of its members and its staff. The staff agreed to wage and benefit givebacks. There was a surcharge on all purchases. Members made loans to the co-op. And though it was a difficult period, the community around the co-op was supportive. Sandra, a board member, reflected on the dynamic in the organization, remembering that members came up with hundreds of thousands of dollars of loans to bail out the co-op. Interim general manager at the time, Charles, was surprised as well by the outpouring of support, noting that he was way too conservative in his budgeting; Weavers Way came out of the crisis financially ahead of the game. Of course, this speaks to both the generosity but also the relative wealth of co-op members, who were able to part, even temporarily, with the sums of money required to keep the co-op afloat. This kind of crisis may have financially sunk a co-op with a less wealthy membership base.

But other members of the co-op community emphasized, as Sandra does here, the responsibility that the co-op had to run like a bigger business and be the stewards of the members' equity:

> We were at a point where, I don't remember what our gross revenues were at that time, but it was up around maybe $4 million or something and we were operating as a small mom and pop where the co-op grew up where the founders did everything and there were really no controls—we trusted each other. We really felt that since we had members' equity that we really needed to act the way that any organization with those revenues would act.

The lesson here is that cooperative organizations can succeed and sustain themselves when they have adequate controls and they disperse organizational responsibilities among the various staff, board, and members. They need to apply sound business practices, like paying vendors in a timely manner and doing audits, and acknowledge that their eclectic and sometimes anticapitalist nature does not excuse them from these core responsibilities. And they have opportunities to build trust based on all of the other elements that are unique about cooperatives: member ownership, one person-one vote governance, lack of pursuit of profit for its own sake, concern for community, and more. It was clear to the members, staff, and vendors that Weavers Way believed in all of its core values and lived by them. Even a crisis of the magnitude that befell the organization in 2002–2003 could not fully shake the trust people felt in Weavers Way. The organization was able to weather it and recover, leading to a renewed vigor, a strengthened board and staff, and ultimately to the expanded operations it currently enjoys.

LATE NIGHTS AT THE REGISTER

Before it expanded to its current location, one of the ways in which Mariposa extended trust to its members was that it allowed after-hours shopping. Members received a key to the store after six months of membership (this was rather loosely enforced) and could let themselves in at any time, day or night, to shop on the honor system. They would simply write down what they purchased and pay for it when they settled their accounts later. Though most members abided by the rules of the co-op during after-hours shopping, a number of problems made the practice untenable. But it continued long after that point. Mariposa discontinued after-hours shopping shortly before the co-op moved to the new location and it does not exist in the expanded co-op.

Talking about after-hours shopping elicited several fantastical stories of malfeasance. These incidents were symbolic of how far Mariposa had moved from conventional business practices in its organizational journey. One co-op member, Jenny, expressed concern about the practice before launching into one representative story:

> I thought it was insane that they let all these people run around in the co-op at night, locking and unlocking doors, relying on them to lock the co-op and not have the co-op be vandalized and ravaged in the middle of the night because someone had not locked the door.
>
> I think it's a magical level of trust in a body of people. I'm on the accountability team, so I have seen that play out in bad ways, where people are stealing from the co-op, and having sex in the bathroom evidently, and my favorite co-op afterhours story is the person who came in after hours, after binge drinking, passed out on the floor, surrounded by Rice Dream ice cream wrappers and cigarette butts. I mean, that should not happen, obviously.

Though it is amusing to picture the person passed out on the floor of the co-op, the real thrust of her story is the "magical level of trust" that Mariposa placed in its members. Of course, there is some upside to endowing members with such privileges. It allows them to feel closely tied to something that they do not have anyplace else in their lives. One interviewee lamented no longer being able to buy the ingredients to make a cake at 2 a.m. whenever the mood struck her. That, to her, made the co-op feel like an extension of home.

But after-hours shopping did not work. Though the co-op did not mean to do it, it was allowing for errors and encouraging stealing. Eventually it had to be discontinued, although the decision to do so was controversial among the Mariposa membership. Sam explains why it was hard to let it go: "Everyone wanted after-hours shopping because it was awesome. It was really empowering on a psychic level that I am trusted to have a key and write down what I buy. [It seemed like] a punishment to have that taken away."

The after-hours shopping dated back to an earlier era when the co-op did not have proper refrigeration for its produce. If there was extra food left after the various members picked up their bulk orders, members could come in and shop what was left on the shelves. But as the co-op grew from a buying club to a membership organization with hundreds, then thousands of stakeholders, this practice was completely

FIGURE 15. A flyer advertises an important meeting to decide the future of Mariposa Food Co-op.

unsustainable. Former board member Merrill ruefully related that coming to terms with the need for co-op expansion meant realizing that her picture of the way things used to function reflected a distorted reality. These trusting but unconventional business practices never really worked in the first place: "[When] we were smaller, the consequences were less significant—and partly we were just kind of used to it."

Before Mariposa went the way of the wilted veggies, it needed to make organizational and operational changes to adapt to its new circumstances. This was not easy for some staff and community members to come to terms with, as they were not comfortable with conventional business practices being employed in the co-op. Staffer Sam was one person who advocated for these practices being adopted, and he ended up leaving the co-op because of intrastaff conflict and a feeling that his vision for the co-op would not be adopted. He talks here about wanting Mariposa to take on conventional business practices:

> Hippies can do it too—just because you are progressive doesn't mean you can't use real business tools. It's not the tools that are the problem; it's the people that are using them. I wanted the co-op to maximize the good it could do, and I didn't see that happening. Systems were really holding back what the co-op could be, even in terms of its own mission statement. We need to stay in business in order to do all these things. We need to be self-sustaining in order to do all the non-grocery-store things we want to do.

Sam did not stay at the co-op long enough to see that the changes he advocated ultimately came into effect. Perhaps his agitation helped catalyze Mariposa to move in this direction, even as he was blamed as the bringer of tidings from the outside world that could no longer go unheeded.

"REALLY FUNNY AND REALLY OPEN"

In one sense, it seems a stretch to talk about Headlong Dance Theater as an exemplar of democracy. Unlike Weavers Way and Mariposa, it is not part of an international movement for consumer cooperation. Unlike the People's Organization of Community Acupuncture, it is not a national network of clinics, patients, and providers all united to transform alternative health care. Yes, I have described in prior chapters how it endorsed democratic decision making with its seven-votes-per-person scheme. Yes, it sought to be radically open and build a community of artists in Philadelphia and beyond. But at the most basic level, Headlong is a tiny arts organization rooted in one city, playing to a relatively constrained audience of lovers of contemporary culture.

Yet I want to claim Headlong as an exemplar of democracy because of its ethic of care, its persistent questioning of the status quo, and its sustained, evolutionary experimentation. All of these are qualities that prefigure a participatory, creative society that I very much want to experience and share with everyone around me. In my time volunteering with Headlong and throughout my research, I found myself wanting to be a part of it, even though I am not an artist. I felt there was a place for me in Headlong, and I suspect that was what attracted many other people to its fold and to loyal devotion to its cause. In the rest of this section, I want to talk about some of these qualities that inhered to Headlong and how they might serve as preconditions for a kind of creative democracy that may be part of a world to come.

In his reading of creative democracy, Lake concludes by exhorting his audience to accord democracy the status of poetry. Like poetry, democracy requires a state of openness to wonder and possibility. It requires an imaginative leap into the unknown. It calls for enchantment and vision, to make possible futures that are currently unknown but not unknowable. It is this energy that I want to capture in these, my last reflections on Headlong for the purposes of this project. In particular, I want to reflect on Headlong's utopianism, its expansive notion of participation, and the way Headlong's values functioned in some ways as a guide for living.

Headlong's aspirations were avowedly utopian, even as the company remained grounded in the messiness of life. In fact, its work explored the contradictions between the world as it is and the world as it should be. That utopian impulse showed up early in Headlong, as the trio of codirectors moved into a shared loft in Philadelphia's Old City in order to unify their lives and work. Francis, an early supporter of the company, drew a through line between their decision to live communally and their utopian ambitions: "Utopianism is actually one of the leitmotifs through the Headlong projects, right? And so, one of the ways that that was articulated was artists living and working in the same space without a lot of division between when they were working and when they were just living their lives." They embodied MacIntyre's notion of the unity of a human life. Early employee Albert felt that Headlong had cracked some sort of code, pursuing their artistic dream: "They're paying themselves a living wage to go into the studio and experiment together on making work that's thoughtful, that response to their local artistic community and that—and that has, you know, a broader audience outside of Philadelphia and I really felt like they were just living the dream for lack of a better way putting it." To be sure, lots of artists live together in their early years, and the cheap rents of Philadelphia in the early 1990s made a lot of art possible. But for Headlong, it was the connection between their living and working, the unity of their lives, that impressed the people around them so deeply.

The second element that stood out to the community that formed around Headlong was its ethic of care toward an expansive and ever-growing group of people. Interviewees recalled with fondness the monthly First Friday performances Headlong used to host (and still does on occasion). Albert recalled that "anyone was welcome, if you had something to teach or something you wanted to learn, you wanted to join a Dance Theater Camp, you wanted to come and see the work at a First Friday performance." In the world of experimental arts, especially in those days, radical inclusion was not a popular attitude. Albert recalled that events that started small, by invitation, and quite intimate grew over time to host a hundred people that regularly interacted with the directors of the company. He went on, emphasizing the relationships that ensued from these initially casual interactions: "Anyone who comes into their circle, they're going to trust. They're not going to wait for people to prove themselves, they are going to really open up and be generous." In reflecting on Headlong's contribution to his life, Albert emphasized that the Headlong values that resonated with him initially have continued to guide his own work as an artist, researcher, and teacher.

The same effect took hold for Suzanna, one of Headlong's later managing directors. She explained that she started to practice using their language and speaking like them. She started to see herself in new ways in the other roles in her life, in family and social circles. She started to ask questions she had not thought to ask before, about the neighborhood she lived in and the community she cultivated:

> I think some friends found me settling into myself, like a truer self, feeling more confident about points of view, and being happy to see that version of me. I think other friends were a little bit more put off by me feeling a little bit more assertive about points of view and

> sounding a bit more like I'm an instigator in certain easy, regular conversations. I think in terms of being around my family and extended family, I felt I had more of a place and a voice at the table, which felt great. Finally, I think they felt like I got serious about the world in a way.

Suzanna's experience was not unique. Other participants told me about ways they found themselves and their voices in the environment Headlong helped to create. These young artists found themselves challenged to a higher level of personal responsibility for questioning the world and for proposing solutions.

Headlong's work itself asked serious (and sometimes silly) questions about how society should function, questioning consumerism and its connection to nature, or the nature of community. Many of these works questioned how people in a city could connect in meaningful ways. This theme was especially present in *Cell,* a dance for one audience member at a time, which I discussed in chapter 3. After maneuvering through the streets of Philadelphia, being prompted by a stranger via cell phone, the audience member enters a private space where they cocreate a spontaneous, private performance within a hive of Headlong dancers. This piece, rather than endorsing a vision of atomistic individualism, fully embraces the social nature of creativity and challenges narratives of the anonymity and danger of the city. In individualism's place, *Cell* proposes a vision of democratic engagement, suffused with poetry and caring, embodied connection.

One of Headlong's last pieces with the founding codirectors, *This Town Is a Mystery,* took place in fall 2012 as part of the annual Fringe Festival. But the work began months before, when Headlong advertised around Philadelphia looking for homes filled by people interested in collaborating on the making of a dance. They ended up identifying four very different households, from an Iranian immigrant family in South Philadelphia, to a Black family poised to move to Florida just after the performance run, to a solo performer in West Mount Airy—the only one to have previously heard of Headlong.[26] These households worked alongside Headlong's choreographers for months in order to put together a show that told a meaningful story about their lives. After showing each piece to a limited public audience, the attendees and the performers ate a communal, potluck meal. They got a chance to debrief the performance or talk about whatever was on their minds. *This Town Is a*

FIGURE 16. Father and daughter dance as part of Headlong's *This Town Is a Mystery.* Photograph copyright Jacques-Jean Tiziou / www.jjtiziou.net.

Mystery pulled back the curtain on life in Philadelphia in all its diversity, offering a tantalizing glimpse of what lies beyond the facades of the countless rowhouses that dot the cityscape. In its attempt to get strangers to break bread together, the show prefigures On the Table Philly, a contemporary project supported by local Philadelphia philanthropies to build community and civility around tables throughout the city, over a meal. But unlike *This Town Is a Mystery,* participants in On the Table do not get the benefit of seeing an intimate, customized performance before breaking bread. *This Town Is a Mystery,* both in its official performance phase and in the informal performance of a communal meal, represents an ideal of cultivating democracy across geographic and demographic distance.

Longtime Headlong collaborator Christopher pointed out that Headlong, in its early days, created work that was "(a) really funny and (b) really open. It was dance that was really open to a nondance crowd. It's like you could appreciate what they were doing as theater or even as standup comedy at that point. But it was also approachable in my opinion like as a—as a critique of dance from inside dance and that there was a way to look at it as dance also." Since its inception, Headlong played with the boundaries of discourse, genre, and performance—all for the sake of asking pressing cultural questions. Dancing with Headlong after a

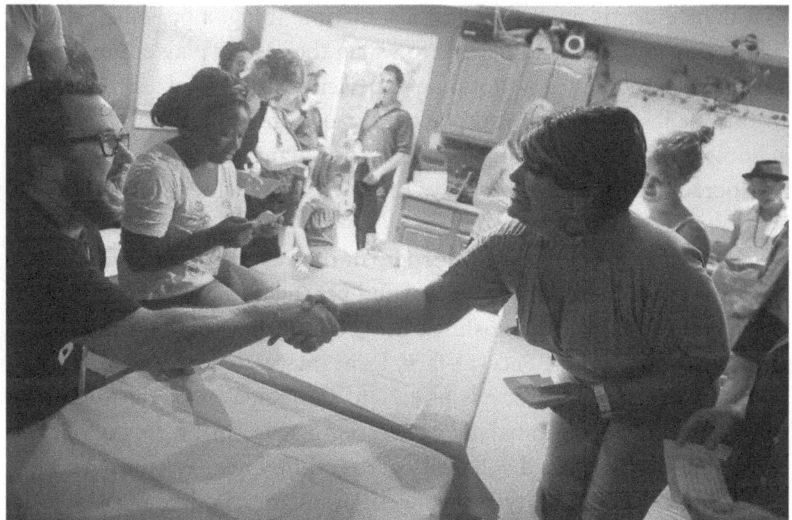

FIGURE 17. Dancer and audience member shake hands after a performance of Headlong's *This Town Is a Mystery.* Photograph copyright Jacques-Jean Tiziou / www.jjtiziou.net.

long hiatus, Jasmine reminisced to me in 2014 that Headlong retained a spirit that was bigger than individual personalities: "It's fun, and challenging, and full of opportunities to rely on instincts and push beyond assumptions and all of this feels like Headlong: The bigger Headlong that is no one person."

Headlong's work, more clearly than the other cases in this book perhaps, speaks to what Lake calls "the urban possibility of creative democracy," in that the work embodies the urban conditions of multiplicity, simultaneity, performativity, and juxtaposition.[27] Headlong, and the best of experimental art in general, opens us to the other in radically generative ways. Using the city as a site of exploration and dramatic potential, Headlong was able to blur the lines between art and life, between audience and performer, between stranger and friend.

CONCLUSION

In this chapter, I sketched out how democracy might be thought of as a practice of cooperation. In undertaking this ambitious effort, I realize that democracy is a world in itself, and no catalog of the efforts of cooperators in and beyond Philadelphia will be able to do justice to the range and variety of possible ways of doing democracy. Still, I maintain that democracy is more than just a sometime thing, a periodic behavior like voting and then sitting back to watch the results play out over time. Instead, democracy is a quotidian experience. It takes place (or it ought to) in our families, our workplaces, our organizations, our streets and schools. Any effort at establishing a thoroughgoing understanding of democracy must catalog the ways in which those who are committed to it put it into practice every day.

Putting democracy into deeper, more sustained practice means avoiding any number of conceptual and practical traps. Principal among these is the embrace of a nostalgic or romantic view of the communities that enact democracy. Face-to-face, local interactions are an important basis on which democracy is built. But these spaces ought to be sites of negotiating power imbalance, overcoming systemic forms of oppression, and forging shared solidarity across difference. We must be careful of reifying community as a concept or an amoeba-like mass of facile agreements. There should be no return to a reflexive understanding of communities as conflict-free zones of agreement. Even within the most seemingly homogeneous collection of individuals, there are differences to be negotiated, as with my example of urban communities that have the right to make demands of the powerful institutions that affect their fates.

At the same time as we understand community in more active and generative ways, we need to recall the shortcomings of both liberalism and communitarianism in framing our understanding of democratic practice. Often these understandings of social and political life have been framed by white men with limited experience of the forms of oppression that have been foisted upon people in other identity groups. Communal institutions like the church, the neighborhood, and the family ought to be valued for the support they can provide to democratic struggles, not for the historic roles they have played, as those roles have had disastrous consequences for some. And we must avoid a temptation to posit an individualist, atomistic self, especially in times of great social, political, and cultural challenges; democracy as a cooperative practice can only function if we understand ourselves as vulnerable and interdependent.

In the cases profiled in this book, small-"d" democracy inheres in the activities they pursue in the work they accomplish in the world. POCA understands care as a collective and communal experience. It seeks to renegotiate complementary and alternative health into a new set of agreements where clinics, providers, and patients all work together to sustain community enterprises of self-help and mutual aid. Its trauma-informed perspective meets patients where they are in life, valuing them as creatures with both needs and challenges, as well as sources of strength and solidarity for the cooperative enterprise. Regard for patients in the fullness of their experience undergirds POCA's philosophy of liberation acupuncture. The challenge of sustaining both the cooperative of clinics as well as POCA Tech will be a continuing source of labor and demands flexibility, ingenuity, and an ongoing pool of dedicated volunteers and staff.

Mariposa and Weavers Way have overcome significant organizational hurdles over the course of the past forty-plus years as they pursue a strategy of collective consumer ownership. While these hurdles may seem operational, they were simultaneously questions of policy and governance along the way to making these co-ops survive as both enterprises and associations. In some ways, they had to get out of their own way and abandon an orientation to professionalization that was overtly antagonistic. In Mariposa's case, the expansion to a bigger store necessitated a reinvention of the shopping and workflow procedures to move away from the honor system to a more conventional operational standard. At Weavers Way, lax oversight of finances resulted in a debilitating shortfall that could have forced the co-op to close. But transparency with its membership and openly asking for help from its stakeholders helped rescue Weavers Way before permanent damage was done. And the resulting tightening of organizational controls led the co-op toward a period of health and sustainable expansion that continues to this day. Collective democratic ownership and stewardship of these cooperatives has resulted in decades of healthy food, good jobs, and profits being recirculated throughout their respective community economies.

Finally, Headlong has plied its unique brand of utopian artistic experimentation for over twenty-five years in an economic environment that is hardly hospitable to such endeavors. Headlong forged a democratic space for artmaking through collectivity by fostering a generation of dancers that shared in the bounty of the structures it built. It has remained a favorite of artists, audiences, and funders because of its stubborn insistence on an expansive ethic of care. Care is evident in the artistic work it has produced, in the talent it has fostered, and the connections it has forged. Even dancers who were unsure at one time where they stood relative to the three founding codirectors (as I discussed in chapter 4) continue to express solidarity and fondness for Headlong's unique role in the Philadelphia dance community. They reflect with deep satisfaction on the fruits of their time in Headlong.

All of these cases reflect the best of what is possible under conditions of creative democracy. They represent a democratic impulse that is collective, relational, and constitutive. None of them fall into the trap of individualism, with the competitive and destructive impulses that can entail. They each feature a relational ethic, with progress being understood as social and collective, hard-fought through sustained engagement with questions of remaking work and the economy as spaces of democracy, spaces of hope. And it is constitutive in its work of building new structures on which to improvise and perfect new structures of democratic engagement.

As in the other chapters, I offer here a few takeaways that seeing democracy as a cooperative practice allows us to envision.

Democracy Is a Communal Experience

Even in times of duress, we have only each other to rely on to solve the pressing issues of the day. An awareness of the social selves we are helps us to move closer to the communities of practice that will enrich and sustain us, not oppress or marginalize us. Even in a divided and polarized political environment, it is necessary to form bonds of solidarity to make possible the kinds of political, economic, social, and cultural transformations we seek.

Democracy Is Built on Trust over Time

The act of showing up for one another, like the people in these organizations continue to do, undergirds the ongoing imperfect practice of democracy. By building trust over time, they forge durable relationships that can withstand stress and discomfort. These relationships prove resilient and can accommodate the inevitable changes that result from long term efforts at cooperation.

Democracy Is Built on Care for Bodies, Hearts, and Minds

The scaled framework of this book began with the body, and it is to the body I want to return. Democracy as cooperative practice should not be about lines on a graph of a public opinion poll or voter survey. It is about the struggles and victories of ordinary bodies striving for health, for nourishment, for collective liberation. When bodies are understood as being put on the line in service of these vital goals, democracy can be realized in its power and its urgency. This is cooperative practice at its most integral and connected: from bodies to society through economy and back again. None of these scales ever operate out of regard or out of connection to one another. This is the challenge and the promise of cooperation as a practice.

CONCLUSION

At the time of this writing, the world is being buffeted by an unprecedented pandemic, COVID-19. It is currently in force throughout the United States, with nearly six hundred thousand casualties as of early May 2021. In some respects, this seems like a strange time to be writing at all, much less writing about the practice of cooperation. And yet, cooperation is emergent around the globe as people seek strategies to combat the effects of this virus. These emergent manifestations of cooperation are very much a bottom-up phenomenon, taking place regardless of the shortcomings and failures of some governments to provide for the welfare of their citizens.

In the early part of the pandemic, diverse economies researchers set out to catalog meaningful examples of cooperation in the face of the pandemic. Dozens of examples surfaced, across many different geographies. These examples are animated by a spirit of social solidarity, in contrast to the advice given by public health officials to practice social distancing to avoid virus transmission. Instead, these groups promote physical distance but social interdependence. Food giveaways have expanded. There have been calls for emergency bail funds to keep people from entering jail in the United States while they await trial, as jails are expected to have higher virus transmission rates. Along these lines, there have been calls to decarcerate prisoners, especially elderly ones, and close immigrant detention centers.

In my own section of Philadelphia, groups formed seeking to establish contact with every single neighbor on each block, especially those who are not on the internet, in order to make sure that there is nobody left behind when providing for basic needs. A Pandemic Free School opened up, which provided three hours of online learning per day, with a rotating cast of parent volunteers serving as instructors of courses as diverse as constitutional rights and how to write a poem. A local bakery has been delivering croissants to frontline health-care workers in order not to idle its own staff.

The organizations and people profiled in this book have moved into coronavirus response mode, as well. Mariposa Food Co-op has become nimble and flexible in the crisis, altering its hours and its store layout to prioritize shopping by the elderly and immunocompromised. It has rapidly built and deployed an online ordering system for curbside food pickup in order to minimize the number of people shopping in the store and risking the health of both shoppers and employees. Former Headlong codirector Amy Smith has been providing virtual guidance to arts communities around the United States, preparing artists to weather the financial shocks of this public health event. She wrote on her Facebook feed:

> Just finished fourth of four webinars I led this week for artists to talk about dealing with the financial aspects of this crisis. Emotionally exhausted but also really grateful that I can be a trusted source and be of service right now in this way. Weirdly it feels like EVERYTHING I have done, working as an artist, running a nonprofit, being freelance, living on $15k per year, living on $60k per year, raising kids as an artist, asking for money, giving away money, doing tax prep for artists, anti-racism trainings, one on one sessions with such a variety of artists have ALL prepared me for this moment.[1]

Clearly, Amy's spirit of cooperation has not been dampened by the crisis, despite the severity of the moment.

Andrew Simonet, Amy's longtime collaborator in Headlong, wrote a blog post in which he calls on artists to see this crisis as an opportunity to make meaning and serve a larger creative purpose.

> I don't know what your art is. I don't know your connections to community. But wherever you are, I call on you to unleash your practice as an artist and maker and re-imaginer.
>
> In this crisis of meaning, you are first responders.
>
> You don't need to save the world. You need only carry your gifts and skills into this present challenge. A concert out your window. A public ritual you and your neighbors can do from your front steps. An expressive moment added to an online conversation. A project to mourn what is lost, a project to invite what is yet to come.
>
> Use your collaboration skills to organize your neighbors, or your D.I.Y. skills to build something from nothing. Or declare these weeks of separation an artist residency.
>
> Make the art this moment needs.
>
> May we be completely safe with our health and bold as all hell in our practice.
>
> This is what we train for.[2]

Andrew, in calling on artists to seize their training and be "bold as all hell" in their practice, continues an unbroken line of loving provocation that he began decades before in the formation of Headlong. Their voices are so urgently needed in a time full of uncertainty and fear.

This book is built on three cardinal assertions. The first is that cooperation is a practice, a form of socially derived, process-based set of actions executed over time. As a practice, cooperation ought to be concerned with internal over external goods, seeking the goals of a just world and a virtuous life for their own sake, not for some form of reward that prioritizes wealth, fame, or anything else. The second assertion of the book is that cooperation is a practice built at multiple scales. In order to completely remake social and economic practice, it is necessary to build cooperation into every aspect of social action. It begins (and ends) with the body; it influences the structure of work and organizations; it catalyzes community economy in a more-than-capitalist framework; it undergirds the work of building a robust and thoroughgoing democracy. Finally, the book's third assertion is that cooperation must address the paradox of exclusivity. Like all participatory projects, cooperatives include some and exclude others. This has a healthy dimension, in that some form of in-group feeling is necessary to sustain interest and dedication to the cooperative project at hand. Absent this feeling, participants might fall away and seek out a less intensive affiliation or no affiliation at all. But if exclusivity is drawn along lines of race, class, ability, gender, sexual orientation, and the like, participants are excluded because of who they are rather than what they prefer to do. I argue throughout the book that this happens more than cooperatives realize and that it is often done inadvertently, as with the story about youth shoppers at Weavers Way that opens the book. Cooperative projects must carefully think through questions of inclusivity and exclusivity as they seek to define their ambit and purview.

Over the course of the book, I have concluded that the two approaches that best explain the goals at hand are those of practice theorists and diverse economy theorists. I believe cooperation in the current U.S. political economy needs to be a form of "diverse practices" that follows from a diverse, noncapitalocentric worldview.[3] This focus on everyday practices allows us to build workplaces, institutions, and economies in new, more generative ways. By incorporating a diverse economies understanding, it is possible to attend to ethics and power dynamics that inhere in the everyday. Together, a diverse practices approach allows for the prefiguration of a more equitable, more just future, infused by cooperation.

Such diverse practices will be undertaken by a group of cooperative subjects. These subjects are attracted to the pragmatism of actually existing cooperation while being simultaneously moved by its emancipatory potential. Cooperative subjects realize that cooperation is appealing to people from different ideological backgrounds and is not beholden to a totalizing economic philosophy, like communism, capitalism, or socialism. The diversity of cooperation is apparent from the variety of projects I showcased in chapter 2. Cooperation, as a form of mutual aid, is flexible and adaptable to different circumstances, hence its presence virtually everywhere on the planet in different forms. Cooperative subjects will advance cooperation through the pursuit of economic democracy and interdependence.

In this book, I have offered a number of takeaways for practice. Here I will revisit and collate them, offering them as a set of guidelines for how to think about advancing cooperation. They speak to the various scales this book has analyzed, but together they form a useful collection.

Demand respect for bodies, building spaces of care: As I have stated throughout this book, the body is a foundational element of cooperation. Bodies are always on the line when it comes to building organizations, movements, and struggles for a more just world. They may seem like containers for our individuality, but bodies are always in relation to one another through biological and social processes that render them mutually interdependent. Cooperation that takes seriously the needs and wants of embodied cooperators will meet them more fully on the journey.

All bodies are welcome: Cooperators must make a thoroughgoing commitment to accepting and celebrating all types of bodies. The white, able, cisgender, straight body is only one among infinite variations and ought not to be made into the normative standard against which all other bodies are judged. This practice needs the active participation of fat bodies, disabled bodies, queer bodies, racially diverse bodies, and many others. All these bodies are welcome in cooperation because a cooperative, creative democracy depends on the participation of all, not a select few.

Nurture the body, do no harm: As we saw in chapter 3, bodies are vulnerable and frequently put in positions of disadvantage. Cooperative projects sometimes demand too much, pushing bodies too far for comfort or safety. In this time of global pandemic, the urgency of keeping every *body* safe feels more pressing than ever. In our rush to keep ourselves safe and whole, we must remember to also prioritize the health of people who need other forms of care. Dependence on other bodies is a condition we all face at some time in life, and we must take responsibility for care as a given, knowing that we have needed care at one time and will need it again. When our bodies are nourished, protected, and cared for, we will be able to do the work of pursuing a more just world.

Resist alienation through cooperation: The world of modernity, particularly the world of work, holds the potential to be deeply alienating. When livelihood and work are unsatisfactory, it is difficult to achieve a sense of self that is congruent with our vision for what life can be. Thinking now of the gig economy workers who keep the gears of contemporary society from locking up, it is clear how urgently they need our support. By organizing themselves and gathering support from people who realize their worth, they can win conditions for their work that overcome some of the alienation they face. And even better: where possible, consumers and workers can seek out cooperative alternatives to capitalist firms to better invest their time, money, and skills.

Balance internal and external goods: MacIntyre's ethical framework for practices seeks the prioritization of internal over external goods. Internal goods are those that advance practices for their own sake, like the chess player who plays to get better rather than to achieve external goods of wealth or fame. In the pursuit of cooperation, it is easy to become distracted by external goods like conventional business success or sales per square foot. These external goods are necessary, and cooperative practices have to succeed as enterprises if they are to stick around at all. But they cannot be the motive force for the practice, which also has to maintain an associational character. The projects profiled in this book maintain a careful balance where internal goods outweigh consideration of external goods, though the balance is tricky and must be calibrated carefully.

Avoid burnout through leadership cultivation and shared responsibility: One of the most important considerations for cooperative enterprises, like any mission-driven project, is concern about burnout. In all of the projects I have profiled, people work extremely hard for relatively modest pay. They often do the equivalent of more than one job. Sometimes there is a lack of security about where the next pool of funding will come from (especially in Headlong's case, where there is not a steady stream of earned revenue from grocery sales or acupuncture treatments). In these organizations, two things are important for reducing burnout: replenishing the supply of labor and creating a livable work/life balance. When it comes to the former, these organizations must engage in constant, deliberate cultivation of new leaders. This can come in the form of board members, staff, volunteers, and even donors. Even when this work seems like one more thing to add to an already overflowing pile of responsibilities, it is one of the best investments of time for a cooperative project. Recently, Mariposa has struggled to seat a large board, probably because the store is operating so effectively and professionally that member owners do not see the need for oversight. In cases like these, the goal is quality over quantity. It is better to have a five-person effective board with fresh energy than a legacy board that is burnt out and tired.

When it comes to work/life balance, the goal is to not penalize and instead to encourage flexible work schedules, comp time, tending to care responsibilities, and the like. Work in many of these organizations can be scheduled around the needs of the workers. For POCA clinics, the hours can be set based on a combination of community needs and practitioner ability. In fact, because the shifts are so tiring for acupunks, POCA clinics tend to schedule practitioners for far less than forty hours per week. This means less income, but provides enough time to bounce back from the challenging work of high-volume group acupuncture provision. Commitments to employee quality of work life need to be written into personnel manuals and enforced by the administrative and governance bodies.

Cultivate a social surplus: In the discussion on ethical coordinates in chapter 5, I discussed the idea of a social surplus. Based on the labor theory of value, surplus is created after labor recoups the cost of paying for itself. In a purely capitalist system, surplus is created for the benefit of the capitalist owner. In cooperative projects, and most projects in the community economy, surplus can be applied socially via a process of collective deliberation. In the case of consumer food co-ops, surplus earnings are often handed out in the form of dividend payments to each member owner. The amount of the payout is based on how much each member owner patronized the co-op, ensuring that owners with the most shopping patronage reap the largest share of the dividend, not the wealthiest or most powerful of the owners. In addition, surplus can be reinvested in the co-op to improve the physical store, to give the workers a raise, or to invest (as Mariposa and other co-ops have done) in a fund to subsidize ownership stakes for low-income members. Weavers Way and Mariposa both use funds to support the existence of the Philadelphia Area Cooperative Alliance.

Surplus works differently in different contexts. In Headlong, the goal was to spend every dollar that came in on creative work or administrative costs; in the nonprofit arts in the United States, there is no surplus as such. Still, Headlong found funds to offer each codirector discretionary artistic funds in order to support their creative vision so that they could incubate new work that was not otherwise budgeted in the organization's multiyear planning. However surplus is conceived, the point of a social approach to surplus is to have an active collective deliberation about how to invest surplus revenues and to strive to affect change in the areas to which the cooperative project is most committed.

Create opportunities for ethical consumption: Ethical consumption was at the heart of the projects of John Ruskin and other moral economists of the nineteenth and early twentieth centuries. This philosophy of ethical consumption is easiest to imagine in the exchange of goods that takes place from consumer or worker cooperatives. The goods ought to be produced with care for the earth, respect for the producers, packagers, and transporters, and adequate compensation for the workers at the point of sale. The food co-ops in this book pay a lot of attention to sourcing ethical, sustainable, often organic products for their member owners and other shoppers. At the same time, co-ops like these need to balance the cost of such items to the consumer so as not to avoid falling into a pattern of exclusivity. Not everything in shoppers' budgets or in their food cultures is manufactured according to the highest standards of production, and it is counterproductive to hold any one fixed notion about what constitutes the best products to sell. The point is to deliberate at a customer, staff, and board levels about what ought to be on the shelves. In the case of the POCA clinics, ethical consumption means paying as much as one can afford on the clinic's sliding scale, volunteering at the clinics when possible to help out the acupunks and owners, and helping out with the broader POCA co-op. Ethical consumption looks different in different cases but can always be a cardinal consideration in market exchange. As co-op pioneer George Jacob Holyoake wrote in the 1890s: "If there are to be moral sellers, there must be moral buyers."[4]

Operate on multiple scales whenever possible: This takeaway comes from my chapter on community economy. While each of the projects I have profiled in this book is intensely grounded in its local community, it has a presence at scales beyond that as well. POCA was birthed out of the needs of locals in Portland, Oregon, and the Working Class Acupuncture clinics there are still very invested in the ongoing urban transformation of that city and their clinic's role in it. Weavers Way is still invested at the corner of Greene and Carpenter, even as its footprint has grown to multiple stores in the region. And Weavers Way continues to be active in food policy conversations in the Delaware Valley region because of its respected position and longevity in the food retail sector of Philadelphia. Even Headlong, an arts group that performs mostly in Philadelphia, is part of a legacy and international conversation about experimental dance. Its company and Headlong Performance Institute alumni are now dancing (and doing a variety of other creative non-dance activities) all over the country and the world. Their sense of a link back to Headlong and its Philadelphia-focused performance practice remains strong even after more than two decades.

Democracy is a communal experience: Democracy is not just about one person, one vote, at least not in the most important ways. It is an ongoing relational process that needs to occur in our everyday interactions and in all cooperative projects. It is a process of continual refinement, as we strive to be more careful and inclusive in our interactions with one another. As we do so, we reform our families, our schools, our institutions, and our workplaces. Especially in the time of duress in which I currently write, the importance of social solidarity and collective decision making becomes even more apparent. When this disaster passes, we must continue to hold the structures of power accountable to be more responsive and responsible when it comes to communal care and democratic governance as an ongoing cooperative practice.

Democracy is built on trust over time: The communal process of democracy is not an instantaneous creation. It needs to be cultivated over time and through relationships. Community organizer adrienne maree brown, in her provocative book *Emergent Strategy,* advises us to "move at the speed of trust."[5] This motto can be contrasted with the malignancy and mistrust of our national political process. Perhaps that process is too flawed to fix (although there are some important reforms, like publicly funded elections, that have been suggested), but at the local level, trust and showing up over time are crucial ingredients in building what Dewey calls a competent democratic public. In the cases in this book, democracy looks like showing up for people over time and remaining consistently accessible and transparent. When these qualities broke down—during Headlong's process for the show *More* or during Weavers Way's financial crisis in the early 2000s—the lack of accessibility and transparency led to existential threats to the integrity of the organizations.

Democracy is built on care for bodies, hearts, and minds: Threats to cooperative projects can be overcome through a careful calibration of multiple factors. But chief among them must be care for the bodies, hearts, and minds of all cooperators. This reflects back to my earliest takeaways in this conclusion about the importance of bodies to cooperative practice. In this moment, I want to link the notions of care for bodies and their people to the notion of democracy. Again, in this recent but devastating pandemic, it is an ethic of care and consideration for physical and emotional health that will not only make people feel more comfortable amid conditions of isolation but also save lives. The terms under which we emerge from this virus will form the template for how humanity thrives under conditions of climate change. In a sense, this tragedy, while shaking us to the core, forces a mass recognition of new priorities, from respect for health-care workers and teachers to acknowledgment of the importance of service workers, concern about the fates of cultural workers suddenly stranded without forms of income, and more. How we care for all of these people over the next months and years will foreshadow the rest of the century and our efforts to manage a series of even more threatening and dire climate-related changes. It is only through prioritizing care that our democracies will continue to thrive.

Looking ahead from today's vantage point, it is hard to predict the future of what might occur regarding the cases that form the substance of this book. For the sake of consistency with what has come before, I will imagine that they will all weather the pandemic and continue on the trajectory they were on before, though it is too soon to tell if that is plausible. However, each of these organizations has proven to meet a need of a community and will hopefully be in a condition to continue to do so over the ensuing months and years.

When it comes to POCA, the clinics have to contend with the widespread occurrence of private acupuncture clinics that also use some form of sliding scale (often in certain locations or on certain days only) and may even call themselves community acupuncture clinics. These clinics are not part of the POCA cooperative and do not contribute directly to the strengthening of the movement POCA spearheads. While it is a healthy development that other acupuncturists see the importance of having more accessible pricing through group treatment, it is possible that these clinics will take business away from nearby POCA clinics. In addition, the POCA cooperative and POCA Tech will have to recruit and retain more talented volunteers and cooperators to continue to move forward with POCA's ambitious agenda to produce the calmest revolution ever staged, as they sometimes call it. The way forward includes more active recruitment of volunteers from the patient population and more clarity that POCA is in fact a volunteer-led cooperative that needs ongoing support. To date, it is not exactly clear when getting a treatment at a POCA clinic that patients can not only join the cooperative but help to run it and determine its future. More urgency and clarity about the importance of the practice of cooperation to keep POCA alive will result in the development of a greater number of willing participants.

For Weavers Way and Mariposa, it seems they are well positioned to ride out the current pandemic, as they are some of the only businesses that are allowed to function amid conditions of self-isolation and stay at home orders from the Commonwealth of Pennsylvania and the City of Philadelphia. Staying open may still result in changes and different sales patterns over the course of the pandemic, forcing the co-ops to revisit staffing levels. That being said, I believe both co-ops will make it through intact and will then have to focus on what serving their member-owners and the general public looks like in the changed landscape that comes after. Under conditions of normalcy, both Mariposa and Weavers Way have to manage the paradox of exclusivity, where the increasing gentrification of Philadelphia may push low-income shoppers and people of color farther away from the neighborhoods served by these stores. In addition, higher-income shoppers who are moving into these neighborhoods may start to demand more expensive, artisanal products that further alienate some shoppers. Finally, the expansion of corporate healthy grocers like Whole Foods (now owned by Amazon) and Trader Joe's (including grocery home delivery from these kinds of stores) will place additional pressure on the co-ops. For both co-ops, it will be important to continue to communicate to their shoppers that they are community-controlled, democratically run stores that pay workers a fair wage and retain profits in the local neighborhood. There is no excuse for these co-ops not to boldly advertise the international cooperative principles in their stores or to openly promote member ownership in the co-op at the checkout counter. At the same time, the stores should consider outreach or partnerships with co-op efforts in low-income areas, making sure that the cooperative model does not become merely an option for the well-to-do.

In some ways, Headlong's future is less certain than the other cooperative projects in this story. Over the past few years, two of the three founding codirectors have left the organization to pursue other projects. There has been no effort to replace them with new codirectors. At this point, Headlong is the project of David Brick and a small staff. David's creativity is limitless, and there is still important work to be done creatively and in incubating artists and students through the Headlong organization. By not carrying the financial burden of a larger organization, it is possible that Headlong will be able to remain nimble and continue to transform itself to meet the needs of the moment. Whatever happens over the next year or two, Headlong's legacy in the Philadelphia and experimental dance universe is assured, and it is my hope that this book serves as partial chronicle of the important work the organization produced over such a long period.

The last question that remains is the future for me and for this research. It feels cliché to say this project is just begun, after all the years that I have devoted to capturing, theorizing, and synthesizing the practice of cooperation. This book represents the closing of a chapter of this inquiry. But as with many such projects, the impact and relevance only become apparent at the end of the process. I look forward to sharing this work with the world and to the conversations that will ensue. And it is clear to me how much learning I still have to do about cooperation, about ethical practice, and about the future we will envision and build together.

NOTES

INTRODUCTION

1. All personal interviews with Weavers Way, Mariposa, and other food co-ops' board, staff, and members were conducted by the author between March 2010 and December 2011 in Philadelphia, Pennsylvania.

2. Joyce Rothschild-Whitt, "The Collectivist Organization: An Alternative to Rational-Bureaucratic Models," *American Sociological Review* 44, no. 4 (1979): 509–27.

3. Jon Elster, "From Here to There; or, If Cooperative Ownership Is So Desirable, Why Are There So Few Cooperatives?," *Social Philosophy and Policy* 6, no. 2 (1989): 93–111, https://doi.org/10.1017/S0265052500000650.

4. bell hooks, "Marginality as Site of Resistance," in *Out There: Marginalization and Contemporary Cultures,* ed. Russell Ferguson et al., Documentary Sources in Contemporary Art (New York, N.Y.: New Museum of Contemporary Art, 1990), 343.

5. There is a vast theoretical literature in the field of geography on scale, with multiple currents of discussion. It is not my intention to wade into it here. But for those who want to learn more about this discussion, I recommend starting with Sallie A. Marston, "The Social Construction of Scale," *Progress in Human Geography* 24, no. 2 (2000): 219–42; A Sayer, "Behind the Locality Debate: Deconstructing Geography's Dualisms," *Environment and Planning A: Economy and Space* 23, no. 2 (February 1991): 283–308, https://doi.org/10.1068/a230283; and Jamie Peck, "Political Economies of Scale: Fast Policy, Interscalar Relations, and Neoliberal Workfare," *Economic Geography* 78, no. 3 (2002): 331–60.

6. Craig Borowiak et al., "Navigating the Fault Lines: Race and Class in Philadelphia's Solidarity Economy," *Antipode* 50, no. 3 (2018): 577–603, https://doi.org/10.1111/anti.12368.

7. Jake Blumgart, "How Redlining Segregated Philadelphia," *Next City* (blog), December 8, 2017, https://nextcity.org/features/view/redlining-race-philadelphia-segregation.

8. John Curl, *For All the People: Uncovering the Hidden History of Cooperation, Cooperative Movements, and Communalism in America* (Oakland, Calif.: PM Press, 2009).

9. Weavers Way Co-op, "Weavers Way Co-op—Employment," accessed January 5, 2013, http://www.weaversway.coop/index.php?page=employment.

10. Nicole Contosta, "Merriment at Mariposa's Groundbreaking Ceremony," *University City Review,* June 29, 2011, http://ucreview.com/merriment-at-mariposas-groundbreaking-ceremony-p2815-1.htm.

11. University City District, *The State of University City 2012/13* (Philadelphia, Penn.: University City District, 2012).

12. Diana Lind, "The Bright Side of Blight," *New York Times,* January 25, 2011;

Caitlin Drummond, "Penntrification," *Philadelphia Weekly*, July 27, 2009, http://www.philadelphiaweekly.com/news-and-opinion/Penntrification-51796462.html.

13. Rothschild-Whitt, "Collectivist Organization"; Joyce Rothschild and J. A. Whitt, *The Cooperative Workplace: Potentials and Dilemmas of Organisational Democracy and Participation* (Cambridge: Cambridge University Press, 1986).

14. Carolyn Dimitri and Catherine Greene, *Recent Growth Patterns in the U.S. Organic Foods Market*, Agriculture Information Bulletin (Washington, D.C.: United States Department of Agriculture Economic Research Service, September 2002), http://www.ers.usda.gov/publications/aib-agricultural-information-bulletin/aib777.aspx; David Browne, *Natural and Organic Food and Beverage: The Market—US—October 2011* (New York: Mintel Group, Ltd., October 2011).

15. Stacey B. Randall, *Millennial Generation Today: Impact of the Economic Environment on Recruitment, Retention, and Engagement* (SBR Consulting, LLC, May 16, 2011).

16. Stuart Reid, "The New Co-op Kids on the Block," *Cooperative Grocer*, June 2011, http://www.cooperativegrocer.coop/articles/2011-04-25/new-co-op-kids-block.

17. Maria T. Chao, Kimberly M. Tippens, and Erin Connelly, "Utilization of Group-Based, Community Acupuncture Clinics: A Comparative Study with a Nationally Representative Sample of Acupuncture Users," *Journal of Alternative and Complementary Medicine* 18, no. 6 (May 2, 2012): 561–66, https://doi.org/10.1089/acm.2011.0128.

18. Chao, Tippens, and Connelly, "Utilization of Group-Based, Community Acupuncture Clinics."

19. Lisa Rohleder, *Fractal: About Community Acupuncture* (People's Organization of Community Acupuncture, 2013).

20. Rohleder, *Fractal*, 32.

21. "Our History," People's Organization of Community Acupuncture, accessed February 10, 2016, https://www.pocacoop.com/our-history.

22. All POCA interviews were conducted by the author between September 2013 and March 2014 in Philadelphia, Pennsylvania, Providence, Rhode Island, and Portland, Oregon.

23. Rohleder, *Fractal*, 68.

24. Charlotte Hess and Elinor Ostrom, eds., *Understanding Knowledge As a Commons: From Theory to Practice* (Cambridge, Mass.: MIT Press, 2005).

25. John Buck and Sharon Villines, *We the People: Consenting to a Deeper Democracy*, 1st ed. (Washington, D.C.: Sociocracy.info Press, 2007).

26. Headlong Dance Theater, "About," LinkedIn, accessed April 19, 2021, https://www.linkedin.com/in/headlong-dance-theater-06a37763/.

1. THE SOCIAL IMPERATIVE OF COOPERATION

1. Niam Yaraghi and Shamika Ravi, "The Current and Future State of the Sharing Economy," *Brookings* (blog), December 29, 2016, https://www.brookings.edu/research/the-current-and-future-state-of-the-sharing-economy/.

2. Rachel Botsman, "Defining the Sharing Economy: What Is Collaborative

Consumption—And What Isn't?," *Fast Company,* May 27, 2015, https://www.fastcompany.com/3046119/defining-the-sharing-economy-what-is-collaborative-consumption-and-what-isnt.

3. Arun Sundararajan, *The Sharing Economy: The End of Employment and the Rise of Crowd-Based Capitalism* (Cambridge, Mass.: MIT Press, 2016).

4. Juliet B. Schor et al., "Paradoxes of Openness and Distinction in the Sharing Economy," *Poetics* 54 (February 1, 2016): 66–81, https://doi.org/10.1016/j.poetic.2015.11.001.

5. Nathan Heller, "Is the Gig Economy Working?," *New Yorker,* May 8, 2017, https://www.newyorker.com/magazine/2017/05/15/is-the-gig-economy-working.

6. Michel Foucault, *The Birth of Biopolitics: Lectures at the Collège de France, 1978–1979* (New York: Palgrave Macmillan, 2011), 230.

7. George Ciccariello-Maher, "My Best Friend Lost His Life to the Gig Economy," *Nation,* July 10, 2018, https://www.thenation.com/article/best-friend-lost-life-gig-economy/.

8. Ciccariello-Maher, "My Best Friend."

9. See Kimberly A. Zeuli and Robert Cropp, "Cooperatives: Principles and Practices in the 21st Century" (Madison: University of Wisconsin Extension, 2004); Stefano Zamagni and Vera Zamagni, *Cooperative Enterprise: Facing the Challenge of Globalization* (Cheltenham, U.K.: Edward Elgar, 2010).

10. International Cooperative Alliance, "Co-operative Facts & Figures," 2012 International Year of Cooperatives, October 27, 2011, http://2012.coop/en/ica/co-operative-facts-figures.

11. Zeuli and Cropp, "Cooperatives," 1.

12. International Co-operative Alliance and International Labour Organization, "The Global Cooperative Campaign Against Poverty," November 2006, www.ica.coop/outofpoverty/documents/summarycampaign.pdf.

13. "Facts and Figures," International Co-operative Alliance, accessed August 8, 2018, https://www.ica.coop/en/facts-and-figures.

14. Dave Grace and Associates, *Measuring the Size and Scope of the Cooperative Economy: Results of the 2014 Global Census on Co-Operatives* (Madison, Wisc.: April 2014), http://www.un.org/esa/socdev/documents/2014/coopsegm/grace.pdf.

15. S. Deller et al., *Research on the Economic Impact of Cooperatives* (Madison: University of Wisconsin Center for Cooperatives, March 2009).

16. Andrew Zitcer and Richardson Dilworth, "Grocery Cooperatives as Governing Institutions in Neighborhood Commercial Corridors," *Urban Affairs Review* (May 18, 2017): https://doi.org/10.1177/1078087417709999.

17. For an alternative categorization of co-op types, see Joyce Rothschild, "Situating the Contemporary Grassroots Cooperatives: Intellectual and Political Origins," in *Community and the World: Participating in Social Change,* ed. Torry D. Dickinson (Hauppauge, N.Y.: Nova Publishers, 2003), 225–26.

18. J. K. Gibson-Graham, *A Postcapitalist Politics* (Minneapolis: University of Minnesota Press, 2006), xxxii.

19. S. Deller et al., *Research on the Economic Impact of Cooperatives* (Madison: University of Wisconsin Center for Cooperatives, March 2009), 2.

20. James DeFilippis, *Unmaking Goliath: Community Control in the Face of Global Capital* (New York: Routledge, 2004).

21. Jon Elster, "From Here to There; or, If Cooperative Ownership Is So Desirable, Why Are There So Few Cooperatives?," *Social Philosophy and Policy* 6, no. 2 (April 1989): 100, https://doi.org/10.1017/S0265052500000650.

22. Catherine Leviten-Reid and Brett Fairbairn, "Multi-stakeholder Governance in Cooperative Organizations: Toward a New Framework for Research?," *Canadian Journal of Nonprofit and Social Economy Research* 2, no. 2 (Fall 2011): 25–36.

23. Marcelo Vieta, "The New Cooperativism," *Affinities: A Journal of Radical Theory, Culture, and Action* (August 25, 2010): https://ojs.library.queensu.ca/index.php/affinities/article/view/6145.

24. Jessica Gordon Nembhard, *Collective Courage: A History of African American Cooperative Economic Thought and Practice* (University Park: Pennsylvania State University Press, 2014).

25. Morris Altman, "Is There a Co-operative Advantage? Experimental Evidence on the Economic and Non-economic Determinants of Demand," *Journal of Co-operative Organization and Management* 4, no. 2 (December 1, 2016): 66–75, https://doi.org/10.1016/j.jcom.2016.08.003.

26. Karl Marx, "The International Workingmen's Association, Instructions for the Delegates of the Provisional General Council," Marxists Internet Archive, 1866, https://www.marxists.org/archive/marx/works/1866/08/instructions.htm.

27. The Webbs' disdain did not extend to consumer-owned cooperatives, which they advocated. Sidney Webb and Beatrice Potter Webb, *The Consumers' Cooperative Movement* (London: Longmans, Green, 1921).

28. David F. Ruccio, "Utopia and the Critique of Political Economy," *Journal of Australian Political Economy* 79 (Winter 2017): 5–20.

29. Ruccio, "Utopia and the Critique of Political Economy," 12.

30. J. K. Gibson-Graham, "Enabling Ethical Economies: Cooperativism and Class," *Critical Sociology* 29, no. 2 (March 1, 2003): 126, https://doi.org/10.1163/156916303769155788.

31. David F. Ruccio, "Cooperatives, Surplus, and the Social," *Rethinking Marxism* 23, no. 3 (July 2011): 340, https://doi.org/10.1080/08935696.2011.583002.

32. Gibson-Graham, "Enabling Ethical Economies," 155.

33. See Johnston Birchall, *The International Co-operative Movement* (Manchester, U.K.: Manchester University Press, 1997); John Curl, *For All the People: Uncovering the Hidden History of Cooperation, Cooperative Movements, and Communalism in America* (Oakland, Calif.: PM Press, 2009); Ellen Furlough and Carl Strikwerda, *Consumers against Capitalism?: Consumer Cooperation in Europe, North America, and Japan, 1840–1990* (Lanham, Md.: Rowman & Littlefield, 1999); John Restakis, *Humanizing the Economy: Co-operatives in the Age of Capital* (Gabriola, B.C: New Society Publishers, 2010).

34. Howard Zinn, *A People's History of the United States: 1492–Present* (New York: HarperCollins, 1995).

35. Michael Menser, *We Decide! Theories and Cases in Participatory Democracy,* Global Ethics and Politics (Philadelphia: Temple University Press, 2018).

36. Peter Kropotkin, *Mutual Aid: A Factor of Evolution* (Courier Corporation, 2012); Matthew Lau, "Remeasuring Stephen Jay Gould," *Jacobin* (blog), May 20, 2017, http://jacobinmag.com/2017/05/stephen-jay-gould-science-race-evolution-climate-change; Stephen Jay Gould, "Kropotkin Was No Crackpot," *Natural History* 7, no. 97 (1988): 12–21.

37. Kimberly A. Zeuli and Robert Cropp, *Cooperatives: Principles and Practices in the 21st Century* (Madison: University of Wisconsin Extension, 2004).

38. T. W. Mercer, *Co-operation's Prophet: The Life and Letters of Dr. William King of Brighton* (Manchester, U.K.: Co-operative Union Ltd., 1947), 99, quoted in Johnston Birchall, *Co-op: The People's Business* (Manchester, U.K.: Manchester University Press, 1994), 1.

39. Karl Polanyi, *The Great Transformation: The Political and Economic Origins of Our Time* (Boston: Beacon Press, 2008), 37.

40. Birchall, *Co-op*.

41. Polanyi, *Great Transformation*, 75–76.

42. Karl Marx and Friedrich Engels, *The Marx-Engels Reader*, ed. Robert C. Tucker (New York: Norton, 1978), 479.

43. Curl, *For All the People*.

44. E. P. Thompson, *The Making of the English Working Class* (Harmondsworth, U.K.: Penguin, 1968), 269.

45. Restakis, *Humanizing the Economy*.

46. George Jacob Holyoake, *Self-Help by the People: The History of the Rochdale Pioneers* (London; New York: G. Allen & Unwin Ltd.; C. Scribner's Son, 1893).

47. Stefano Zamagni and Vera Zamagni, *Cooperative Enterprise: Facing the Challenge of Globalization* (Cheltenham, U.K.: Edward Elgar, 2010).

48. "Annual Results 2017," Co-operative Group, accessed August 21, 2018, https://www.co-operative.coop/investors/annual-results.

49. Birchall, *International Co-operative Movement*.

50. Ramon Flecha and Pun Ngai, "The Challenge for Mondragon: Searching for the Cooperative Values in Times of Internationalization," *Organization* 21, no. 5 (September 1, 2014): 666–82, https://doi.org/10.1177/1350508414537625.

51. Stephen Healy, "Cooperation, Surplus Appropriation, and the Law's Enjoyment," *Rethinking Marxism* 23, no. 3 (July 1, 2011): 364–73, https://doi.org/10.1080/08935696.2011.583012.

52. Birchall, *International Co-operative Movement*.

53. Birchall, 100.

54. Flecha and Ngai, "Challenge for Mondragon."

55. Gibson-Graham, *Postcapitalist Politics*, 121.

56. Healy, "Cooperation, Surplus Appropriation, and the Law's Enjoyment," 365.

57. Gibson-Graham, *Postcapitalist Politics*, 102.

58. Anne Meis Knupfer, *Food Co-ops in America: Communities, Consumption, and Economic Democracy* (Ithaca, N.Y.: Cornell University Press, 2013).

59. Laura Hanson Schlachter, "Stronger Together? The USW-Mondragon Union Co-op Model," *Labor Studies Journal* 42, no. 2 (June 2017): 124–47, https://doi.org/10.1177/0160449X17696989.

60. Gibson-Graham, "Enabling Ethical Economies."

61. Daniel Ozarow and Richard Croucher, "Workers' Self-Management, Recovered Companies, and the Sociology of Work," *Sociology* 48, no. 5 (October 1, 2014): 989–1006, https://doi.org/10.1177/0038038514539064.

62. Ozarow and Croucher, "Workers' Self-Management."

63. Restakis, *Humanizing the Economy.*

64. Restakis.

65. Peter Ranis, *Cooperatives Confront Capitalism: Challenging the Neo-liberal Economy,* reprint ed. (London: Zed Books, 2016), 66.

66. Restakis, *Humanizing the Economy.*

67. Ranis, *Cooperatives Confront Capitalism.*

68. Ozarow and Croucher, "Workers' Self-Management."

69. Camille Kerr, *Investing in Worker Ownership* (Oakland, Calif.: Democracy at Work Institute, 2015), https://institute.coop/sites/default/files/CapitalAccess.pdf.

70. Stacey A. Sutton, "Cooperative Cities: Municipal Support for Worker Cooperatives in the United States," *Journal of Urban Affairs* (May 14, 2019): 1–22, https://doi.org/10.1080/07352166.2019.1584531.

71. Healy, "Cooperation, Surplus Appropriation, and the Law's Enjoyment."

72. Sutton, "Cooperative Cities," 6.

73. Johnson Birchall and Lou Hammond Ketilson, *Resilience of the Cooperative Business Model in Times of Crisis* (brochure) (International Labor Organization, June 10, 2009), http://www.ilo.org/empent/Publications/WCMS_108416/lang--en/index.htm.

74. Japanese Consumers' Cooperative Union, *2017–2018 Profile of Japanese Consumers' Co-operative Union* (Tokyo: Japanese Consumers' Cooperative Union, September 2017).

75. David Thompson, "Japan: Land of Cooperatives," *Cooperative Grocer,* March 2008, https://www.grocer.coop/articles/japan-land-cooperatives.

76. Ruth Grubel, "The Consumer Co-op in Japan: Building Democratic Alternatives to State-Led Capitalism," in *Consumers against Capitalism?: Consumer Cooperation in Europe, North America, and Japan, 1840–1990,* ed. Ellen Furlough and Carl Strikwerda (Lanham, Md.: Rowman & Littlefield, 1999), 303–30.

77. Restakis, *Humanizing the Economy.*

78. Robin M. LeBlanc, *Bicycle Citizens: The Political World of the Japanese Housewife* (Berkeley: University of California Press, 1999).

79. Steve Dubb, "Seikatsu Club Consumers' Co-operative Union," Community-Wealth.org, October 9, 2012, https://community-wealth.org/content/seikatsu-club-consumers-co-operative-union.

80. "To Create an Alternative Economy," Seikatsu Club, accessed July 12, 2018, http://www.seikatsuclub.coop/about/economy_e.html.

81. Restakis, *Humanizing the Economy,* 127.

82. Caroline Shenaz Hossein, *The Black Social Economy in the Americas: Exploring Diverse Community-Based Markets* (New York: Palgrave Macmillan, 2017).

83. Gordon Nembhard, *Collective Courage;* Jessica Gordon Nembhard, "Cooperative Ownership in the Struggle for African American Economic Empow-

erment," *Humanity & Society* 28, no. 3 (August 1, 2004): 298–321, https://doi.org/10.1177/016059760402800307; Jessica Gordon Nembhard, "Cooperatives and Wealth Accumulation: Preliminary Analysis," *American Economic Review* 92, no. 2 (May 1, 2002): 325–29, https://doi.org/10.2307/3083425.

84. Joshua L. Carreiro, *Consumers' Cooperation in the Early Twentieth Century: An Analysis of Race, Class, and Consumption* (Amherst: University of Massachusetts Amherst, 2015).

85. Gordon Nembhard, *Collective Courage.*

86. Hossein, *Black Social Economy in the Americas.*

87. Caroline Shenaz Hossein and Ginelle Skerritt, "Drawing on the Lived Experience of African Canadians: Using Money Pools to Combat Social and Business Exclusion," in *The Black Social Economy in the Americas: Exploring Diverse Community-Based Markets,* ed. Caroline Shenaz Hossein (New York: Palgrave Macmillan, 2017), 41–58.

88. Steve Dubb, "Worker Co-ops Gain Ground in Communities of Color," *Shelterforce* (blog), July 7, 2016, https://shelterforce.org/2016/07/07/co-ops-gain-ground-in-communities-of-color/.

89. Kali Akuno and Ajamu Nangwaya, *Jackson Rising: The Struggle for Economic Democracy and Black Self-Determination in Jackson, Mississippi* (Montreal: Daraja Press, 2017).

90. Steve Dubb, "Co-op Movement Confronts Its Complicated Relationship with Racial Equity," Nonprofit Quarterly, August 26, 2019, https://nonprofitquarterly.org/co-op-movement-racial-equity/.

91. Gordon Nembhard, *Collective Courage.*

92. Eillie Anzilotti, "More U.S. Businesses Are Becoming Worker Co-ops: Here's Why," Fast Company, May 21, 2018, https://www.fastcompany.com/40572926/more-u-s-businesses-are-becoming-worker-co-ops-heres-why.

93. Knupfer, *Food Co-ops in America.*

94. George Cronk, "George Herbert Mead," in *Internet Encyclopedia of Philosophy,* accessed January 23, 2018, http://www.iep.utm.edu/mead/.

95. George Herbert Mead, *Mind, Self & Society* (Chicago: University of Chicago Press, 1934), 309.

2. TOOLS FOR THE JOURNEY

1. Sean Safford, "Challenging the Supremacy of Economics," *Orgtheory.Net* (blog), December 3, 2014, https://orgtheory.wordpress.com/2014/12/03/challenging-the-supremacy-of-economics/.

2. Robert Axelrod and William D. Hamilton, "The Evolution of Cooperation," *Science* 211, no. 4489 (1981): 1390–96.

3. Michael Taylor, *Rationality and the Ideology of Disconnection,* Contemporary Political Theory (Cambridge: Cambridge University Press, 2006), 54.

4. Mustafa Ongun, "Reappraising Neoliberalism: *Homo Economicus,* Practitioners, and Practices," in *Virtue and Economy: Essays on Morality and Markets,* ed. Andrius Bielskis and Kelvin Knight, Rethinking Political and International Theory (Farnham, U.K.: Routledge, 2015), 110–33.

5. Taylor, *Rationality and the Ideology of Disconnection,* 62.

6. Alasdair MacIntyre, *Whose Justice? Which Rationality?*, 1st ed. (Notre Dame, Ind.: University of Notre Dame Press, 1989).

7. Karl Polanyi, *The Great Transformation: The Political and Economic Origins of Our Time* (Boston: Beacon Press, 2008); Tim Rogan, *The Moral Economists: R. H. Tawney, Karl Polanyi, E. P. Thompson, and the Critique of Capitalism* (Princeton, N.J.: Princeton University Press, 2018).

8. John Dewey, *Individualism Old and New* (Prometheus Books, 1999), 8.

9. George Herbert Mead, *Mind, Self & Society* (Chicago: University of Chicago Press, 1934).

10. Catriona Mackenzie and Natalie Stoljar, "Introduction: Autonomy Reconfigured," in *Relational Autonomy: Feminist Perspectives on Automony, Agency, and the Social Self* (London: Oxford University Press, 2000), 3–31.

11. John Christman, "Relational Autonomy, Liberal Individualism, and the Social Constitution of Selves," *Philosophical Studies* 117, no. 1 (2004): 143–64.

12. J. K. Gibson-Graham, *A Postcapitalist Politics* (Minneapolis: University of Minnesota Press, 2006), 82.

13. Jean-Luc Nancy, *Being Singular Plural,* trans. Robert D Richardson and Anne Elizabeth O'Byrne (Stanford, Calif.: Stanford University Press, 2000).

14. Dewey, *Individualism Old and New,* 41.

15. Alasdair C. MacIntyre, *After Virtue: A Study in Moral Theory,* 3rd ed. (Notre Dame, Ind.: University of Notre Dame Press, 2007), 221.

16. James Baldwin, *The Fire Next Time* (New York: Vintage International, 1993), 81.

17. Taylor, *Rationality and the Ideology of Disconnection.*

18. Joan Didion, *The White Album* (New York: Simon and Schuster, 1979).

19. J. K. Gibson-Graham, "Enabling Ethical Economies: Cooperativism and Class," *Critical Sociology* 29, no. 2 (March 1, 2003): 126, https://doi.org/10.1163/156916303769155788.

20. J. K. Gibson-Graham, *The End of Capitalism (as We Knew It): A Feminist Critique of Political Economy* (Malden, Mass.: Blackwell, 1996), xxv.

21. Jeff Popke, "Geography and Ethics: Non-representational Encounters, Collective Responsibility, and Economic Difference," *Progress in Human Geography* 33, no. 1 (February 1, 2009): 88, https://doi.org/10.1177/0309132508090441.

22. Peter North, "Ten Square Miles Surrounded By Reality?: Materialising Alternative Economies Using Local Currencies," *Antipode* 46, no. 1 (2014): 247–48, https://doi.org/10.1111/anti.12039.

23. North, "Ten Square Miles."

24. Amanda Fickey, "'The Focus Has to Be on Helping People Make a Living': Exploring Diverse Economies and Alternative Economic Spaces," *Geography Compass* 5, no. 5 (2011): 237–48, https://doi.org/10.1111/j.1749-8198.2011.00418.x.

25. Gibson-Graham, *Postcapitalist Politics,* 71.

26. Amanda Fickey and Kelsey B. Hanrahan, "Moving beyond Neverland: Reflecting upon the State of the Diverse Economies Research Program and the Study of Alternative Economic Spaces," *ACME: An International E-Journal for Critical Geographies* 13, no. 2 (May 2014): 398–99.

27. Fickey and Hanrahan, "Moving beyond Neverland."

28. Gibson-Graham, *Postcapitalist Politics,* 82.

29. Gerda Roelvink, *Building Dignified Worlds: Geographies of Collective Action* (Minneapolis: University of Minnesota Press, 2016).

30. Janelle Cornwell, "Worker Co-operatives and Spaces of Possibility: An Investigation of Subject Space at Collective Copies," *Antipode* 44, no. 3 (2012): 725–44, https://doi.org/10.1111/j.1467-8330.2011.00939.x; Ken Byrne and Stephen Healy, "Cooperative Subjects: Toward a Post-Fantasmatic Enjoyment of the Economy," *Rethinking Marxism* 18, no. 2 (April 2006): 241–58, 345.

31. Gerda Roelvink, "Performing Posthumanist Economies in the Anthropocene," in *Making Other Worlds Possible: Performing Diverse Economies,* ed. Kevin St. Martin, J. K. Gibson-Graham, and Gerda Roelvink (Minneapolis: University of Minnesota Press, 2015), 232.

32. Barry Barnes, "Practice as Collective Action," in *The Practice Turn in Contemporary Theory,* ed. Theodore R. Schatzki, Karin Knorr Cetina, and Eike von Savigny (London: Routledge, 2001), 27.

33. Benedikt Schmid and Thomas S. J. Smith, "Social Transformation and Postcapitalist Possibility: Emerging Dialogues between Practice Theory and Diverse Economies," *Progress in Human Geography* (February 20, 2020): 6, https://doi.org/10.1177/0309132520905642.

34. Schmid and Smith, "Social Transformation and Postcapitalist Possibility."

35. Schmid and Smith, 15.

36. MacIntyre, *After Virtue,* 151.

37. MacIntyre, 187.

38. Gibson-Graham, "Enabling Ethical Economies," 130.

39. Johnson Birchall and Lou Hammond Ketilson, *Resilience of the Cooperative Business Model in Times of Crisis* (brochure) (International Labor Organization, June 10, 2009), http://www.ilo.org/empent/Publications/WCMS_108416/lang--en/index.htm.

40. MacIntyre, *After Virtue,* 232.

41. Gibson-Graham, *End of Capitalism,* 21–22.

42. MacIntyre, *After Virtue,* 221.

43. MacIntyre, 222.

44. Alasdair C. MacIntyre, *The MacIntyre Reader* (Notre Dame, Ind.: University of Notre Dame Press, 1998), 226.

3. PRACTICES OF THE BODY

1. All interviews associated with Headlong were conducted by the author between September 2013 and July 2014 in Philadelphia, Pennsylvania.

2. I have changed names for all interviewees, with the exception of the three founding codirectors of Headlong and the founder of POCA. Those four names are so closely associated with the organizations that it would be impossible to disguise their identities.

3. Robert E. Stake, "Qualitative Case Studies," in *The SAGE Handbook of Qualitative Research,* ed. Norman K. Denzin and Yvonna S. Lincoln, 3rd ed.

(Thousand Oaks, Calif.: Sage Publications, 2005), 443–66; Bent Flyvbjerg, "Five Misunderstandings about Case-Study Research," *Qualitative Inquiry* 12, no. 2 (April 1, 2006): 219–45, https://doi.org/10.1177/1077800405284363.

4. Mac McClelland, "I Was a Warehouse Wage Slave," *Mother Jones* (blog), April 2012, https://www.motherjones.com/politics/2012/02/mac-mcclelland-free-online-shipping-warehouses-labor/.

5. Roberto A. Ferdman, "'I Had to Wear Pampers': The Cruel Reality the People Who Bring You Cheap Chicken Allegedly Endure," Wonkblog, *Washington Post,* May 11, 2016, https://www.washingtonpost.com/news/wonk/wp/2016/05/11/i-had-to-wear-pampers-many-poultry-industry-workers-allegedly-cant-even-take-bathroom-breaks/.

6. Michelle Alexander, *The New Jim Crow: Mass Incarceration in the Age of Colorblindness* (New York: New Press, 2012).

7. Susan Hekman, "The Embodiment of the Subject: Feminism and the Communitarian Critique of Liberalism," *Journal of Politics* 54, no. 4 (November 1992): 1098, https://doi.org/10.2307/2132110.

8. Diana Meyers, "Feminist Perspectives on the Self," in *The Stanford Encyclopedia of Philosophy,* ed. Edward N. Zalta, Spring 2010 ed., http://plato.stanford.edu/archives/spr2010/entries/feminism-self/.

9. J. K. Gibson-Graham, *The End of Capitalism (as We Knew It): A Feminist Critique of Political Economy* (Minneapolis: University of Minnesota Press, 2006), 95; Judith Butler, *Bodies That Matter: On the Discursive Limits of Sex* (Abingdon, U.K.: Taylor & Francis, 2011); J. Jack Halberstam, *In a Queer Time and Place: Transgender Bodies, Subcultural Lives* (New York: NYU Press, 2005).

10. Martha C. Nussbaum, *Women and Human Development: The Capabilities Approach* (Cambridge: Cambridge University Press, 2000).

11. J. K. Gibson-Graham, *A Postcapitalist Politics* (Minneapolis: University of Minnesota Press, 2006), 16.

12. Alasdair C. MacIntyre, *Dependent Rational Animals: Why Human Beings Need the Virtues* (Chicago: Open Court, 1999), 2. See Iris Marion Young, *On Female Body Experience: "Throwing Like a Girl" and Other Essays* (Oxford: Oxford University Press, 2005); Judith Butler, *Gender Trouble: Feminism and the Subversion of Identity* (New York: Routledge, 2011); Aimi Hamraie, "Enlivened City: Inclusive Design, Biopolitics, and the Philosophy of Liveability," *Built Environment* 44, no. 1 (2018): 77–104.

13. MacIntyre, *Dependent Rational Animals,* 120.

14. Olena Hankivsky, "Rethinking Care Ethics: On the Promise and Potential of an Intersectional Analysis," *American Political Science Review* 108, no. 2 (2014): 252–64.

15. Carol Gilligan, "Hearing the Difference: Theorizing Connection," *Hypatia* 10, no. 2 (May 1995): 120–27, https://doi.org/10.1111/j.1527-2001.1995.tb01373.x.

16. Marion Barnes, "Beyond the Dyad: Exploring the Multidimensionality of Care," in *Ethics of Care: Critical Advances in International Perspective,* ed. Marion Barnes and Tula Brannelly (Bristol, U.K.: Policy Press, 2015), 31–43.

17. Kimberlé Crenshaw, *On Intersectionality: Essential Writings* (New York: New Press, 2017); Ina Kerner, "Relations of Difference: Power and Inequality in

Intersectional and Postcolonial Feminist Theories," *Current Sociology* 65, no. 6 (2017): 846–66, https://doi.org/10.1177/0011392116665152; S. Maddison and E. Partridge, "Agonism and Intersectionality: Indigenous Women, Violence, and Feminist Collective Identity," in *Intersectionality and Social Change*, vol. 37 (Bingley, U.K.: Emerald Publishing, 2014), 27–52.

18. Hankivsky, "Rethinking Care Ethics"; Parvati Raghuram, "Race and Feminist Care Ethics: Intersectionality as Method," *Gender, Place & Culture* 26, no. 5(2019): 613–37.

19. Hankivsky, "Rethinking Care Ethics."

20. Nicki Ward, "Care Ethics, Intersectionality, and Poststructuralism," in *Ethics of Care: Critical Advances in International Perspective*, ed. Marion Barnes and Tula Brannelly (Bristol, U.K.: Policy Press, 2015), 57–68.

21. Gibson-Graham, *Postcapitalist Politics*, 32.

22. Stephen Healy, "Caring for Ethics and the Politics of Health Care Reform in the United States," *Gender, Place & Culture* 15, no. 3 (2008): 267–84, https://doi.org/10.1080/09663690801996270.

23. Gibson-Graham, *Postcapitalist Politics*, 77.

24. Stephen Healy, "Caring for Ethics and the Politics of Health Care Reform in the United States," *Gender, Place & Culture* 15, no. 3 (2008): 267–84, https://doi.org/10.1080/09663690801996270.

25. Liz Bondi, Joyce Davidson, and Mick Smith, "Introduction: Geography's 'Emotional Turn,'" in *Emotional Geographies* (Aldershot, U.K.: Ashgate, 2005), 16–31.

26. Bondi, Davidson, and Smith, "Introduction," 18.

27. Steve Pile, "Emotions and Affect in Recent Human Geography," *Transactions of the Institute of British Geographers* 35, no. 1 (January 1, 2010): 16, https://doi.org/10.1111/j.1475-5661.2009.00368.x.

28. Bondi, Davidson, and Smith, "Introduction," 20.

29. Kirsten Simonsen, "Practice, Spatiality, and Embodied Emotions: An Outline of a Geography of Practice," *Human Affairs* 17, no. 2 (January 1, 2007), https://doi.org/10.2478/v10023-007-0015-8; Kirsten Simonsen, "Encountering O/other Bodies: Practice, Emotion, and Ethics," in *Taking-Place: Non-representational Theories and Geography*, ed. Paul Harrison and Ben Anderson (Farnham, U.K.: Ashgate, 2010), 221–39.

30. Simone de Beauvoir, *The Second Sex* (New York: Vintage Books, 1989).

31. Simonsen, "Practice, Spatiality, and Embodied Emotions," 173.

32. Joan S. M. Meyers and Steven Peter Vallas, "Diversity Regimes in Worker Cooperatives: Workplace Inequality under Conditions of Worker Control," *Sociological Quarterly* 57, no. 1 (December 1, 2016): 98–128, https://doi.org/10.1111/tsq.12114.

33. All POCA interviews were conducted by the author between September 2013 and March 2014 in Philadelphia, Pennsylvania, Providence, Rhode Island, and Portland, Oregon.

34. Maria T. Chao, Kimberly M. Tippens, and Erin Connelly, "Utilization of Group-Based, Community Acupuncture Clinics: A Comparative Study with a Nationally Representative Sample of Acupuncture Users," *Journal of Alternative*

and Complementary Medicine 18, no. 6 (May 2, 2012): 561–66, https://doi.org/10.1089/acm.2011.0128.

35. Aimi Hamraie, *Building Access: Universal Design and the Politics of Disability* (Minneapolis: University of Minnesota Press, Minnesota Scholarship Online, 2018), https://doi.org/10.5749/minnesota/9781517901639.001.0001.

36. Simonsen, "Practice, Spatiality, and Embodied Emotions," 178; Iris Marion Young, *Justice and the Politics of Difference* (Princeton, N.J.: Princeton University Press, 1990).

37. Bondi, Davidson, and Smith, "Introduction," 20.

38. Nigel Thrift, "The Still Point: Resistance, Expressive Embodiment, and Dance," in *Geographies of Resistance,* ed. Steve Pile and Michael Keith (London: Routledge, 1997), 145.

39. Alan Radley, "The Elusory Body and Social Constructionist Theory," *Body & Society* 1, no. 2 (1995): 3–23, https://doi.org/10.1177/1357034X95001002001, 9, as cited in Thrift, "Still Point," 150.

40. Tim Cresswell, "'You Cannot Shake That Shimmie Here': Producing Mobility on the Dance Floor," *Cultural Geographies* 13, no. 1 (January 1, 2006): 55–77, https://doi.org/10.1191/1474474006eu350oa.

41. Stephen Fineman, *Understanding Emotion at Work* (London: SAGE, 2003).

42. Martha C. Nussbaum, "Emotions and Women's Capabilities," in *Women, Culture, and Development: A Study of Human Capabilities,* ed. Martha C. Nussbaum and Jonathan Glover (Oxford: Oxford University Press, 1995), 360–95; bell hooks, *Sisters of the Yam: Black Women and Self-Recovery* (New York: Routledge, 2014).

43. Elizabeth A. Hoffmann, "Emotions and Emotional Labor at Worker-Owned Businesses: Deep Acting, Surface Acting, and Genuine Emotions," *Sociological Quarterly* 57, no. 1 (December 1, 2016): 152–73, https://doi.org/10.1111/tsq.12113.

44. David F. Ruccio, "Utopia and the Critique of Political Economy," *Journal of Australian Political Economy* 79 (Winter 2017): 5–20.

45. George Lipsitz, *How Racism Takes Place* (Philadelphia: Temple University Press, 2011).

46. Joyce Rothschild, "The Logic of a Co-operative Economy and Democracy 2.0: Recovering the Possibilities for Autonomy, Creativity, Solidarity, and Common Purpose," *Sociological Quarterly* 57, no. 1 (Winter 2016): 7–35, https://doi.org/10.1111/tsq.12138.

4. PRACTICES OF WORK AND ORGANIZATION

1. All personal interviews with Weavers Way, Mariposa, and other food co-ops' board, staff, and members were conducted by the author between March 2010 and December 2011 in Philadelphia, Pennsylvania.

2. International Cooperative Alliance, "Co-operative Identity, Values & Principles," International Co-operative Alliance, accessed January 28, 2013, http://ica.coop/en/whats-co-op/co-operative-identity-values-principles.

3. Rahel Jaeggi, *Alienation,* trans. Alan E. Smith and Frederick Neuhouser (New York: Columbia University Press, 2014).

4. Alasdair C. MacIntyre, *Marxism: An Interpretation* (London: SCM Press, 1953), cited in Jaeggi, *Alienation,* 3.

5. Karl Marx and Friedrich Engels, *The Marx-Engels Reader,* ed. Robert C. Tucker (New York: Norton, 1978), 72.

6. David Harvey, "Universal Alienation," *TripleC: Communication, Capitalism & Critique* 16, no. 2 (May 1, 2018): 424–39.

7. David Graeber, "On the Phenomenon of Bullshit Jobs," *STRIKE! Magazine,* August 2013, http://www.strikemag.org/bullshit-jobs/.

8. Harvey, "Universal Alienation."

9. Jaeggi, *Alienation.*

10. Marx and Engels, *Marx-Engels Reader,* 76.

11. Harvey, "Universal Alienation," 437.

12. J. K. Gibson-Graham, *A Postcapitalist Politics* (Minneapolis: University of Minnesota Press, 2006), 67.

13. Jaeggi, *Alienation,* 14–15.

14. Kelvin Knight, *Aristotelian Philosophy: Ethics and Politics from Aristotle to MacIntyre* (Malden, Mass.: Polity, 2007), 107.

15. Niko Noponen, "Alienation, Practices, and Human Nature : Marxist Critique in MacIntyre's Aristotelian Ethics," in *Virtue and Politics: Alasdair MacIntyre's Revolutionary Aristotelianism,* ed. Paul Blackledge and Kelvin Knight (Notre Dame, Ind.: University of Notre Dame Press, 2011).

16. Ron Beadle and Geoff Moore, "MacIntyre on Virtue and Organization," *Organization Studies* 27, no. 3 (March 1, 2006): 334, https://doi.org/10.1177/0170840606062425.

17. Beadle and Moore, "MacIntyre on Virtue and Organization," 330.

18. Incite! Women of Color Against Violence, *The Revolution Will Not Be Funded: Beyond the Non-profit Industrial Complex* (Cambridge, Mass.: South End Press, 2007).

19. Alasdair C. MacIntyre, *After Virtue: A Study in Moral Theory,* 3rd ed. (Notre Dame, Ind.: University of Notre Dame Press, 2007), 187.

20. Ron Beadle and Geoff Moore, "MacIntyre, Neo-Aristotelianism, and Organization Theory," in *Philosophy and Organization Theory,* ed. Haridimos Tsoukas and Robert Chia, vol. 32, Research in the Sociology of Organizations (Bingley, U.K.: Emerald Group Publishing Limited, 2011), 97.

21. MacIntyre, *After Virtue,* 194.

22. Alasdair C. MacIntyre, *After Virtue: A Study in Moral Theory,* 2nd ed. (London: Duckworth, 1985), 196, cited in Beadle and Moore, "MacIntyre on Virtue and Organization," 331.

23. Beadle and Moore, "MacIntyre, Neo-Aristotelianism and Organization Theory," 101.

24. Brett Fairbairn, "Keepin' It Real: Co-ops in Turbulent Times," presented at 55th Annual Consumer Cooperative Management Association, June 18, 2011, San Diego, Calif., posted by Joel Brock, "CCMA 2011: Brett Fairbairn," December 4, 2011, YouTube video, 57:13, https://www.youtube.com/watch?v=GHOYJP_OTpQ&feature=youtu.be&ab_channel=JoelBrock.

25. Stefano Zamagni and Vera Zamagni, *Cooperative Enterprise: Facing the Challenge of Globalization* (Cheltenham, U.K.: Edward Elgar, 2010), 1.

26. Beadle and Moore, "MacIntyre, Neo-Aristotelianism, and Organization Theory," 106.

27. Andrew Zitcer, "Food Co-ops and the Paradox of Exclusivity," *Antipode* 47, no. 3 (June 1, 2015): 812–28, https://doi.org/10.1111/anti.12129.

28. Jade Barker and Patricia Cumbie, "Everyone Welcome: Personal Narratives about Race and Food Co-ops" (CDS Consulting Co-op, 2017), http://library.cdsconsulting.coop/everyone-welcome-personal-narratives/.

29. Thane Joyal, "Who's Watching Member Labor in Retail Food Cooperatives?," *Cooperative Grocer*, January 2012, http://www.cooperativegrocer.coop/articles/2012-01-18/who%E2%80%99s-watching-member-labor-retail-food-cooperatives; Dave Gutknecht, "The Good Old Days," *Cooperative Grocer*, March 1987, http://www.cooperativegrocer.coop/articles/index.php?id=37; David Barry, "Managing Working Members," *Cooperative Grocer*, January 1987, http://www.cooperativegrocer.coop/articles/2004-01-09/managing-working-members.

30. The dynamics of labor are very different in these consumer-owned co-ops than they are in worker cooperatives. Though there are no worker cooperatives in my study, there are several scholars devoted to understanding them in depth. Janelle Cornwell, "Worker Co-operatives and Spaces of Possibility: An Investigation of Subject Space at Collective Copies," *Antipode* 44, no. 3 (2012): 725–44, https://doi.org/10.1111/j.1467-8330.2011.00939.x; Joan S. M. Meyers and Steven Peter Vallas, "Diversity Regimes in Worker Cooperatives: Workplace Inequality under Conditions of Worker Control," *Sociological Quarterly* 57, no. 1 (December 1, 2016): 98–128, https://doi.org/10.1111/tsq.12114; Stacey A. Sutton, "Cooperative Cities: Municipal Support for Worker Cooperatives in the United States," *Journal of Urban Affairs* 41, no. 8 (May 14, 2019): 1–22, https://doi.org/10.1080/07352166.2019.1584531.

31. It bears mentioning that there have been controversies in the past at Park Slope where members have sent their nannies to work their shifts for them based on a loose interpretation of the rules. See Anemona Hartocollis and Juliet Linderman, "At a Food Co-op, a Discordant Thought: Nannies Covering Shifts," *New York Times*, February 17, 2011, https://www.nytimes.com/2011/02/18/nyregion/18coop.html.

32. Beadle and Moore, "MacIntyre on Virtue and Organization," 330.

33. Lisa Rohleder, *Fractal: About Community Acupuncture* (Portland, Ore.: People's Organization of Community Acupuncture, 2013), 68.

34. I should clarify that it is POCA the *movement* that is committed to democratic governance. Individual clinics vary in their ownership and governance, with a range of management styles. "POCA FAQ," People's Organization of Community Acupuncture, accessed February 10, 2016, https://www.pocacoop.com/faq.

35. Charlotte Hess and Elinor Ostrom, eds., *Understanding Knowledge as a Commons: From Theory to Practice* (Cambridge, Mass.: MIT Press, 2005).

36. Rohleder, *Fractal*, 32.

37. MacIntyre, *After Virtue*, 195.

38. Joyce Rothschild, "Creating a Just and Democratic Workplace: More Engagement, Less Hierarchy," *Contemporary Sociology* 29, no. 1 (January 1, 2000): 195–213.

39. This calls to mind the voting schemes proposed in Lani Guinier, *Tyranny of the Majority: Fundamental Fairness in Representative Democracy* (New York: Free Press, 1995).

40. Joyce Rothschild and J. A. Whitt, *The Cooperative Workplace: Potentials and Dilemmas of Organisational Democracy and Participation* (Cambridge: Cambridge University Press, 1986).

41. Jaeggi, *Alienation*, 220.

5. PRACTICES OF COMMUNITY ECONOMY

1. John Ruskin, *Unto This Last, and Other Writings*, ed. Clive Wilmer, Penguin Classics (New York: Penguin Books, 1985), 222.

2. David Melville Craig, *John Ruskin and the Ethics of Consumption*, Studies in Religion and Culture (Charlottesville: University of Virginia Press, 2006).

3. Craig, *John Ruskin*, 2.

4. Christopher May, "John Ruskin's Political Economy: 'There Is No Wealth but Life,'" *British Journal of Politics and International Relations* 12, no. 2 (May 1, 2010): 189–204, https://doi.org/10.1111/j.1467-856X.2010.00406.x.

5. Frank Trentmann, "Citizenship and Consumption," *Journal of Consumer Culture* 7, no. 2 (2007): 147–58.

6. Craig, *John Ruskin*, 19.

7. Tim Rogan, *The Moral Economists: R. H. Tawney, Karl Polanyi, E. P. Thompson, and the Critique of Capitalism* (Princeton, N.J.: Princeton University Press, 2018).

8. J. K. Gibson-Graham, *The End of Capitalism (as We Knew It): A Feminist Critique of Political Economy* (Minneapolis: University of Minnesota Press, 2006), 6.

9. J. K. Gibson-Graham, *A Postcapitalist Politics* (Minneapolis: University of Minnesota Press, 2006), 56.

10. Gibson-Graham, *Postcapitalist Politics*, 70–71.

11. She is careful to assert that such seemingly negative behaviors need to be understood in context; there are times when theft may be morally justified in a context of unjust laws, for example.

12. J. K. Gibson-Graham, "Diverse Economies: Performative Practices for 'Other Worlds,'" *Progress in Human Geography* 32, no. 5 (October 1, 2008): 628, https://doi.org/10.1177/0309132508090821.

13. Ethan Miller, "Community Economy: Ontology, Ethics, and Politics for Radically Democratic Economic Organizing," *Rethinking Marxism* 25, no. 4 (October 2013): 518–33, https://doi.org/10.1080/08935696.2013.842697.

14. Gibson-Graham, *End of Capitalism*, chap. 6.

15. Miller, "Community Economy," 521.

16. Miller, 524.

17. Miller, 525.

18. J. K. Gibson-Graham and Gerda Roelvink, "An Economic Ethics for the Anthropocene," *Antipode* 41 (2010): 320–46, https://doi.org/10.1111/j.1467-8330.2009.00728.x; Gibson-Graham, *Postcapitalist Politics*.

19. Amanda Huron, *Carving Out the Commons: Tenant Organizing and Housing*

Cooperatives in Washington, D.C., Diverse Economies and Livable Worlds 2 (Minneapolis: University of Minnesota Press, 2018).

20. Incite! Women of Color Against Violence, *The Revolution Will Not Be Funded: Beyond the Non-profit Industrial Complex* (Cambridge, Mass.: South End Press, 2007).

21. Morgan Williams, "Are Diversity, Equity, and Inclusion Statements Effective Tools for Foundations?," *GIA Reader* 30, no. 2 (Summer 2019): https://www.giarts.org/article/are-diversity-equity-and-inclusion-statements-effective-tools-foundations.

22. Gibson-Graham and Roelvink, "Economic Ethics for the Anthropocene," 333.

23. J. K. Gibson-Graham, "An Ethics of the Local," *Rethinking Marxism* 15, no. 1 (January 2003): 55, https://doi.org/10.1080/0893569032000063583.

24. Laura Brzyski, "Food Co-ops Are on the Rise in Philly," *Philadelphia Magazine* (blog), October 23, 2019, https://www.phillymag.com/be-well-philly/2019/10/23/philly-food-co-ops/.

25. Andrew Zitcer and Richardson Dilworth, "Grocery Cooperatives as Governing Institutions in Neighborhood Commercial Corridors," *Urban Affairs Review* 55, no. 2 (March 1, 2019): 558–90, https://doi.org/10.1177/1078087417709999.

26. Cassidy Hartmann, "Greene and Carpenter Lane Inc.," *Philadelphia Weekly*, November 23, 2005, http://www.philadelphiaweekly.com/news/greene-and-carpenter-lane-inc/article_1de01db8-c933-5fc3-8e5c-222fb7a8cd8f.html.

27. Hartmann, "Greene and Carpenter Lane Inc."

28. Weavers Way Co-op, *Weavers Way Customer Survey 2013* (Philadelphia: December 2013), 5.

29. Brzyski, "Food Co-ops Are on the Rise in Philly."

30. "If You're Thinking of Applying," POCA Tech, accessed March 23, 2020, http://pocatech.org/if-youre-thinking-applying.

31. Marcelo Vieta and Doug Lionais, "Editorial: The Cooperative Advantage for Community Development," *Journal of Entrepreneurial and Organiational Diversity* 4, no. 1 (August 13, 2015): 1–10.

6. PRACTICES OF DEMOCRACY

1. Ann Markusen, "Fuzzy Concepts, Scanty Evidence, Policy Distance: The Case for Rigour and Policy Relevance in Critical Regional Studies," *Regional Studies* 37, no. 6/7 (August 2003): 702, https://doi.org/10.1080/0034340032000108796.

2. Iris Marion Young, "The Ideal of Community and the Politics of Difference," in *Feminism and Community*, ed. Penny A. Weiss and Marilyn Friedman (Philadelphia: Temple University Press, 1995), 233–58.

3. Iris Marion Young, *Inclusion and Democracy* (Oxford: Oxford University Press, 2000).

4. Miranda Joseph, *Against the Romance of Community* (Minneapolis: University of Minnesota Press, 2002).

5. James DeFilippis, Robert Fisher, and Eric Shragge, *Contesting Community: The Limits and Potential of Local Organizing* (New Brunswick, N.J.: Rutgers University Press, 2010).

6. MacIntyre is often lumped together with the communitarian school of political philosophy, a categorization he strenuously rejects throughout his work. He maintains that there is nothing inherently liberating about a given community. Rather, local communities support human flourishing only when they actively support "the virtues of just generosity and shared deliberation." He supports a standard of mutually acknowledged dependence. Communities do not and should not support the status quo of the state: "It is . . . a mistake, the communitarian mistake, to attempt to infuse the politics of the state with the values and modes of participation in local community." See Alasdair C. MacIntyre, *Dependent Rational Animals: Why Human Beings Need the Virtues* (Chicago: Open Court, 1999), 142.

7. Marilyn Friedman, "Feminism and Modern Friendship: Dislocating the Community," in *Feminism and Community,* ed. Penny A. Weiss and Marilyn Friedman (Philadelphia: Temple University Press, 1995), 187–208.

8. Young, "Ideal of Community."

9. DeFilippis, Fisher, and Shragge, *Contesting Community.*

10. Charles Wade Mills, *Black Rights/White Wrongs: The Critique of Racial Liberalism* (New York: Oxford University Press, 2017), 195–96.

11. Joseph, *Against the Romance of Community,* chap. 1.

12. DeFilippis, Fisher, and Shragge, *Contesting Community,* 17.

13. DeFilippis, Fisher, and Shragge.

14. DeFilippis, Fisher, and Shragge.

15. Iris Marion Young, *Justice and the Politics of Difference* (Princeton, N.J.: Princeton University Press, 1990).

16. John Dewey, *The Public and Its Problems* (Athens: Swallow Press/Ohio University Press, 1991).

17. Robert W. Lake, "On Poetry, Pragmatism, and the Urban Possibility of Creative Democracy," *Urban Geography* 38, no. 4 (April 21, 2017): 479–94, https://doi.org/10.1080/02723638.2016.1272195.

18. Astra Taylor, *Democracy May Not Exist, but We'll Miss It When It's Gone* (New York: Metropolitan Books, 2019), 11.

19. John Dewey, *The Public and Its Problems* (Athens, Ohio: Swallow Press/Ohio University Press, 1991), 143.

20. Benedikt Schmid and Thomas S. J. Smith, "Social Transformation and Postcapitalist Possibility: Emerging Dialogues between Practice Theory and Diverse Economies," *Progress in Human Geography* 45, no. 2 (February 20, 2020): https://doi.org/10.1177/0309132520905642.

21. Darcy K. Leach, "Prefigurative Politics," in *The Wiley-Blackwell Encyclopedia of Social and Political Movements,* ed. David A. Snow et al. (Oxford: Blackwell, 2013).

22. Helen Scharber, "Innovation in Community Acupuncture Education at People's Organization of Community Acupuncture Technical Institute," *Journal of Alternative and Complementary Medicine* 25, no. 7 (July 2019): 681–82, https://doi.org/10.1089/acm.2019.0069.

23. Mary Milstead, "In a Room Made for Bodies," *Gay Mag,* September 5, 2019, https://gay.medium.com/in-a-room-made-for-bodies-64cc6a9fd68.

24. Jon Steinman, "Who Owns Your Grocery Store?" *Yes! Magazine,* December 6, 2019, https://www.yesmagazine.org/opinion/2019/12/06/grocery-store-own.

25. Joyce Rothschild and J. A. Whitt, *The Cooperative Workplace: Potentials and Dilemmas of Organisational Democracy and Participation* (Cambridge: Cambridge University Press, 1986).

26. Amy S. Rosenberg, "Now This Is Home Staging," *Philadelphia Inquirer,* September 2, 2012, https://www.inquirer.com/philly/entertainment/20120902_Now_this_is_home_staging.html.

27. Lake, "On Poetry," 486.

CONCLUSION

1. Amy Smith, "Just finished fourth of four webinars I led this week for artists to talk about dealing with the financial aspects of this crisis," Facebook, March 27, 2020, https://www.facebook.com/headlongamy/posts/10218812692923269.

2. Andrew Simonet, "This Is What We Train For," ArtPlace, March 25, 2020, https://www.artplaceamerica.org/blog/what-we-train.

3. Benedikt Schmid and Thomas S. J. Smith, "Social Transformation and Postcapitalist Possibility: Emerging Dialogues between Practice Theory and Diverse Economies," *Progress in Human Geography* 45, no. 2 (February 20, 2020): 253–75, https://doi.org/10.1177/0309132520905642.

4. George Jacob Holyoake, *Self-Help by the People: The History of the Rochdale Pioneers* (London; New York: G. Allen & Unwin Ltd.; C. Scribner's Son, 1893), 15.

5. Adrienne M. Brown, *Emergent Strategy* (Chico, Calif.: AK Press, 2017), sec. 3.

INDEX

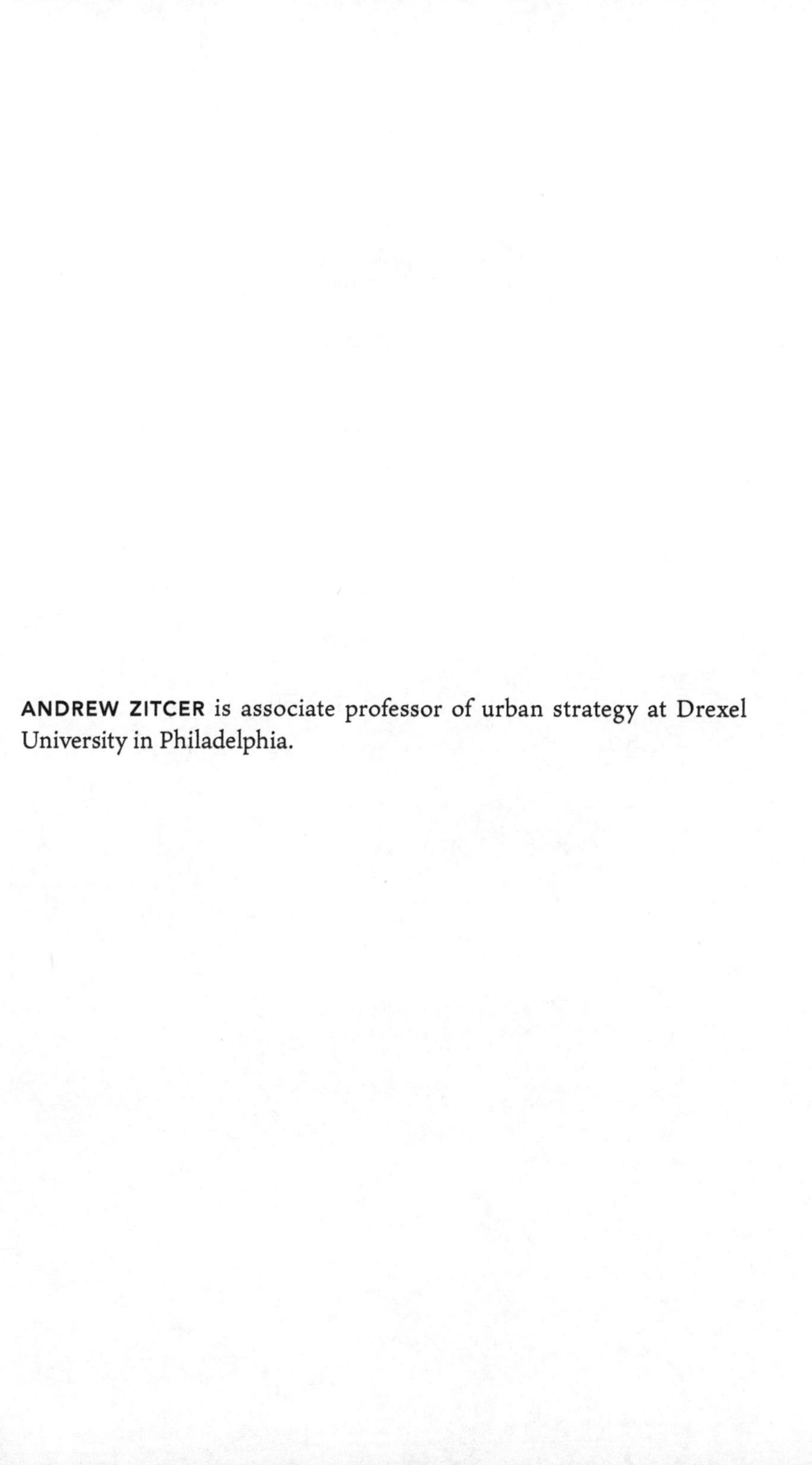

ANDREW ZITCER is associate professor of urban strategy at Drexel University in Philadelphia.

Zeitfracht Medien GmbH
Ferdinand-Jühlke-Straße 7
99095 Erfurt, Deutschland
produktsicherheit@kolibri360.de